Winning Legally

Winning Legally

*How to Use the Law to
Create Value, Marshal Resources,
and Manage Risk*

Constance E. Bagley

HARVARD BUSINESS SCHOOL PRESS
BOSTON, MASSACHUSETTS

Library of Congress Cataloging-in-Publication Data
    Bagley, Constance E.
    Winning legally: how to use the law to create value, marshal resources, and manage risk / Constance E. Bagley.
        p.   cm.
    Includes bibliographical references and index.
    ISBN 1-59139-192-X
    1. Business law—United States. 2. Executives—United States—
Handbooks, manuals, etc. I. Title.
    KF390.B84B347 2005
    346.7307—dc22

                                                            2005007403

To Christoph

Contents

Acknowledgments   *ix*

1. Maximizing Value While Managing Risk   1

2. Playing by the Rules   21

3. Cultivating Compliance for Strategic Strength   47

4. Using Contracts to Define and Strengthen Relationships   87

5. Capturing the Value of Intellectual Capital   117

6. Protecting Brand Equity   153

7. Unleashing the Power of Human Capital   175

8. Managing Disputes   203

9. Achieving the Advice Advantage   223

Notes   *247*
Index   *269*
About the Author   *283*

Acknowledgments

A NUMBER OF MY COLLEAGUES at the Harvard Business School were most generous in offering encouragement and providing suggestions for this book. They include Teresa Amabile, Lynda Applegate, Srikant Datar, Bill Fruhan, Geoff Jones, Bob Kaplan, David Moss, Lynn Paine, Joel Podolny, Kash Rangan, Hank Reiling, Bill Sahlman, and Debora Spar. I thank each of them. Any inaccuracies are my own.

I also thank Arthur McCaffrey, who provided research support, and Mark Lamoureux, who did his usual great job of preparing the manuscript. Good luck, Mark, as you pursue your literary calling. I'll miss you.

I would like to thank Harvard Business School Press executive editor Kirsten Sandberg and developmental editor Colleen Kaftan for helping me to bring this project to fruition. Thanks also to John Allison, Rahul Mehendale, and the four anonymous reviewers who provided excellent feedback on the manuscript during its development. The Harvard Business School Division of Research and Faculty Development provided research support for this project, for which I am most grateful.

Thanks to Michael Watkins for helping to keep me on course when the going got tough and to Liz Smith, former vice president of investor relations and shareholder services at Texaco, Inc., for introducing me to her former boss, Texaco CEO and chairman James Kinnear, and for being such a great coach.

Thanks also to Arleen Ashjian, Mary Harvey, Christy Haubegger, Brian King, Jeffrey and Kathleen Pfeffer, Kent and Teddy Portney, and Marilyn Santiesteban for their ongoing love and support. Finally, thanks to my son Christoph for putting up with all the late nights and for making each day a joy and a delight. You rule.

—C.E.B.

1

Maximizing Value While Managing Risk

I N APRIL 1998, Sanford Weill of Travelers Insurance and John Reed of Citicorp stunned the business community by announcing the merger of their two giant institutions. But there was a problem. The Glass-Steagall Act and the Bank Holding Company Act prohibited Citibank, one of the world's largest commercial banks, from merging with Smith Barney and Salomon Brothers, the insurance arm and investment banking powerhouses of Travelers.

Instead of accepting the regulatory environment as permanent, Weill and Travelers' general counsel, Charles Prince, worked with a handful of executives and lawyers at Travelers and Citicorp to create a bold legal and business strategy that would enable the merger.[1] First, they asked Alan Greenspan, head of the Federal Reserve Board, whether he would support or oppose such a marriage. After Greenspan indicated that he would view the proposed combination favorably, they met with lobbyists to gauge which reforms were in the realm of the possible, given the evolution of the global banking environment since the middle of the twentieth century.

In structuring the merger, they ultimately relied on a previously unexploited provision in the acts that gave firms two to five years to persuade Congress to change the law. Both Reed and Weill thought they could achieve their legal strategy within the allotted time, but neither would have bet their companies on that possibility. Instead, the executives and lawyers developed contingency plans, ways of combining certain assets from the two firms and selling others, to create a business entity that made economic sense even if the restrictions in Glass-Steagall and the Bank Holding Company Act remained on the books when the five-year honeymoon ended.

One year after the merger became official, Congress repealed the provisions prohibiting banks from issuing securities and underwriting insurance. Weill, Prince, and Reed not only succeeded in creating and capturing tremendous value for the new firm but also helped reshape the regulatory environment for the entire U.S. financial services industry. In so doing, they brought U.S. banks and banking law into line with global competition.

When Sandy Weill handed the reins to his former general counsel, Chuck Prince, in 2003, Citigroup was the most profitable company in the world, with $15.3 billion in profits and assets of $1.1 trillion.[2] It was also seen as a great place to work for smart, ambitious men and women from many backgrounds, cultures, and countries. The company had a reputation for creating innovative solutions to customers' needs, which required employees to develop a nuanced understanding of the law across many specialty areas and in many jurisdictions.

Yet Citigroup has also run afoul of the law on many occasions over the years, destroying considerable shareholder value along the way. In May 2004 the Federal Reserve Board fined CitiFinancial, Citigroup's consumer finance subsidiary, $70 million, its largest fine ever, for predatory lending practices and trying to mislead bank examiners.[3] In the same month Citigroup agreed to pay $2.65 billion to settle class action securities fraud lawsuits filed by investors who bought WorldCom shares and bonds underwritten by Citigroup between 1999 and WorldCom's collapse in 2002. It set aside another $6.7 billion in reserves to resolve suits related to Enron and other clients. In 2003, Citigroup's Salomon Smith Barney unit paid $400 million in state and federal fines to settle charges that their research analysts published false and misleading market research reports to curry favor with the firm's investment banking clients.[4]

A scathing article in the *Houston Chronicle* characterized this $9 billion total in settlement payments and reserves as "the price of greed."[5] In contrast, Charles Prince called Citigroup's settlement with the Federal Reserve Board "another important step in our continuing efforts to address the issues of the past and move forward with standards that define best practices in our business."[6] The *Houston Chronicle* pointed out that writing a big check was "the easy part, an obligatory penance," and cautioned that the settlements "aren't a guarantee investors won't be abused again in the next round of hot deals." If Prince "really wants to close this chapter," the *Houston Chronicle* asserted, "it will take more than $9 billion. He'll have to change the moral compass of the company."[7] To build a truly great and enduring firm, Prince must combine Weill's audacity and vision with integrity and respect for law.

Citigroup's story illustrates two key messages of this book: At any moment, employees at any level of the corporate hierarchy and at any point in the value chain may discover opportunities to capture value by harnessing the power of the law. At any other moment, any of these same people can jeopardize the entire franchise by misunderstanding, ignoring, or flouting the law. Remember that a sole rogue trader—Nick Leeson—brought down Barings Bank, Britain's oldest merchant bank, in 1995.

Examples of such compliance failures abound. The spectacle of handcuffed corporate executives on the perp walk after the collapse of Enron, WorldCom, and Adelphia Communications, the criminal conviction and demise of Arthur Andersen, the payment of record fines by Wall Street firms and other companies, the parade of top executives refusing to answer questions before Congress on the grounds that their answers might incriminate them, and the sentencing of the founder and former CEO of ImClone Systems to more than seven years in prison for insider trading all serve as stark reminders of the consequences of failing to comply with the law. An unprecedented series of accounting scandals in the late 1990s shook public confidence in the U.S. capital markets. WorldCom lost $200 billion of shareholder value in fewer than twelve months, making it the largest corporate fraud in history.[8]

But there are many examples of companies winning legally, and there could be more if managers became more adept at harnessing the empowering nature of law. Thus, avoiding trouble is only part of the picture. Managers who view the law purely as a constraint, something to comply with and react to rather than to use actively, will miss opportunities to use the law and the legal system for increasing the total value created and the firm's share of that value.

This book uses the term *law* to encompass policy and government as well. Like James Willard Hurst, we use the term *law* to refer to "all formal and informal aspects of political organized power," including "the functions of all legal agencies (legislative, executive, administrative, or judicial)."[9] Accordingly, this book addresses not only the effects of constitutions and statutes but also judicial decisions, regulations, and statutory interpretations by administrative agencies (such as the Securities and Exchange Commission) and enforcement policies.

In short, law matters in the management of business—it is not separate and apart from what managers do. Instead of viewing law as an outside force that constrains the manager, this book reframes the relationship of law to business and explains how legally astute managers can both help shape the legal environment in which they do business and embrace the law and the tools it offers to manage the business enterprise more effectively.

Mastering the Legal Aspects of Business

Understanding the legal dimensions of business is essential to successful management in today's global marketplace. As managers rise in the corporate hierarchy, they increasingly face legal issues they are ill-equipped to handle. Most managers do not have a legal background, and less seasoned managers often do not understand how law affects the risk/reward ratio of the firm. They may not know the right answers or even the right questions to ask. Nor do many managers know how to select and work with a good legal adviser.

Worse, managers often view the law as an arcane set of rules designed to impede, not facilitate, value creation. Under that assumption, they may want to skirt—and occasionally to break—the rules designed to provide a level playing field for all competitors.

Managers must ensure that their legal strategy aligns with their business strategy. Like information technology[10] and human resource practices,[11] the legal strategy must be integral to and inseparable from the business strategy. The legal dimensions should not be treated as an afterthought or an add-on to the business strategy development process.

Legal astuteness requires the management team to learn about the law that affects their business and to adopt a more proactive approach to managing the legal dimensions of business. It also requires the lawyers to learn about the business so that they can participate actively in each stage of strategy formulation and execution.

Before committing resources to new opportunities, legally astute managers evaluate the business and legal opportunities and risks at each phase of development.[12] Decisions made in the early phases can dramatically affect the alternatives available later, so a developmental strategy must make sense at each stage and also promise a successful result. Proper use of the law and the legal system in the planning stages can increase the realizable reward and limit a firm's downside risk.

Some business people naively believe that they need not learn about specific laws and the legal environment because they can hire lawyers to handle all the "legal stuff." Yet few would argue that they need not understand an income or cash flow statement because they can hire certified public accountants to handle the "financial stuff." To paraphrase Clemenceau, legal matters are too important to leave to the lawyers. As we'll see, managers can and should seek legal counsel to understand their legal and strategic alternatives, but ultimately they must make the hard decisions.

Managers must also learn to spot legal issues before they become legal problems. If managers are not sensitive to the legal issues that might arise, then they will not know when to call in the lawyers. Once an issue has become a problem, managers have little recourse except damage control.

At the same time, managers usually lack the time and the resources to seek legal advice on every matter, especially when they must act quickly on market opportunities.[13] A basic awareness of the law enables them to move fast and appropriately.

Partnering with Legal Counsel

Ideally, managers work with counsel as partners to craft business solutions that maximize the possible reward while minimizing (and eliminating entirely all unnecessary) legal and business risk. Managers must understand the legal nomenclature and principles most relevant to their business as much as lawyers must sufficiently understand the business model and its execution.

Managers can and should work with counsel to design strategies for achieving the core business objectives without breaking the rules. If a client proposes an action that would violate the law, then the lawyer needs the independence and courage to advise the client in no uncertain terms that what he has proposed is illegal. The manager, in turn, should heed the advice. That may seem obvious, but a host of managers at firms ranging from Putnam Investments and Health-South to Cendant appear to have forgotten this basic tenet.

But relatively few decisions are binary, zero for illegal and one for legal. Although Congress and the U.S. Supreme Court have declared certain conduct, such as horizontal price-fixing between direct competitors, to be clearly illegal, the legal analysis of most courses of action is far more subtle. There are large gray areas. The law is rarely applied in a vacuum and its application to a given set of facts is often not clear-cut. As U.S. Supreme Court Justice Oliver Wendell Holmes explained, legal advice is often just a prediction of what a judge and jury will do in a future case.[14]

At the end of the day, as long as counsel has not advised that a particular course of action is illegal, the management team must decide whether a particular risk is worth taking or a particular opportunity is worth pursuing. Individual managers must determine which course of conduct is ethical.

To choose wisely, managers must understand the legal and ethical ramifications of their actions and factor them into business decisions just as they factor other elements, such as currency fluctuations or raw materials availability, into the risk/reward calculation. Chapter 3 offers tools for doing so more effectively.

For example, suing a supplier for late delivery of goods may mean losing the supplier forever. Instead, alternative dispute resolution techniques, such as negotiation and mediation, might yield a better long-term outcome for both parties. Similarly, refunding an unhappy customer's money might preserve a company's reputation for treating customers fairly even if the customer has no legal right to a refund. Indeed, some retailers, such as Nordstrom, differentiate themselves from their competitors by their exemplary ethics and customer service.

Learning to Communicate

To work together effectively, the lawyer and the business leader must understand the other's concerns. Unfortunately, managers and lawyers employ distinct mental models,[15] which impede their ability to leverage each other's professional expertise.

First, managers and lawyers often have different objectives that are a product of their training. Managers often focus on value creation and capture, that is, maximizing the potential upside. Lawyers usually focus on risk management, minimizing the potential downside.[16] Lawyers strive to keep their clients out of jail and out of court and are consequently more risk averse than are managers.

Managers learn to focus on identifying opportunities and analyzing risk/reward profiles and on devising strategies for executing their business plans.[17] Lawyers, for their part, study discrete areas of the law such as contracts, torts, and antitrust. Relatively few courses in law school even attempt to explore messy business problems, which usually include a combination of legal subjects and a variety of business considerations. Although several law schools now offer courses in accounting and finance, law students rarely study business strategy, and most lawyers are not skilled managers.

Second, managers and lawyers speak distinct professional dialects, further enhancing the potential for misunderstanding. To achieve legal astuteness, lawyers and managers must develop a common language.[18]

Consider Arthur Andersen's conviction for obstruction of justice after shredding boxes of documents relating to its audit of Enron Corporation. The shredding began right after one of Arthur Andersen's attorneys, Nancy Temple, sent an e-mail to the Andersen employees working on the Enron audit admonishing them to comply with Andersen's document retention policy. At trial, the Andersen partner in charge of the Enron account testified that he interpreted the e-mail as a call to start shredding documents. Temple claimed that her e-mail was misconstrued, that she was not recommending the shredding of documents.[19]

The expression "document retention policy" is a euphemism for destroying classes of documents, including documents that could later prove difficult to explain.[20] By merely parroting to the Houston employees that Andersen had such a policy, Temple failed to alert the Houston employees that destroying documents in the face of an existing or imminent governmental investigation or lawsuit is illegal.

This book strives to create a common language that will enable managers and lawyers to communicate more effectively. Just as managers should not remain hostage to their information technology experts, neither should they depend entirely on their lawyers.

Linking Law and Legal Astuteness to Competitive Strategy

In some respects, the law's impact on competition and business is akin to the role that a physical force, such as gravity, plays in determining the behavior of particles and waves in the physical world. Like gravity, law affects everything. It is pervasive and shapes the space within which bodies interact.

Law affects the internal organization of the firm,[21] including the choice of business entity and the internal relationships with employees, officers, directors, and investors. It affects the firm's resources, whether physical, human, or organizational, that have the potential of providing sustained competitive advantage.[22] Failure to implement appropriate legal measures can prevent firms from fully realizing the benefits of the other resources they control. In particular, law affects:

- The allocation of firm resources among stakeholders (for example, by allocating power between the directors and shareholders in constituency statutes), discussed in chapter 3.

- The environment in which resources are converted into products (for example, by imposing strict product liability on each firm in the chain of distribution), discussed in chapter 6.

- The marshaling of human resources (for example, by providing damages for wrongful termination and banning employment discrimination), discussed in chapter 7.

- The marshaling of physical capital (for example, by offering limited liability to investors, by offering entrepreneurs fresh starts under the bankruptcy laws, and by promoting transparency in the capital markets under the federal and state securities laws), discussed in chapter 3.

- The uniqueness of resources (for example, by providing patent and trade secret protection and by enforcing certain noncompete agreements), discussed in chapter 5.

Indeed, under the resource-based view of the firm,[23] legal astuteness may itself be a dynamic capability[24] offering competitive advantage. As Tom Hinthorne explained, "[L]awyers and corporate leaders who understand the law and the structures of power in the U.S.A. have a unique capacity to protect and enhance share-owners wealth."[25]

Forging the relationships necessary for a legally astute management team is not easy, which may explain why legal astuteness appears to be rare. It is also firm-specific and path-dependent, so is not easily transferable to rivals. There are also no strategically equivalent substitutes.

Law helps shape the firm's external relationships with customers, suppliers, competitors, and complementors, that is, players who cause customers to value another firm's products and services more.[26] It also enables managers to use properly structured contracts to better define and strengthen business relationships (discussed in chapter 4).

As we'll see, law affects each of the five forces Michael E. Porter identified as determining the attractiveness of an industry: buyer power, supplier power, the competitive threat posed by current rivals, the availability of substitutes, and the threat of new entrants.[27] There are legal aspects to each of the "generic" strategies Robert Kaplan and David Norton describe in *Strategy Maps:* (1) low total cost, characterized by "highly competitive prices combined with consistent quality, ease and speed of purchase, and excellent, though not comprehensive, product selection";[28] (2) product leadership, characterized by superior performance along dimensions such as speed, accuracy, size, or power consumption that leading-edge customers value and are willing to pay more to receive;[29] (3) complete customer solutions, characterized by long-lasting, quality relationships with customers to whom the company sells multiple, bundled products and services tailored to their needs and provides exceptional service, both before and after the sale;[30] and (4) customer lock-in, characterized by high switching costs, low prices to attract customers, and complementors with high-margin revenues from selling secondary products and services to users of the basic product.[31]

Building on the examples contained in *Strategy Maps* and elsewhere, one can generate table 1-1. Table 1-1 identifies several of the legal aspects of each strategy and indicates the chapter in this book in which it is discussed.

Law affects each activity in the value chain. Table 1-2 summarizes the types of legal issues managers should consider at every step.

Unlike gravity or other physical forces, human law is mutable; it can be changed by legislators, judges, and voters. In contrast, natural laws do not change over time. Our understanding of them may change, as when Copernicus demonstrated that the sun, not Earth, was at the center of the planets and when Newtonian physics encountered quantum mechanics and special relativity, but the underlying forces remain constant.

Furthermore, and perhaps most problematic in our discussion of business risk and reward, human laws can be violated. The violation may result in punishment, but humans may still choose to break the law. Some break laws they believe to be unjust, as when

TABLE 1-1

Legal aspects of strategy

Strategies	Legal aspects
Low total cost	Protect low-cost innovative production processes by using process patents and trade secret protection (chapter 5).
	Establish long-term relationships with excellent suppliers and distributors through contracts (chapter 4).
	Manage disputes (chapter 8).
	Reduce safety hazards to employees and communities and avoid accidents and environmental incidents by involving marketers and lawyers in product development process and operations management (chapters 6 and 7).
	Use information technology to enhance customer's buying experience but respect customer privacy and ensure integrity of customer data (chapter 6).
Product leadership	Obtain rapid regulatory approval for new offerings (chapter 2).
	Maintain excellent government relations to reduce total environmental impact (chapters 2 and 3).
	Improve product safety and employee and customer health (chapter 6).
	Obtain strong intellectual property protection (chapter 5).
	Require employee assignments of inventions and nondisclosure agreements (chapters 5 and 7).
Complete customer solutions	Gain regulatory approval for new offerings (chapter 2).
	Protect customer lists as trade secrets (chapter 5).
	Protect customer data and privacy (chapter 6).
	Restrict employees' ability to compete (chapter 7).
	Use contracts to strengthen customer relationship (chapter 4).
	Manage disputes (chapter 8).
	No illegal tying (chapter 3).
	Offer bundled products that provide greater functionality than two products bolted together (chapter 3).
	Secure intellectual property protection (especially patents, copyrights, and trade secrets) so can deny competitors the right to offer postsale service even if have market power in primary market (chapter 5).
Lock-in	Defend proprietary position (chapter 5).
	Expand use of standard in communities. Use patents, licensing agreements, or copyrights to preclude competitors from offering postsale products and services. Protect trade secrets (chapter 5).
	Enforce contracts to ensure customers, suppliers, and complementors do not deviate from proprietary standard or rules of exchange (chapter 4).
	Educate all employees about actions that can lead to litigation and government restraints (chapter 3).
	Avoid illegal bundles and potential antitrust litigation (chapter 3).

TABLE 1-2

Law's role in the value chain

Support activities		
Firm infrastructure	*Limited liability, corporate governance, choice of business entity, tax planning*	
Human resource management	*Employment contracts, at-will employment, wrongful termination, bans on discrimination, equity compensation, Fair Labor Practices Act*	
Technology development	*Intellectual property protection, nondisclosure agreements, assignments of inventions, covenants not to compete, licensing agreements*	
Procurement	*Contracts, Uniform Commercial Code, Convention on the International Sale of Goods, bankruptcy, securities regulation*	

Primary activities				
Inbound logistics	Operations	Outbound logistics	Marketing and sales	Service
• *Contracts* • *Antitrust limits on exclusive dealing contracts* • *Environmental compliance*	• *Workplace safety* • *Environmental compliance*	• *Contracts* • *Environmental compliance*	• *Contracts* • *UCC* • *CISG* • *Consumer protection laws* • *Bans on deceptive or misleading advertising or sales practices* • *Antitrust limits on vertical and horizontal market division, tying, and predatory pricing* • *Import/export* • *World Trade Organization*	• *Strict product liability* • *Warranties* • *Waivers* • *Doctrine of unconscionability*

Source: The framework (including the text in roman) is from Michael E. Porter, "How Competitive Forces Shape Strategy," in Michael E. Porter, *On Competition* (Boston: Harvard Business School Press, 1996), 77. I have added the words in italics to Porter's framework.

Rosa Parks violated the segregation laws that required African Americans to sit in the back of the bus by instead sitting up front with the whites. Others believe that they are clever enough not to get caught, as when executives from Hoffman-La Roche met with their direct competitors in the Black Forest in Germany to fix the prices for wholesale vitamins. As we'll see in chapter 3, the violation did come to light and resulted in stiff criminal penalties and civil damages.

Defenders of corporate America blamed "a few bad apples" for the massive defense procurement scandals of the 1970s and 1980s (remember the $900 hammers?), the bribery and insider trading scandals of the 1980s (remember "Greed is good"?), and the epidemic of accounting fraud and executive compensation excesses of the late 1990s—implying that these behaviors were exceptions in an otherwise compliant world. The evidence suggests, however, that a significant number of large and small firms do indeed pursue a strategy of noncompliance.

A study of criminal violations by *Fortune* 500 firms in the period between 1970 and 1980 revealed that "a surprising number of them have been involved in blatant illegalities."[32] Fifty-eight percent of the *Fortune* 500 firms engaged in criminal antitrust, 18 percent in bribery, 15 percent in illegal political contributions, 5 percent in tax evasion, and 4 percent in criminal fraud. Although some violations may be inadvertent, "a goodly number of violations are probably the result of conscious deliberation on the part of corporate executives who believe the benefits to be obtained from violating the law outweigh the costs that might accrue to themselves and the corporation. It would be naïve to think otherwise."[33]

Often such egregious behavior leads to stricter and more costly regulations for all firms, as we will see in chapter 2. And when individual violators are brought to justice, the resulting loss of value—in civil and punitive fines, criminal convictions, and even corporate bankruptcies—ultimately hurts all players. Over time, the system adapts as it reacts to successive waves of scandal, responds to stakeholders' demands for change, incorporates technological developments, and evolves to protect the public's interests.

A Systems Approach to Business Regulation

This book takes a systems approach to business regulation. That is, it recognizes the impact that law and government have on market forces,[34] the competitive environment, and the firm's resources and capabilities, but also explains how managerial actions and decisions affect the public rules and society at large. It shows how legally astute management teams can use legal tools to increase the total value created and the portion of that value captured by the firm, while managing the attendant risks and keeping legal costs under control. This system is depicted in figure 1-1.

At the center is the management team, which evaluates and pursues opportunities and manages the risk/reward ratio of the firm. Public law helps shape and affects the competitive environment,

FIGURE 1-1

A systems approach to business regulation

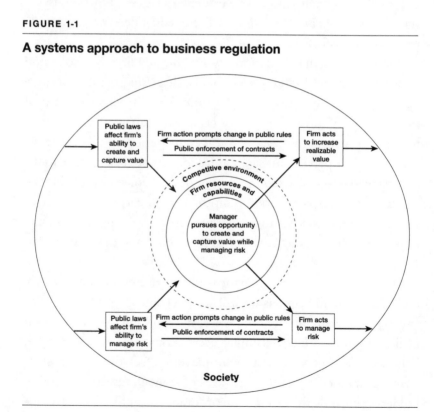

each activity in the value chain, and firm resources and capabilities. Courts enforce the private rules (so-called private law) embodied in contracts between the firm and its employees, customers, investors, suppliers, and others, as long as they do not conflict with the public policies embodied in the public law. Given the public law constraints and the firm's strategic position within the competitive environment and its resources, the legally astute management team can use a variety of legal tools to increase the firm's realizable value and to reduce risk.

The system is not static, however. Public laws change in response to corporate lobbying, firm action, especially unethical behavior or managerial misconduct, and societal pressures. In other words, instead of viewing law as just an external force acting on managers, this book views law and the tools it offers as an enabling force that legally astute management teams can help shape and direct.

The framework outlined in figure 1-1 can help managers in established businesses as well as managers in pursuit of new opportunities. Table 1-3 shows how various legal tools can support the twin objectives—creating and capturing value and managing risk—during five stages of business development:

- Evaluating the opportunity and defining the value proposition, which includes developing the business concept for exploiting the opportunity

- Assembling the team

- Raising capital

- Developing, producing and marketing the product or service

- Harvesting the opportunity, through sale of the venture, an initial public offering of stock (IPO), or reinvestment and renewal[35]

Table 1-3 does not purport to be an all-inclusive list of techniques for using the law to increase realizable value while managing risk. Rather, it is intended to suggest both the variety and the pervasive nature of the tools available.

TABLE 1-3

Legal tools for increasing realizable value while managing risk

| | | | STAGES OF BUSINESS |
MANAGERIAL OBJECTIVES	Evaluating opportunity and defining value proposition	Assembling team	Raising capital
Create and Capture Value	• Ask whether idea is patentable or otherwise protectable. • Examine branding possibilities.	• Choose appropriate form of business entity and issue equity to founders early. • Structure appropriate equity incentives for employees. • Enter into non-disclosure agreements and assignments of inventions. • Secure intellectual property protection.	• Be prepared to negotiate downside and sideways protection and upside rights for preferred stock.* • Be prepared to subject at least some founder stock to vesting. • Sell stock in exempt transaction.
Manage Risk	• Ask whether anyone else has rights to opportunity.	• Document founder arrangements and subject their shares to vesting. • Analyze any covenants not to compete or trade secret issues. • Require arbitration or mediation of disputes. • Comply with antidiscrimination laws in hiring and firing. Institute harassment policy. • Avoid wrongful termination by documenting performance issues. • Caution employees on discoverabilityof e-mail. • Provide whistleblower protection.	• Be prepared to make representations and warranties in stock purchase agreement with or without knowledge qualifiers. • Choose business entity with limited liability. • Respect corporate form to avoid piercing of corporate veil.

*These and other rights and privileges commonly accorded preferred share holders are discussed in detail in Constance E. Bagley and Craig E. Dauchy, *The Entrepreneur's Guide to Business Law,* 2d ed. (Mason, OH: West Legal Studies in Business, 2003).

Development, production, marketing, and sale of product or service	Harvest
• Implement trade secret policy. • Consider patent protection for new business processes and other inventions. • Select a strong trademark and protect it. • Register copyrights. • Enter into licensing agreements. • Create options to buy and sell. • Secure distribution rights. • Decide whether to buy or build, then enter into contracts.	• If investor, exercise demand registration rights or board control to force initial public offering or sale of company. • Rely on exemptions for sale of restricted stock. • Ask whether employee vesting accelerates on an initial public offering or sale. • Negotiate and document arrangements with underwriter or investment banker.
• Enter into purchase and sale contracts. • Impose limitations on liability and use releases. • Buy insurance for product liabilities. Recall unsafe products. • Create safe workplace. • Install compliance system. • Do due diligence before buying or leasing property to avoid environmental problems. • No tying or horizontal price fixing. Integrate products; no bolting. • Be active in finding business solutions to legal disputes. • Avoid misleading advertising. • Do tax planning. File tax returns on time and pay taxes when due.	• Be mindful of difference between letter of intent and contract of sale. • If buyer, consider entering into no-shop agreement to preclude seller from soliciting other bidders. If seller, negotiate fiduciary out to pursue right to accept a better offer and be prepared to pay a breakup fee. • Disclose fully in prospectus or acquisition agreement. Secure indemnity rights. • Perform due diligence. • Allocate risk of unknown. • Make sure board of directors is informed and disinterested. • Ban insider trading and police trades.

How This Book Is Organized

Chapter 2 outlines the key public policies underlying business regulation in the United States, including the Sarbanes-Oxley Act of 2002. It also explains the mechanisms by which managers can help shape the regulatory environment to their advantage.

Chapter 3 shows how managers can practice what I call "strategic compliance management," which goes beyond mere compliance with law to embrace organizational integrity and to seek out and exploit business opportunities provided by regulation and deregulation. A fundamental premise of this book is that compliance with law is just the baseline for winning legally. Just because something is legal does not mean that it makes good business sense to do it or that an individual of good conscience should do it. Successful managers go beyond what the law requires to ensure that the firm conducts business in an ethical manner with due regard not just to shareholders but also to other stakeholders, such as employees, customers, suppliers, the community, and the environment.

Chapter 4 identifies the web of relationships inherent in any business, which can affect both the amount of value that can be created in a given industry (the size of the pie) and the portion of the value captured by any given firm (splitting up the pie).[36] The chapter explains how managers can structure contracts to increase predictability, to define and strengthen relationships, to allocate risk and reward, to create and retain options, and to align incentives.

Chapter 5 offers another key strategic benefit of harnessing the law: the ability to use the intellectual property laws to capture the value of the firm's inventions, proprietary information, and other intangible assets. It shows managers how to use patents, copyrights, trade secrets, and trademarks both *offensively* to differentiate their products, to command premium prices, to erect barriers to entry, to maintain first-mover advantage, to generate licensing revenue, and to reduce costs, and *defensively* as bargaining chips to resolve disputes.

Chapter 6 explores ways to protect brand equity from erosion due to product defects, unfair trade practices, deceptive advertising, and invasions of customer privacy.

Chapter 7 explains how to unleash the power of human resources by treating workers fairly, addressing performance issues, adopting appropriate written policies, embracing diversity, and preventing harassment. Chapter 8 offers suggestions for dealing with business disputes, including the role top management should play in overseeing litigation and the advisability of using alternative dispute resolution mechanisms.

The book concludes with a discussion in chapter 9 of ways that managers can work more effectively with counsel to create legally astute management teams capable of crafting strategies that maximize the likelihood of creating and capturing value while managing the attendant risks and keeping legal costs under control.

2

Playing by the Rules

P UBLIC LAW—the constitutions, statutes, regulations, and judicial decisions that reflect society's definition of acceptable behavior—is essential for economic prosperity.[1] In the absence of law and order, property rights, and enforceable contracts, "few people will habitually take risks to improve on what they have."[2]

The legal system embodies the rules of the game within which managers work to create value and manage risk. It also provides a variety of tools managers can use to manage the firm more effectively. The legally astute manager embraces these rules and tools and takes pains to avoid overstepping the legal limits.

Law makes the world more *predictable* by increasing "the likelihood of things happening in the way we expect they'll happen."[3] It provides "a structure to everyday life" by defining and limiting the set of choices available.[4] At the same time, law *evolves* continuously to reflect a nation's needs, norms, and capabilities. Legally astute managers understand these underlying priorities and the mechanisms by which they change. Armed with this knowledge, they think and act proactively to help shape the legal environment within which they do business. As good corporate citizens, they recognize the importance of honoring both the letter and the spirit of the law. As strong competitors, they respect the positive economic force of a level playing field. As forward-thinking executives, they take steps to harness and shape the law. And as prudent businesspeople, they

21

manage risk by ensuring that their companies comply with the laws applicable to their business.

This chapter begins with a discussion of the dynamic nature of law and the forces that shape the rules governing business activities. It then presents a framework for understanding the public policies behind the laws regulating business in the United States in the early twenty-first century. The chapter concludes with a discussion of the manager's role in advocating responsibly for changes to the legal environment.

The Dynamic Nature of Law

There is no such thing as law with a capital "L." Laws change: Congress enacts new statutes, the courts make new law, and regulatory agencies adopt new regulations and revoke others. As society's public priorities and its notion of fairness evolve, so in turn does the law.

Changing Public Priorities

During the nineteenth and early twentieth centuries in the United States, Congress and the state legislatures focused on spurring investment for major manufacturing facilities and public works. Provisions granting bankruptcy protection and limiting liability for passive investors literally helped build the railroads and other major industries.[5]

After the stock market crash in 1929, Congress enacted the first federal statutes relating to the offer and sale of securities. Congress also created a new administrative agency, the Securities and Exchange Commission, and gave it broad power to protect investors from abuse by corporate insiders and to regulate the securities markets.

Protecting workers also became a priority during the first half of the twentieth century.[6] Employers became obligated to pay for workplace injuries and to make Social Security payments on behalf of their workers.[7] Starting in the early 1960s, the focus shifted to protecting consumers,[8] first by imposing strict liability for defective products then by enacting a flurry of consumer protection laws designed to regulate everything from the interest rate charged on loans to the flammability of nightclothes worn by children.

Although Congress had responded to incidents of rancid and contaminated foods by establishing the Food and Drug Administration in 1930, the consumer protection laws enacted in the 1960s were far more sweeping and comprehensive. They had the effect of replacing the doctrine of *caveat emptor*—buyer beware—with the doctrine of *caveat venditur*—seller beware.[9]

In the 1970s, concerns about clean air and water and the dumping of hazardous waste sparked sweeping federal and state environmental legislation designed not only to make the polluter pay but also to require those unfortunate enough to have acquired contaminated property to clean it up. Concerns about preserving the oceans and sustaining fish and other ocean life have transcended national borders as countries work together to create a new law of the sea. As more countries send objects and humans into space, international regulation of space has become more important.

Law will evolve to address new technologies, such as the Internet. As Professor Debora Spar explained in *Ruling the Waves*,[10] government influences which standards dominate and how they are developed. The Electronic Signatures in Global and National Commerce Act, adopted by Congress in 2000, gave most contracts executed electronically the same legal effect as physical paper contracts with a manual signature. The U.S. Supreme Court held that human-made living organisms were patentable, thereby spawning the biotechnology industry.[11]

Regulating Corporate Behavior

Legislatures and regulatory bodies often react to unethical conduct in violation of societal expectations by enacting new rules that are harsher than rules businesses might have been subject to if they had exercised more self-restraint. The Foreign Corrupt Practices Act, which prohibits the payment of bribes to government officials and requires accurate financial record keeping, was enacted in 1978 in response to the widespread use of corporate slush funds as bribes to obtain lucrative defense contracts and other favorable treatment from U.S. and foreign government officials.

The Sarbanes-Oxley Act of 2002,[12] the most comprehensive set of federal regulations concerning corporate governance, public company accounting, and securities fraud since the Securities Exchange Act of 1934, was a direct result of massive corporate misbehavior at the end of the twentieth century. The act:

- Mandates the composition and authority of audit committees at public companies.

- Requires corporations to disclose whether or not they have a financial expert on their audit committee.

- Prohibits the provision of nonaudit services to audit clients in all but very limited circumstances.

- Makes it illegal to attempt to influence auditors.

- Requires CEO and CFO certification of public company periodic reports.

- Mandates enhanced financial disclosures in periodic reports.

- Requires the CEO, CFO, and auditors to certify the adequacy of the firm's internal controls to facilitate accurate financial reporting and disclosure.

- Provides for enhanced Securities and Exchange Commission review of periodic reports.

- Requires additional disclosures of transactions involving directors, officers and principal stockholders.

- Prohibits many types of personal loans to executives.

- Orders that CEOs and CFOs forfeit certain bonuses and profits if their employer is required to restate its financial statements due to material noncompliance with securities laws.

- Generally prohibits insiders from trading during pension fund blackout periods.

- Requires corporations to disclose whether or not they have a code of ethics applicable to senior financial officers.

- Gives the SEC the power to prohibit "unfit" persons from serving as officers or directors of a public company.

- Increases maximum fines by tens of millions of dollars and increases maximum durations of imprisonment by as much as tenfold.

- Creates the Public Company Accounting Oversight Board (PCAOB) to regulate, inspect and adjudicate issues involving public accounting firms that provide audit reports for public companies.

Revising the Law Through the Courts

Sometimes judges, not legislators, shape the legal environment. Judges in a common law system (such as the systems of the United States and England) have the authority to interpret the constitution, the statutes enacted by the legislature, and regulations promulgated by administrative agencies and executive departments, such as the Department of Labor. They also can create new law in the course of deciding a particular case. For example, the adoption by the state of California of the doctrine of strict liability for product defects resulted not from any new statutes passed by the California legislature but from a case in which the California Supreme Court concluded that strict liability was good public policy.[13]

By contrast, in civil law countries, such as France and Germany, courts have the power to interpret existing laws but not to create new laws. Several finance scholars have suggested that the flexibility inherent in common law jurisdictions promotes economic growth.[14] Although this flexibility introduces an element of uncertainty, the judges' ability to make common law permits courts to act more quickly than legislatures to regulate innovations, such as videocassette recorders, MP3 music players, and genetically modified microorganisms.

Creating "Private" or "Manager-Made" Law

In many situations, managers can use contracts to make their own private law. By enforcing contracts, the state gives private parties the power to structure many of their relationships and to specify their respective rights and obligations to best suit their wishes and needs. U.S. courts generally enforce contracts as long as they are reasonable and consistent with public law.

Managers can also create their own governance structure by choosing a particular form of business unity and electing to organize under the laws of a particular jurisdiction. For example, the state of Delaware offers managers more flexibility and protection than the state of California.[15]

Shaping the Legal Environment

Managers can also help shape the public laws that govern the conduct of business, as we saw in the Citigroup example that opened this book. Because a regulatory change can affect an industry's structure, "a company must ask itself, 'Are there any government actions on the horizon that may influence . . . the structure of my industry? If so, what does the change do for my relative strategic position, and how can I prepare to deal with it effectively now?'"[16] Put another way, how are society's expectations for my business apt to change, and what should I do about it?

Public Policy Objectives and the Law: A Framework for the Twenty-First Century

To benefit from the law, managers need to understand its overall structure and the policy objectives that underlie it. Figure 2-1 groups the laws and regulations applicable to U.S. business in the early twenty-first century under four primary public policy objectives: promoting economic growth, protecting workers, promoting consumer welfare, and promoting public welfare.

FIGURE 2-1

Underlying rationales of U.S. public law governing business

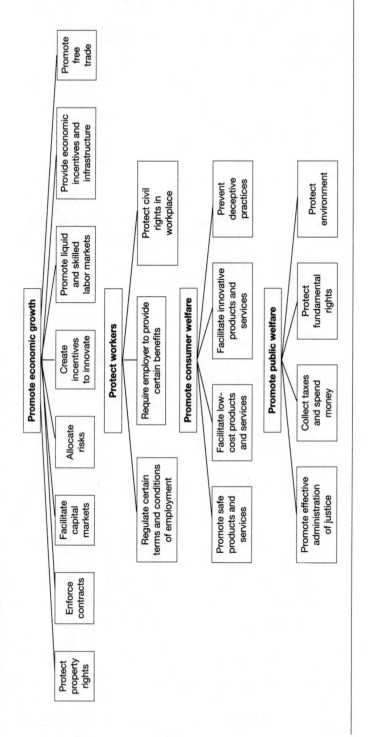

Other major economic powers tend to have laws that further the same objectives, albeit with varying degrees of emphasis on the different objectives and varying ways of furthering them.[17] Indeed, much of the current debate on what constitutes good corporate governance turns on how much weight each country gives to the interests of shareholders, debtholders, employees, customers, and suppliers and to the protection of the environment.

Managers should be mindful of these broad objectives for several reasons. First, the objectives provide a framework for understanding the multitude of local, state, and federal laws governing business. Second, if applied appropriately, the objectives enhance the firm's ability to create and protect a profitable business. Third, the objectives reflect modern society's values and expectations, which, if violated, are likely to result in more onerous regulation or even a challenge to the current economic system.[18] Finally, even if a clever lawyer is able to craft a strategy that fits within the letter of the law, the company may still be hauled before an administrative agency, the Congress, a court of law, or the court of public opinion if it engages in conduct that violates the spirit of the law.[19] As a result, managers are usually well advised to comply with both the letter and the spirit of the law.

First Broad Objective: Promote Economic Growth

The first objective is to promote economic growth. As shown in figure 2-2, this is done by protecting private property rights enforcing private agreements; facilitating the raising of capital; allocating risks; creating incentives to innovate;[20] promoting liquid and skilled labor markets; providing subsidies, tax incentives, and infrastructure; and promoting free trade in the global markets.

Protect Property Rights

Scholars have concluded that although there is no "one best way" to organize a capitalist system, "there are a few essentials, such as private property and the rule of law."[21] Economist Hernando de Soto asserts in *The Mystery of Capital* that the inability of many poorer

FIGURE 2-2

How U.S. law promotes economic growth

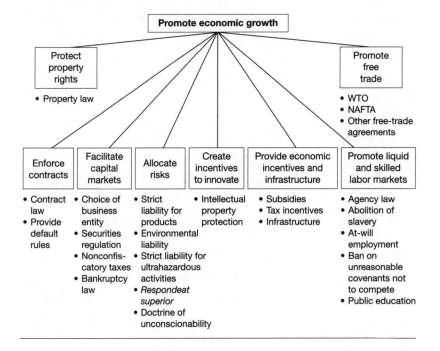

non-Western countries to produce capital for investment and growth is not attributable to a lack of assets or savings but rather to a "bad legal and administrative system"[22] that "lacks ways to represent the invisible potential that is locked up in the assets we accumulate."[23] According to de Soto, the "implicit legal infrastructure hidden deep within [the American, European, and Japanese] property systems" is the mechanism whereby assets and labor are converted into capital.[24] If ownership rights are not adequately recorded, then assets "cannot be traded outside of narrow local circles where people know and trust each other, cannot be used as collateral for a loan, and cannot be used as a share against an investment."[25]

Enforce Contracts

Although sometimes a person is willing to rely on another's word and a handshake, often managers seek more certainty in their business dealings and want the assurance of performance provided by a legally enforceable contract. Indeed, "the ability to engage in secure contracting across time and space" is a necessary condition for the creation of modern economies.[26] To facilitate the creation of contracts, state and federal laws provide a variety of default rules that apply unless the parties expressly agree to be bound by their own mutually agreed upon terms. We'll explore contracts in detail in chapter 4.

Facilitate Capital Markets

Businesses need capital to grow. Many attribute the size and success of the U.S. capital markets to the flexibility of its business formation laws, the transparency and perceived fairness of its securities markets, and the nonconfiscatory nature of the tax system.

Choice of Business Entity. Most state laws offer a variety of ways in which to organize a firm. At one extreme is a sole proprietorship: the business is owned by a single individual who has unlimited liability for the obligations of the business. At the other extreme is a corporation, managed by a board of directors and owned by shareholders who put only their invested capital at risk. The choice of business entity determines whether the investors have limited or unlimited liability. It also defines the scope of investors' rights to transfer their interests to others.

Corporate law determines when management may block a hostile takeover of the firm, even if it is in the shareholders' short-term interest. In addition, state laws, in conjunction with the federal Internal Revenue Code, determine whether the business enterprise pays taxes or "passes through" its income and losses to the tax accounts of its owners.

Securities Regulation. The federal and state securities laws prescribe what information must be disclosed to potential investors. They require securities offerings (such as stock or investment contracts) to be registered with the Securities and Exchange Commission or, alternatively, to be offered without registration if they qualify for an exemption. Companies may sell risky securities, but the risks must be fully disclosed to the potential purchasers.

As we'll see in chapter 3, the securities laws prohibit managers from lying about the business or its prospects and from telling half-truths. Corporate insiders are prohibited from trading using material nonpublic information.

Nonconfiscatory Taxes. Investors' willingness to buy securities and make other investments depends in part on the after-tax returns available. Although tax planning is beyond the scope of this book, suffice it to say that managers should never do tax planning in a vacuum.[27] A particular structure might reduce taxes but increase risk or reduce cash flow.

Bankruptcy Laws. Even if a business fails or incurs liabilities in excess of its assets, bankruptcy laws often give founders and entrepreneurs a second chance. Bankruptcy laws help preserve the going concern value of the firm by preventing the piecemeal dismemberment of a company seeking to reorganize. If reorganization is not feasible, the laws ensure an orderly liquidation. They also protect lenders by generally requiring that creditors be paid in full before assets or ownership interests may be distributed to equity holders of a bankrupt company.

The United States has perhaps the most debtor-friendly bankruptcy provisions in the world. Business historian Thomas McCraw characterized the lenient American approach to bankruptcy as "one of the hidden reasons why the American business system has tended to be more entrepreneurial than that of other countries."[28] McCraw went on to note, "Many American entrepreneurs whose names became household words, such as R. H. Macy and H. J. Heinz, suffered repeated business failures before achieving breakthrough success."[29]

Allocate Risks

The law mandates certain risk allocations while giving private parties the right to allocate others by contract.

Strict Product Liability. Everyone in the chain of distribution has strict liability for defective products, that is, liability regardless of fault. Manufacturers and other firms in the chain of distribution are deemed best equipped to bear the risk of injury caused by defective products. They can insure against it or self-insure and then pass the costs along to consumers in the form of higher prices.

The policy protects consumers against unsafe products, and it prevents manufacturers from escaping liability simply because they typically do not have a contract with the user of the product or nonusers who might be injured by the product. Imposing strict liability also gives wholesalers and retailers an incentive to select more reliable manufacturers and suppliers of components. In short, strict liability forces companies to internalize the costs of product-caused injuries.

As we'll see in chapter 6, the use of due care is not a defense to a claim of strict product liability. Nonetheless, the availability of punitive damages in egregious cases gives manufacturers an incentive to make their products safer.

Environmental Liability. The environmental laws impose liability not only on the persons responsible for operating facilities involving hazardous waste but also on the current owners and operators of properties contaminated by hazardous waste.

The Comprehensive Environmental Responsibility Compensation and Liability Act (CERCLA, or Superfund) fundamentally changed the risk/reward profile for companies buying or leasing real property. The current owner or operator is required to pay the cost of cleaning up hazardous waste on the property even if the owner was in no way responsible for its being there and, in fact, was unaware of its existence when the property was acquired.[30] CERCLA has been applied retroactively so that owners and competitors can be required to clean up sites even if the waste was handled in accordance with the laws applicable at the time of disposal. For example, the Environmental Protection Agency ordered General Electric to spend roughly $460 million to dredge the Hudson River to remove

PCBs GE had legally dumped there in the period from 1940 until the dumping was banned in the 1970s.[31]

Liability for Ultrahazardous Activities. Strict liability is also imposed in cases involving ultrahazardous activities, such as storing large quantities of flammable materials in an urban area. An activity is *ultrahazardous* if it necessarily involves a risk of serious harm to persons or property that cannot be eliminated by the exercise of utmost care *and* if it is not a matter of common usage.

Once the court determines that the activity is abnormally dangerous, it is irrelevant that the defendant observed a high standard of care. Evidence of due care would, however, prevent an award of punitive damages. Managers of companies engaged in ultrahazardous activities should ensure that a risk management officer or other person regularly reviews the firm's activities and insurance to ensure that the firm has adequate liability coverage.

Respondeat Superior. Under the doctrine of *respondeat superior*—"let the master answer"—the employer is liable for any crimes or civil wrongs (torts) committed by employees acting within the scope of their employment. Underlying the doctrine of *respondeat superior* is the policy of allocating the risk of doing business to those who stand to profit from the undertaking. Because the employer benefits from the business, it is deemed more appropriate for the employer to bear the risk of loss than for the innocent bystander. The employer is in a better position to absorb such losses or to shift them, through liability insurance or price increases, to customers and insurers and thus to the community in general.

The employer is liable even if the employee was acting contrary to company policy, as long as the employee was, at least in part, engaged in the employer's business. The employer is also liable for acts outside the scope of employment if the employer gave the employee the authority or instrumentality that made the acts possible. The employer is liable even if it had no knowledge of the wrongful acts and in no way directed them.

Doctrine of Unconscionability. Although the law generally permits parties to agree privately on their own risk allocations, courts will not enforce unconscionable agreements that allocate risk in an objectively unreasonable manner or hide onerous terms in fine print. Courts are most likely to invoke this doctrine when the parties have unequal bargaining power, as is often the case with consumer contracts.

Create Incentives to Innovate

By copyrighting or patenting their inventions or protecting their trade secrets, inventors attain the right to exclude others from making or marketing the invention for specified periods of time. This opportunity to charge monopoly prices serves as an incentive to take the risk of creating something new.[32] The ability to trademark a product enables firms to create brand equity. We will explore the protection of intellectual property in chapter 5.

Promote Liquid and Skilled Labor Markets

The law of agency makes it possible to marshal the human resources necessary to pursue business opportunities. The most common agency relationship is the employment relationship, whereby employees are agents of their employer. Agency law also makes it possible for individuals to operate in the name of an entity, such as a corporation.

The abolition of slavery in the Thirteenth Amendment to the U.S. Constitution and bans on unreasonable noncompete covenants enable workers to change jobs and to seek the employer who most highly values the employee's service. As we'll see in chapter 7, at-will employment gives employers flexibility in hiring. Public education, funded by taxes, provides the skills and training needed for competing in the knowledge economy.

Provide Subsidies, Tax Incentives, and Infrastructure

By providing subsidies and tax incentives, federal, state, and local governments seek to encourage research and development and to attract and retain businesses and thereby create jobs. Government-funded economic and physical infrastructure can also make it more attractive for a company to locate in a particular area.

Promote Free Trade

Free-trade agreements, which are normally ratified as treaties, reduce tariffs on goods sold overseas. By eliminating government-controlled or government-induced regulatory rules or practices (such as tariffs, quotas, or discriminatory practices) that distort trade flows in goods and services, these treaties seek to ensure that market outcomes reflect the real costs of goods and services and the resources used to produce them. Some countries employ protectionist measures to limit imports and shield domestic industries from foreign competition, ideally on a temporary basis, as the domestic economy shifts resources from noncompetitive sectors to those where domestic firms are more competitive. The agreements that created the World Trade Organization established an international body with the power to resolve trade disputes and impose penalties for treaty violations, while also reducing tariffs.

Second Broad Objective: Protect Workers

Worker protection constitutes a major public policy underlying U.S. business law. As depicted in figure 2-3, worker protection is accomplished by regulating certain terms and conditions of employment, requiring the employer to provide certain benefits, and protecting workers' civil rights. Complying with these requirements imposes costs on employers that society, acting through the legislature, has deemed it appropriate for employers to bear.

Regulate Certain Terms and Conditions of Employment

Minimum wage laws ensure that employees receive a fair wage. Federal and state workplace safety laws (such as the Occupational Health and Safety Act or OSHA) ensure that workers are not required to work in unduly unsafe conditions. Serious violations resulting in the death of an employee may lead to criminal prosecution of the responsible manager, and some states punish offenders

FIGURE 2-3

How U.S. law protects workers

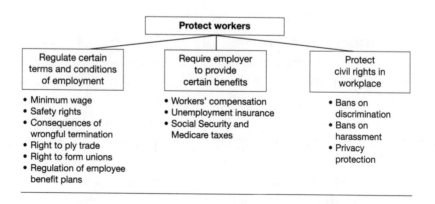

more harshly than the federal law does. Managers can also be prosecuted for crimes such as battery and reckless endangerment if they require employees to work in unsafe conditions.

Although employees in the United States can be hired at-will and thus may be terminated for any or no reason, employers are prohibited from discharging an employee for *bad* reasons, such as because the employee refused to perform an illegal act. Bans on unreasonable covenants not to compete preserve workers' ability to ply their trade, and the National Labor Relations Act gives workers the right to bargain collectively and to form unions.

Congress and the Department of Labor have promulgated extensive rules and regulations governing virtually every aspect of employee benefit plans, including pensions, profit sharing, life insurance, and medical and dental insurance, under the Employee Retirement Income Security Act (ERISA). In response to the millions of dollars Enron employees lost when their 401(k) and other pension accounts became worthless when Enron declared bankruptcy, Congress included in the Sarbanes-Oxley Act a provision making fraud in connection with an ERISA plan a federal offense punishable by up to twenty years in prison.

Require Employer to Provide Certain Benefits

Federal and state laws require employers to provide unemployment insurance and workers' compensation to cover the cost of workplace injuries regardless of fault. Some states may impose substantial fines or shut down companies that fail to properly maintain workers' compensation insurance. Employers must also pay Social Security and Medicare taxes on behalf of their employees to mitigate the costs of retirement, disability, and medical care.[33]

Protect Civil Rights in the Workplace

As discussed more fully in chapter 7, federal and state laws prohibit discrimination in hiring, firing, promotion, or any other term of employment based on race, color, religion, gender, national origin, citizenship, age, or disability. Further, they require the employer to provide a workplace free of sexual and other types of harassment and racial or religious hostility. These laws reflect a public policy in favor of making employment a viable option for as many people as possible, both to prevent a drain on public resources (such as welfare) and to enable each person to achieve his or her full potential. In addition, employers must respect employees' reasonable expectations of privacy.

Third Broad Objective: Promote Consumer Welfare

As shown in figure 2-4, business regulation is designed to protect consumers by encouraging the sale of safe and innovative products and services at a fair price.

Promote Safe Products and Services

As noted earlier, each firm in the chain of distribution has strict liability for defective products. Product safety requirements (such as Food and Drug Administration approval of new drugs and medical devices and the National Highway Traffic Safety Administration's motor vehicle safety standards) promote the sale of safe products. The law of unconscionability restricts the types of agreements that

FIGURE 2-4

How U.S. law promotes consumer welfare

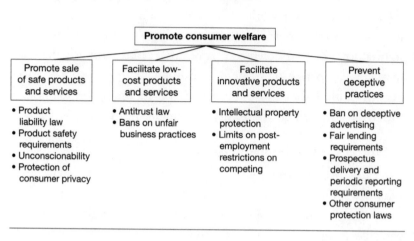

sellers can require a customer to sign as a condition of buying their product. Federal and state laws protect medical records and other sensitive confidential information.

Facilitate Low-Cost Products and Services

As discussed further in chapter 3, the antitrust laws promote competition by banning price fixing and other unreasonable restraints on trade as well as monopolization and attempts to monopolize. State law also bans unfair business practices, such as deceptive comparative advertising and raiding a competitor's workforce.

Facilitate Innovative Products and Services

Intellectual property laws spur innovation. Laws limiting an employer's right to prevent an employee from working for a competitor promote innovation by permitting employees to leave established firms to work for a start-up or another firm trying to enhance its position in a particular market. A number of scholars have attributed the explosive growth of firms and new technologies in Silicon Valley in part to Section 16600 of the California Business and Professions Code, which prohibits postemployment covenants not to compete except in connection with the sale of a business as a going concern.

Prevent Deceptive Practices

As discussed further in chapter 6, the Federal Trade Commission Act prohibits misleading or deceptive trade practices, including false advertising. The Truth-in-Lending statutes require lenders to disclose the costs of credit, and other laws regulate consumer credit, debt collection activities, and credit reporting. The Securities Act of 1933 requires the delivery of a prospectus in connection with public offerings of securities. The Securities Exchange Act of 1934 requires publicly traded companies to file periodic reports and prohibits fraud in connection with the purchase or sale of securities. A host of other consumer protection laws prohibit consumer deception and fraud and promote consumer health and safety.

Fourth Broad Objective: Promote Public Welfare

As depicted in figure 2-5, business regulation promotes public welfare by promoting the effective administration of justice, collecting taxes and spending money, protecting fundamental rights, and protecting the environment.

Promote Effective Administration of Justice

Statutes specify which conduct is criminal and prescribe the consequences of failing to meet society's expectation of what constitutes

FIGURE 2-5

How U.S. law promotes public welfare

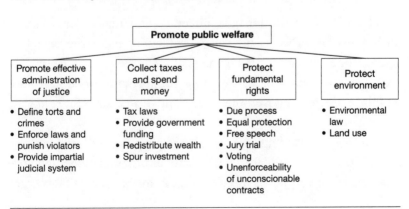

acceptable behavior. Tort law, which can be embodied in statutes or created by judges as common law, defines the duties members of society owe to each other and the interests entitled to protection from infringement by others. The state prosecutes crimes, but tort cases are civil actions brought by the injured party to obtain compensation for the wrong done. Certain types of conduct, such as battery (a harmful or offensive physical contact with the body of another individual), can give rise to both criminal prosecution and tort liability. For example, if a manager knows that serious injury or death will result if workers continue to work in a foundry with faulty venting of hazardous gasses, then the manager would be liable in a civil suit for battery and could be prosecuted in a criminal case as well.

Lifetime tenure for federal judges, rules of evidence, and laws making perjury and obstruction of justice criminal are designed to help ensure impartial judicial rulings. The Sarbanes-Oxley Act made selective destruction of documents and other evidence a federal offense even if there is no government investigation or court case pending or imminent at the time of destruction. Chapter 8 discusses document retention policies in more detail.

Collect Taxes and Spend Money

The government imposes and collects taxes to fund government spending, redistribute wealth, and spur investment. Favorable tax treatment for employee incentive stock options promotes entrepreneurship.

Protect Fundamental Rights

The U.S. Constitution guarantees certain fundamental rights, including due process and equal protection under the law; free speech; one person, one vote; and trial by a jury of one's peers. For example, some form of notice and an opportunity to be heard are required before the government can deprive a person of life, liberty, or property.

Considerations of due process also require that a defendant have certain "minimum contacts" with a state or other jurisdiction before the defendant can be required to appear in its court.[34] Significant contacts include doing business in the state, locating employees there, or owning property there. Most courts have concluded that having a Web site viewable in a particular state is not enough to confer personal jurisdiction over a defendant if the defendant sells no products and enters into no contracts in the jurisdiction.

In a decision heralded by litigation-weary business leaders, the U.S. Supreme Court ruled that excessive awards of punitive damages violate the defendant's right to due process.[35] The Court explained that, in practice, "few awards exceeding a single-digit ratio between punitive and compensatory damages" satisfy due process. Private property may not be taken for public use without just compensation. A more complex situation arises when the government does not physically take the property but imposes regulations that restrict its use. Conditions to land-use approval will be upheld if they are reasonably related to the burdens on the community created by the development being approved.

If a development will result in an influx of workers, a fee to fund traffic improvements will be upheld. On the other hand, a regulation will constitute a taking requiring just compensation if it denies the owner all economically viable use of its land. For example, although ordinary rent control statutes are generally upheld as constitutionally permissible exercises of governmental authority, a rent control regime will be struck down if it deprives the landlord of a fair rate of return.

The right to free speech extends not only to individual speech but also to commercial speech, whether in the form of advertising or images on the Internet.[36] The U.S. Constitution also prohibits federal or state governments from impairing the obligation of existing contracts. However, the courts will not enforce unconscionable contracts or those procured by fraud.

Protect the Environment

Environmental laws are designed to promote human health and welfare as well as to protect natural assets for the benefit of future generations. For example, the Clean Water Act[37] requires all industrial and municipal entities to obtain a permit from the Environmental

Protection Agency before discharging specified pollutants into a water source. The Resource Conservation and Recovery Act assigns cradle-to-grave responsibility for the storage, transport and disposal of hazardous waste.[38]

Zoning and other land use laws, which restrict commercial and residential buildings and developments, are designed to ensure not only that the structures being built are sound but also that they are aesthetically pleasing. As the U.S. Supreme Court explained:

> The concept of the public welfare is broad and inclusive. . . . The values it represents are spiritual as well as physical, aesthetic as well as monetary. It is within the power of the Legislature to determine that the community should be beautiful as well as healthy, spacious as well as clean, well-balanced as well as carefully patrolled.[39]

Under this broad reading of public welfare, regulations as varied as architectural review, rent control, limitations on condominium conversions, and restrictions on off-site advertising signs have all been upheld as being appropriate uses of a city's police power.

Overlaps and Conflicts: Predicting and Promoting Change

Sometimes a single set of laws furthers more than one objective. For instance, intellectual property laws promote both economic growth and consumer welfare by encouraging innovation. In other cases, the underlying public policy objectives may conflict with each other. For example, the antitrust laws are designed to promote competition with the objective of providing consumers better products at lower prices. In general, companies are discouraged from exploiting a monopoly position in a particular industry. Yet in some ways a patent, which denies others the right to use the invention for twenty years after the date the patent application is filed, creates a legally sanctioned type of monopoly. Thus, an ongoing debate rages over just how to reconcile the special rights granted a company by intellectual property laws with the laws banning unreasonable restraints of trade and monopolization.[40]

Similarly, there is a conflict between setting a higher minimum wage, which may improve employee well-being, and the consumer's interest in less expensive products and services. Likewise, permitting employers to restrict former employees' ability to work for competitors helps preserve the value of trade secrets and thereby promotes innovation, but it interferes with workers' ability to ply their trade. Free trade agreements may encourage exports of U.S. goods and services, but they result in lost jobs when companies outsource manufacturing and other labor-intensive work to facilities outside the United States.

Often these conflicts are resolved through the political process. A liberal candidate supported by organized labor is more likely to push for a higher minimum wage than is a conservative supported by big business who is concerned about the ability of U.S. companies to compete with firms using cheap overseas labor.

It is important for managers to be aware of these fault lines because they point to an area of instability that is susceptible to political pressure. For example, managers of drug companies need to be sensitive to the tension between granting patents to spur the discovery of new, safe and effective drugs and the public's interest in alleviating human suffering. As the pharmaceutical companies selling HIV drugs discovered, they risk having a country eliminate patent protection altogether if they are not sensitive to those human needs. Similarly, proponents of free trade need to be mindful of the plight of workers who are laid off when manufacturing is moved offshore lest the displaced workers become vocal advocates for political candidates who promise to stop the flood of "American jobs" moving offshore.

Practicing Responsible Advocacy

As with other aspects of the competitive landscape that are subject to change, managers should not passively await regulatory change. Instead, they should act responsibly to influence the legislators and

administrative agencies responsible for shaping the legal environment of business.[41] Successful lobbying requires managers to understand the laws regulating their business and industry and the policies
behind them. For example, Federal Express has been highly successful lobbying Congress to obtain favorable changes in the postal laws
that permit Federal Express to compete more effectively with the
U.S. Postal Service.

Neither Cisco Systems nor Dell Computer initially did much
lobbying at the state or federal level. Eventually, however, they both
realized the importance of proactively influencing their regulatory
environment. Both companies gained leading positions in the high-
tech sector in part because they stepped up their government affairs
activities.

At other times a particular constituency may lobby for new rights,
as happened when groups representing the disabled lobbied for legislation banning employment discrimination based on disability.
Often an industry group seeks new laws to erect barriers to entry, as
happened when the major record labels and other media companies
lobbied to include provisions in the Digital Millennium Copyright
Act of 1998 prohibiting firms from selling products that circumvent
copy-control technologies designed to prevent illegal copies of
music and movies.

Occasionally one particular company leads the charge to enact
new rules, as Walt Disney Company did when it persuaded Congress to extend the term for copyrights by twenty-five years, thereby
keeping its rights to the first Mickey Mouse film, *Steamboat Willy*,
which was released in 1928.

Sometimes socially responsible firms lobby for new regulations to
prevent unscrupulous firms from taking advantage of existing loop-
holes. For example, a firm that is committed to disposing of all its
hazardous waste in a responsible manner might lobby for tighter
environmental controls in a country where it does business so that
its responsible but more costly practices do not put it at a competitive disadvantage.

Indeed, companies spend millions of dollars on lobbyists and
campaign contributors in hopes of influencing the content of legis-

lation and the selection of the persons (from the President of the United States on) responsible for administering and enforcing the law. As Michael Watkins explains in *Winning the Influence Game: What Every Business Leader Should Know about Government*: "Both to gain a competitive advantage and to avoid harm . . . businesses must know how to influence government. . . . Because if *you* do not organize to influence the rules of the game, *others* surely will."[42] Thus, managers should never take existing law as a given. Instead, companies should look for ways to help shape the rules that govern their business.

As with any managerial action, lobbying (whether through direct contact with lawmakers, the provision of expert testimony and other information, or the payment of campaign contributions) must be conducted with due regard for the letter and spirit of the law, ethical considerations, and the social responsibility of for-profit firms to all stakeholders, including society at large. Managers should consider both the propriety of their goals and the means they employ to reach them.[43]

The joint collapse of Enron and Arthur Andersen illustrates the peril of crossing the line. Both companies and many of their peers were major campaign contributors. One of their biggest lobbying successes was derailing efforts by SEC Chairman Arthur Levitt to end the incestuous relationships between accountants and the firms they audited. These incestuous relationships led directly to the Enron/Andersen debacle and other scandals when accounting firms traded their independence for lucrative consulting work.[44] In the aftermath, many of the transgressors were punished. Unfortunately, their misconduct also burdened law-abiding firms with the costs of complying with the legislation enacted in response—the Sarbanes-Oxley Act.

Executive Summary

Every market participant has a stake in preserving the rule of law. The World Economic Forum reported in 2002 that for all 75 countries studied there was a statistically significant relationship between a country's gross domestic product (GDP) per capita—"the best single, summary means of current competitiveness available across all countries"—and each of the following:

- Judicial independence

- The adequacy of legal recourse

- Police protection of business

- Demanding product standards

- Stringent environmental regulations

- Quality laws relating to information technology

- The extent of intellectual property protection

- The effectiveness of the antitrust laws[45]

Managers who violate society's expectations face criminal prosecution and civil lawsuits and the prospect of even harsher government regulation. On the other hand, as discussed further in the next chapter, prosecutors and courts may grant leniency to companies that have effective compliance systems in place and discipline wrongdoers.

Furthermore, responsible advocacy can lead to a more level playing field for all market participants. For example, a socially responsible firm with a manufacturing plant in a country with lax environmental laws might lobby for tighter rules so that less scrupulous firms cannot attain a competitive cost advantage by dumping their waste in a nearby river instead of treating it properly. Responsible advocacy can also unleash the power of new technologies, such as voice over Internet protocol (VOIP), which the Federal Communications Commission hailed as a breakthrough technology worthy of protection from overzealous state regulators.[46]

3

Cultivating Compliance for
Strategic Strength

C OLUMBIA/HCA Healthcare Corporation, the largest for-profit
hospital company in the United States, paid $1.7 billion in civil
fines and criminal penalties after pleading guilty in 2001 to massive
Medicare fraud.[1] Its "profit-at-any-cost" culture cost top management their jobs, landed several executives in jail, and nearly destroyed the firm.

Scorecards sent out monthly by HCA headquarters rated and
ranked each hospital on nearly a dozen measures, from costs of supplies to number of surgeries—but not on quality of care.[2] It was
therefore not surprising that former employees declared that patient
care was not an HCA priority. As one employee remarked, "Columbia hospitals exist to make money—period." Another reported that
he "committed felonies every day."[3]

The scorecards set a lofty "budgeted" case mix index that meas-
ured the severity of the procedures each hospital billed to Medicare
and thus the reimbursement level. If a hospital coded its procedures
to indicate additional problems, enough to meet the index, its managers received additional compensation.

Former HCA managers testified that they faced pressure to illegally "upcode" their Medicare cases to generate far higher collec-
tions from Medicare. Some claimed that HCA headquarters set

"impossible, insane" goals for what portion of Medicare cases should carry medical "complications," which result in higher reimbursement.[4] Health-care industry analysts estimate that community hospitals typically have complications in about 40 to 60 percent of cases; large teaching hospitals with more patients who require specialized treatment might hit complication rates of 80 percent. At HCA, however, some former executives were told to try to ensure that 97 or 98 (in one case even 100) percent of their Medicare patients were coded as having complications.[5] Health-care consultants called this practice "unbelievable," and one remarked, "My first question to Columbia is: Are you asking for trouble? This is a red flag. It is saying, 'Here I am, come look at my records.'"[6]

As it turned out, federal regulators had noticed. By July 1997, HCA had become fully embroiled in the Justice Department's largest health-care fraud investigation ever. In an affidavit filed as part of a grand jury investigation, the federal government stated that the FBI and other investigative agencies had uncovered a "systemic corporate scheme perpetrated by corporate officers and managers" of HCA facilities to improperly inflate the amount of reimbursement it received each year from federal programs such as Medicare, Medicaid, and the military health-care program.[7] Witnesses cited in the affidavit testified that HCA officers made an effort to hide from federal regulators internal documents that could have disclosed fraud. They also claimed that HCA's executive in charge of internal audits told his employees to "soften" the language used in internal financial audits and to delete the word "fraud" from any reports.[8]

HCA soon realized that the federal government's wide-ranging investigation was not going away. The board ousted its top management and several HCA executives were convicted of Medicare fraud.[9] The new management team decided that Columbia's corporate culture had to be reformulated from the ground up. In October 1997, they took a substantial step in that direction by hiring attorney Alan Yuspeh to take charge of Columbia's ethics overhaul.[10]

Yuspeh had played a key role in the defense industry's efforts to rebound from the procurement scandal in the 1980s. At a time when the defense industry was under fire for billing the government $9,000 for wrenches and \$1,500 for toilet seats, Yuspeh set up a framework for defense contractors and government compliance officers to discuss how to do business properly. In this process, leading defense contractors pledged to strictly enforce their individual codes of ethics and to alert government authorities if they found evidence of impropriety.

Yuspeh quickly announced a plan to create at HCA "the finest compliance program in the country."[11] As part of the overhaul, HCA created audit teams that would be dispatched to hospitals to review the coding of patients' illnesses and generally ensure that the company did not take advantage of the "ambiguities" in Medicare rules.[12] If "playing the system" had been the strategy of the past, playing by the rules became the strategy for the future.

Compliance Is a Strategic Issue

Columbia/HCA is hardly alone in revisiting the value of compliance. In the post-Enron era, scores of surviving companies have come to recognize compliance and good governance as key to attracting the best employees, investors, customers, suppliers and other partners.

Firms whose names were stained in the most recent wave of scandals—Tyco, WorldCom, Boeing, and many others—have installed new management with the specific task of creating new cultures of compliance and risk management. Indeed, we may be experiencing an unprecedented opportunity to reinforce the rules and reestablish widespread respect for the level playing field.

To be sure, many organizations have long recognized the importance of their reputation for legal and ethical behavior. Notable examples include Johnson & Johnson and Berkshire Hathaway. But for others, legal compliance has apparently not been a strategic priority. Yet when one considers the demise of Drexel Burnham in the wake of the insider trading scandals of the 1980s, the collapse of the savings and loan industry as a result of massive fraud, the Treasury bond auction scandal that brought Salomon Brothers to its knees, not to mention the demise of Arthur Andersen and Enron, it becomes clear that strategies of noncompliance can threaten the very existence and continued viability of a firm.

In contrast, practicing strategic compliance management can be a source of competitive advantage.[13] Like trustworthiness,[14] the ability to comply with the law and conduct business in an ethical manner is a valuable internal capability that can be developed only over long periods of time. Such a capability is path dependent yet also dynamic and is not a resource that can be readily bought and sold. Because it is often not clear how to develop a culture of compliance in the short to medium term, it is difficult for competitors to replicate it. Nor are there ready substitutes.[15] In addition, failure to implement appropriate compliance measures can prevent firms from fully realizing the benefits of the other resources they control.[16]

So what can managers do to promote legal compliance as a source of strategic strength? This chapter lays out a nine-step program for strategic compliance management:

- Start with ethics and start at the top.

- Understand duties and exposure to risk.

- Implement appropriate controls and processes.

- Prevent securities fraud.

- Compete hard but fairly.

- Convert constraints into opportunities.

- Play it safe in the gray areas.

- Educate all employees and distribute written policies.

- Be prepared to deal with compliance failures.

Start with Ethics and Start at the Top

Every company should develop a code of ethics that defines the firm's "guiding values, aspirations, and patterns of thought and conduct" and "combines a concern for the law with an emphasis on managerial responsibility for ethical behavior."[17] The policy should stress the importance of honesty and integrity. Managers should require employees to sign a yearly statement stating that they have read and abided by the code of ethics.

A code of conduct is not sufficient in itself, however. It simply provides a solid foundation from which compliance values are continuously imparted to employees. Adequate supervisory and enforcement mechanisms are needed as well, particularly in the vast gray area of uncertainty. Managers at every level must embrace the policy and model its required behaviors, both professionally and in their personal lives.

It is much harder for an employee to justify unethical or illegal behavior when he or she cannot claim that the top management is also guilty of improper conduct. Employees are far more likely to steal from their employer if they see officers flying their girlfriends around in the corporate jet or tapping the corporate treasury to fund over-the-top birthday parties. After reading about Dennis Kozlowski spending more than $1 million of the Tyco International shareholders' money on his wife's forty-fifth birthday party in Sardinia, complete with "an ice sculpture of Michelangelo's David urinating vodka,"[18] one must ask, "What were they thinking? Were they even thinking?"

The code of ethics should state clearly that violations will result in sanctions, such as salary reductions, poor performance ratings, and, in extreme cases, termination of employment. And the sanctions must be enforced, no matter the stature or the earning power of the violator. If the head of sales gets away with cheating on expense reports, then employees quickly become cynical about management's professed concerns about honesty.

The board of directors and senior management must do their best to empower every employee to be ethical. Just as total quality management calls on managers to empower each employee to stop the production line if there is a quality defect, so should top management and the board of directors empower any manager or other employee to come forward without fear of retaliation if the person believes that something is not right. Warren Buffett did exactly that, after the treasury auction scandal at Salomon Brothers, when he gave managers his home phone number and told them to call him if they spotted a problem.

Creating the Code

Figure 3-1 depicts the range of approaches companies can take in defining their approach to ethics and legal compliance. It summarizes the key reasons for building a heightened sense of corporate responsibility and ethics that goes beyond the letter of the law.

Some organizations may situate themselves toward the legalistic pole and others closer to the ethical pole on the continuum shown in figure 3-1. All, however, must address the risk of "slippery slope" behavior, the ways of interpreting gray areas of the law, and the threat of legal and societal backlash when things go wrong.

Evaluating the Ethics of Specific Decisions

The decision tree in figure 3-2 provides a tool business leaders and their counsel can use as they develop a corporate code of ethics and adopt policies for employees to use when making daily decisions. To

FIGURE 3-1

Range of approaches to legal compliance

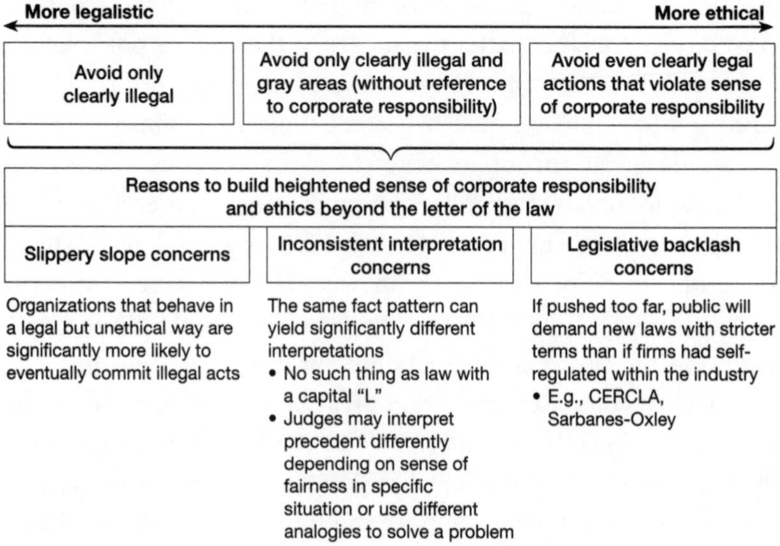

More legalistic		More ethical
Avoid only clearly illegal	Avoid only clearly illegal and gray areas (without reference to corporate responsibility)	Avoid even clearly legal actions that violate sense of corporate responsibility

Reasons to build heightened sense of corporate responsibility and ethics beyond the letter of the law		
Slippery slope concerns	Inconsistent interpretation concerns	Legislative backlash concerns
Organizations that behave in a legal but unethical way are significantly more likely to eventually commit illegal acts	The same fact pattern can yield significantly different interpretations • No such thing as law with a capital "L" • Judges may interpret precedent differently depending on sense of fairness in specific situation or use different analogies to solve a problem	If pushed too far, public will demand new laws with stricter terms than if firms had self-regulated within the industry • E.g., CERCLA, Sarbanes-Oxley

FIGURE 3-2

Ethical business leader's decision tree

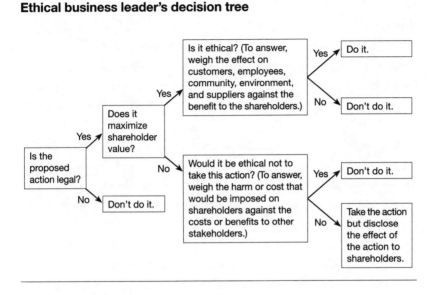

evaluate a specific business decision, first ask whether the proposed action is legal. Legality is addressed first to reinforce the notion that legal compliance is the baseline standard. If an action is not in accordance with the letter and the spirit of the law, then, regardless of the likely effect on shareholder value, the action should not be taken.

Next, the filter for shareholder value requires managers to consider early on the interests of those with ultimate authority over corporate leadership. The inquiry does not stop there, however. Even if taking a proposed action (or refraining from acting) would increase shareholder value, business leaders must still ask whether the proposed action is ethical and whether it would be unethical not to act. If the board decides to take an action that will have a material adverse effect on shareholders, then that decision and the reasons for it should be disclosed to the shareholders.[19]

Contrary to popular belief, directors are not legally required to maximize shareholder value without regard for the effect on employees, customers, suppliers, the environment, or the communities in which the corporation does business. Thus the CEO who asserted, "I have a duty to maximize value for my shareholders. I can't let my own sense of right and wrong get in the way," is just plain wrong as a matter of law. A CEO or board member may *choose* to do things in the name of the corporation that they would feel wrong doing in their personal life, but they are not legally *required* to do so. In the same way that medical ethics do not compel a physician to do something that violates his or her own personal ethics, corporate law does not require managers to check their sense of right and wrong outside the executive suite.

A myopic focus on shareholder value can not only result in the unfair treatment of nonshareholder constituencies but can even end up hurting the shareholders in the long run. As Robert Kaplan and David Norton, inventors of the Balanced Scorecard Management system, put it:

> We recognize companies' responsibilities to employees, citizens, and their communities because failure to perform adequately on regulatory and social processes puts at risk the company's ability to operate, grow and deliver future value to shareholders. Even more important, many companies believe that achieving excellence in such processes enhances long-term shareholder value.[20]

In the age of the Internet and 24/7 cable news, misdeeds in far away places are often featured on the evening news in the home country that same day. Nongovernment organizations (NGOs) and other interest groups track and report on working conditions in overseas factories, the dumping of hazardous waste and spoliation of forests and rivers, the exploitation of indigenous peoples, and the sale of shoddy and dangerous products. Maintaining a reputation for integrity and honesty is more important than ever as customers vote with their feet and boycott clothing made in sweatshops in the Mauritius Islands or gasoline made from oil transported in pipelines built with slave labor in Myanmar.

Moreover, when we call on managers and directors to check their personal ethics at the door of the executive suite or the boardroom, we desensitize the ethical trip wire that is often triggered before a person crosses the line and violates the law. A manager who becomes accustomed to disregarding his or her inner voice in the name of the shareholders is more likely to rationalize other actions to the ultimate detriment of everyone, including the shareholders.

For instance, managing earnings to meet analyst expectations may start out being rationalized as necessary to avoid undue volatility in the stock price. Over time, it may end up being used to artificially pump up the stock price so executives can exercise their stock options, then dump the stock at an artificially high price. To put it differently, if we try to make individuals' ethical systems overly plastic, they will crack or shatter, leaving the person on the slippery slope to illegality.

In many cases, it is possible to both maximize shareholder value and be a good corporate citizen. Indeed, managers should search for the "sweet spot" where their actions generate a robust return for their shareholders without exploiting others. Great business leaders formulate creative strategies that are fair to nonshareholder constituencies and still generate a handsome return to shareholders.

For example, executives often consider proposals to establish offshore manufacturing facilities in countries where environmental laws are much less stringent than they are in the United States. Executive decisions should address the possibility that the laws might later be tightened and applied retroactively, requiring costly cleanups that will adversely affect shareholder value. There may in fact be a strategic advantage to being proactive, to developing techniques to reduce the production of waste before a country imposes more costly "end-pipe" controls.[21] Managers should also weigh the cost of installing pollution control equipment against the harm that might occur if the equipment is *not* installed.

Thus, top management might feel ethically compelled to install $5 million worth of pollution control equipment in a country that does not require such equipment if a failure to do so would cause $100 million dollars worth of damage or certain loss of life or serious physical injury. If the company elects to spend a material amount of the shareholders' money for such equipment, the board should disclose its decision and the reasons for it in its periodic reports to shareholders. That way, social responsibility does not become a fig leaf for poor performance. In addition, the company should consider whether to lobby for new regulations that would level the playing field so all competitors compete on a more ethical plane.

Understand Duties and Recognize Risks

All managers need to understand their legal duties to the firm and its employees, investors, customers, and suppliers, as well as to third parties who might be injured by the firm or those acting on its behalf. At a minimum, as we noted in chapter 2, managers need to learn about the laws relevant to their business and the specific legal risks that are likely to arise. Some firms, for instance, may be more likely than others to encounter the risks of securities fraud or price-fixing.

Individuals are always liable for their own actions. Even if a manager believed that he or she was acting in the best interest of the employer, the manager is still individually responsible for his or her criminal acts. Under certain circumstances, a supervisor may also be held responsible for failure to exercise adequate supervision over lower-level employees who break the law. In such cases the crucial questions are often "How much did the manager know?" and "How much does the statute require that the manager know before he or she can be held criminally liable?"

Under the *responsible corporate officer doctrine*, a corporate officer can be convicted of a crime involving human health and safety if he or she bore a "responsible relationship" to the violation of the statute. For example, as discussed further in chapter 6, the Supreme Court upheld the criminal conviction of the CEO of Acme Markets, a national retail food chain, for distributing "adulterated" food in violation of the Food, Drug, and Cosmetic Act.[22] The court explained that the act requires executives to exercise "foresight and vigilance" and "to implement measures that will insure that violations will not occur." Although in theory a corporate officer might avoid liability by showing that he or she did everything possible to avoid the violation of law, establishing the impossibility defense is very difficult. The corporate officer must introduce evidence that he or she exercised "extraordinary care" and still could not prevent the violations of law."[23]

As noted earlier, under the doctrine of *respondeat superior*, a corporation (or other business entity) can be held liable for crimes and torts committed by employees acting within the scope of their employment even if the employee acted without the approval or even the knowledge of top management.

Negligence and the Duty to Use Reasonable Care

A person is liable to anyone injured by intentional misconduct. But a person is not liable for negligence unless there was a duty to use reasonable care. The existence of this duty often depends on the relationship between the parties, and it may change over time.

For example, historically, an employer had no liability for torts committed by employees driving their own car to or from home and their place of employment. In 1983, the Texas Supreme Court held for the first time that an employer could be held liable for injury to third parties caused by an intoxicated employee sent home by his supervisor.[24] In imposing a duty to act responsibly to protect third parties from intoxicated employees, the Texas Supreme Court explained that "changing social conditions lead constantly to the recognition of new duties. . . . [T]he courts will find a duty where, in general, reasonable men would recognize it and agree that it exists." A dissenting judge argued that in "an attempt to do justice in this one case, the majority has placed an impractical and unreasonable duty upon all employers." He also faulted the majority for eroding "the concept that an individual is responsible for his or her own actions."

Although critics lament that such decisions are turning the United States from a "country of pioneers to one of plaintiffs,"[25] managers ignore judicial developments at their peril. Legally astute managers refrain from doing anything that foreseeably will result in harm to others and instruct their subordinates to do the same. They also procure adequate insurance to protect their companies from suits not only by customers who slip on an icy sidewalk but also by trespassers who enter the property without permission.

Fiduciary Duties

Directors, officers, and most managers are *fiduciaries* with obligations that hold them to "something stricter than the morals of the market-place."[26] They have a duty of loyalty (which includes a duty to act in good faith) and a duty of care.

Avoiding Conflicts of Interest and
Conflicts with the Duty of Loyalty

The *duty of loyalty* requires fiduciaries to act in the best interests of the corporation and to refrain from putting their own interests ahead of those of the corporation. Using the corporate till as a personal piggy bank, as Adelphia Communications founder and CEO John Rigas and his son were convicted of doing, is a clear breach of this duty.

If a manager learns of a business opportunity that is in the corporation's line of business, the insider may not exploit the opportunity for personal gain.[27] Further, when a manager has a personal stake in a corporate decision or any other potential conflict of interest, the manager must fully disclose the conflict to an officer or, if the manager is an officer, to the board of directors. Any transactions in which an officer or director has a personal interest should, after full disclosure, be approved by the disinterested directors or by the shareholders. After approval, the arrangement must be subjected to ongoing scrutiny.

In an example that later proved particularly painful and embarrassing, the Enron directors approved giving the chief financial officer, Andy Fastow, an ownership stake in certain special-purpose off-balance sheet entities with which Enron traded. As a condition of their approval, they resolved that the Enron compensation committee should take into account the money Fastow received from the special-purpose entities when setting his compensation. Unfortunately, the compensation committee never did this, leaving Fastow with tens of millions of dollars from the entities in addition to his regular executive compensation package.

The Delaware Court of Chancery surprised many in 2003 when it permitted a lawsuit against the directors of the Walt Disney Company to go forward notwithstanding the provision in Disney's charter that eliminated personal liability for negligence and failures to use due care. The plaintiffs alleged that the directors had approved CEO Michael Eisner's decision to pay $140 million in no-fault severance to Michael Ovitz, Eisner's friend of twenty-five years, barely one year after Eisner had hired Ovitz for a position that Ovitz himself conceded he was unqualified to fill. The directors never reviewed the final package Eisner negotiated with Ovitz or even questioned whether Ovitz was legally entitled to receive any severance. The court stated that if the plaintiffs could prove the directors' supine acceptance of Eisner's will, then that constituted bad faith for which the directors could be held personally liable.[28]

Reaching an Informed Business Judgment and Satisfying the Duty of Care

The *duty of care* requires fiduciaries to act with the same degree of care a reasonably prudent person would use in similar circumstances. Managers should be familiar with the firm's charter documents and understand the scope of their authority to act on behalf of the company. Managers should also identify and make sure they understand the contracts relevant to their area of responsibility, as discussed in detail in chapter 4.

The duty of care requires fiduciaries to be informed: they may not blindly rely on what they are told by other managers or even by experts.[29] To illustrate, in one case a Goldman Sachs partner told the directors of SCM that an option being given Merrill Lynch to buy two of SCM's divisions was priced at fair market value.[30] The directors never asked why the two divisions—which they knew contributed two-thirds of SCM's total earnings—were being sold for less than one-half of the total purchase price for all of SCM. Had they asked, they would have learned that the Goldman partner had not actually calculated fair value and was talking off the cuff. The U.S. Court of Appeals for the Second Circuit ruled that the directors were derelict in exercising their duty of care. Similarly, the SEC has cautioned directors that they cannot blindly accept assurances from company counsel that certain information may be excluded from a proxy statement or other SEC filing.[31]

In deciding whether a board of directors has satisfied its duty of care, courts usually defer to the directors' business judgment. Under the *business judgment rule*, as long as the directors have no personal interest in the decision at hand and inform themselves before acting, courts presume that they acted in good faith and in the honest belief that their decisions were in the best interests of the corporation. This presumption can be rebutted only by showing that the directors engaged in willful misconduct, acted in bad faith, or were grossly negligent.[32]

The duty of care includes a duty of oversight. Directors are required to ensure that adequate internal policies and procedures are in place to prevent and immediately correct violations of law.[33] Failure to put these mechanisms in place or to monitor them to ensure that they are effective can make the directors personally liable for the illegal activities of managers and others acting on behalf of the corporation.

Implement Appropriate Internal Controls and Processes

All companies should institute effective internal controls and implement appropriate processes to reinforce the code of ethics and ensure compliance with law. A detailed discussion of internal controls is beyond the scope of this book. Readers are encouraged to read *Levers of Control*, Harvard Business School professor Robert Simons's excellent book on the subject.[34] This section illustrates several of the key components of an effective compliance program.

Institute Good Corporate Governance Practices

Companies should have in place a system of corporate governance featuring several critical elements: a board comprising primarily independent and informed directors, independent and conscientious internal and external auditors, and honest and forthright in-house counsel.

Lavish executive compensation and perks not only drain the corporate treasury and dilute the shareholders, but perhaps even more important, they can lead the recipients to believe that they really are worth 500 times more than the average worker. This belief in turn can breed a sense of entitlement, a belief that they are special, that the rules that apply to mere mortals don't apply to them.

This is just one of the reasons why separating the role of CEO and chair of the board or at least appointing a lead director is so important.[35] We all need to feel accountable to a higher authority. The appointment of a nonexecutive chair or a lead director, coupled with regular meetings of the independent directors, is critical to the independent directors' ability to function effectively as a counterweight to management.

Self restraint is key. Consider Dick Grasso's fall from grace as head of the New York Stock Exchange after he negotiated a pay package worth more than $100 million, or consider the public outrage at Jack Welch's retirement package from General Electric. Contrast either case with Thomas Watson Jr.'s decision to surrender some of his IBM stock options because he felt that the rise in the value of the IBM stock price had caused his compensation package to be unduly rich.

Ideally, the general counsel should report to the board of directors to ensure a clear line of communications. Managers should do their best to hire lawyers who will not succumb to pressure from division managers to approve an action that counsel believes may violate a criminal statute. Just as the audit committee meets privately with the internal and external auditors, so too should it meet with the general counsel.

Design a Compliance Program to Fit the Business Risk Profile

Every manager has a role to play in creating a corporate culture that respects the rule of law. Firms should have a comprehensive program in place to ensure compliance with the applicable laws and regulations. The audit committee of the board should usually have overall oversight responsibility.

Although organizations are generally liable for the criminal actions of their employees and agents, the existence of a meaningful voluntary-compliance program is a mitigating factor that will reduce otherwise applicable fines under the Federal Sentencing Guidelines for Organizations. For a compliance program to be effective, the company must do the following:

- Adopt standards and procedures to reduce criminal conduct. A viable code of conduct tailored to the legal risks of the company is a good starting point.

- Appoint high-level personnel to take charge of program. A designated compliance officer should oversee the program and report directly to the audit committee of the board of directors.

- Exercise due care in delegating authority. The fox can't guard the hen house—for example, the person authorized to write the checks should not be responsible for reconciling the bank statements.

- Engage in effective communication and training. A well-designed video can help ensure ongoing training about the standards. There are also good interactive online training tools available.

- Adopt mechanisms for monitoring and reporting criminal misconduct. Whistleblowers should be protected through the use of ombudspersons, anonymous hot lines, and access to internal counsel.

- Enforce standards consistently. Investigate and discipline all employees in a uniform manner regardless of their rank or history of generating profits for the firm. Days before the merger of Texaco and Chevron, Texaco fired a manager for cheating on his expense reports, causing him to lose two years worth of severance pay. Although Texaco's management could have just let the incident slide, the chief compliance officer made the decision to fire to preserve Texaco's culture of compliance.[36]

- Establish procedures for feedback and correction. If there is a compliance failure, the compliance officer should investigate its causes; identify the flaws in the compliance system that permitted it to happen; and then correct them to prevent the same problems from arising in the future. It is also prudent to hire an outside firm to audit the compliance program and to suggest ways to strengthen it.

Top management should resist the temptation to settle for "the appearance of a compliant reputation."[37] As Richard S. Gruner warns: "Compliance programs that are treated by management as a sham tend to encourage cynicism by employees. Such cynicism, in turn, tends to cause employees to pay less attention to legal requirements and to be more willing to commit offenses."[38]

Create Proper Incentives

The design of performance measures and incentive systems requires particular care. Criminal misconduct within a corporation is often a function of performance measures and goal setting that induces people to do what they should not do. Even if a company adopts all the compliance "bells and whistles," the result will not be a more law-compliant and ethical work force if managers send out conflicting— "wink and nod"—signals to employees that reward performance at all costs. Inappropriate incentives were a key factor in Columbia/HCA Healthcare's fall from grace and in the automobile repair scandal that rocked Sears when authorities discovered that the Sears mechanics were charging customers for unnecessary repairs to meet sales targets. Indeed, 70 percent of the employees who responded to a 2000 KMPG survey attributed employee misconduct to pressure to meet schedules, and 65 percent blamed pressure to hit unrealistic earnings goals.[39]

Perform Due Diligence to Uncover Potential Liabilities

Before acquiring property or stock, the manager in charge of the deal should ensure that there has been adequate due diligence. Because the environmental laws impose liability not only on the persons responsible for operating facilities involving hazardous waste but also on the current owners and operators of such properties, adequate

environmental due diligence is particularly important. It is also critical to understand the possible product liability and tax risk associated with an acquisition.

Benchmark to Expose Potential Trouble Spots

By benchmarking product liability claims, worker injuries, customer
complaints, consumption of water and other natural resources, and
releases of carbon dioxide and other waste, managers can more readily address potential trouble spots.[40] Outside evaluations of the firm's
risk exposure and its compliance programs can identify areas for
improvement.

Prevent Securities Fraud

Securities fraud undermines investor confidence, makes it more difficult and expensive for honest businesses to raise capital, and spawns
even more onerous government regulation. This is particularly the
case when investors feel that insiders are profiting at their expense.
As the U.S. Supreme Court warned, no one "would knowingly roll
the dice in a crooked crap game."[41]

It also taints the reputation of the firms involved, drives away
clients, and destroys shareholder value. Boston's Putnam Investments saw its long-term mutual fund assets fall by $13 billion in
November 2003, a 9 percent decline, after institutional investors
withdrew their capital in the wake of civil charges that Putnam illegally permitted hedge funds and other favored clients to market time
investments in their funds and thereby profit at the expense of individual fund participants.[42]

Cendant paid $3.19 billion in 2000 to settle securities fraud cases
against it arising out of its fraudulent financial reporting. The market cap of the firm dropped $14 billion in one day after the fraud
came to light.[43]

Most managers who end up committing securities fraud do not
wake up one morning and decide to risk imprisonment by breaking
the law. As Martin L. Grass, the founder and former CEO of Rite-

Aid Corporation, testified before being sentenced to eight years in prison for accounting fraud, "In early 1999, when things started to go wrong financially, I did some things to try to hide that fact. Those things were wrong. They were illegal. I did not do it to line my own pockets."[44]

It starts small. Perhaps there is a shortfall in orders that will cause the company to miss analysts' quarterly earnings estimates. The stock price will get hammered and the company may lose its best engineers if their stock options are underwater. So the VP of marketing persuades a customer to accept an early shipment of goods not needed until the next quarter. The manager robs Peter to pay Paul, assuming that he or she can make up the shortfall the next quarter. But the economy takes a downturn and orders are down again. So this time the manager ships product to an independent warehouse and invoices a nonexistent customer. Before you know it, the company is doing what computer disk drive maker Miniscribe did: shipping boxes filled with bricks instead of disk drives to nonexistent customers. Admonish your employees: "Don't start down that slope. It's not worth it."

Ignorance of these laws is no excuse. As the U.S. Court of Appeals for the Seventh Circuit put it: "No one with half a brain can offer 'an opportunity to invest in our company' without knowing that there is a regulatory jungle out there."[45]

Disclose Fully and Carefully

Investors are entitled to full and accurate disclosure. As Linda Chatham Thomsen, deputy director of enforcement for the Securities and Exchange Commission, cautioned executives in the wake of the 2004 indictment of Kenneth L. Lay, former chair and CEO of Enron, on charges that he deceived Enron's accountants, investors, and employees in the months preceding the company's collapse into bankruptcy in 2001, "It is our sincere hope that others who might someday be tempted to dissemble the investing public—and improperly place their personal interests ahead of those of their shareholders—will be deterred by the specter of a determined and multifaceted prosecution."[46]

Before making any statement about a company's performance or plans, the corporate representative should ascertain the facts. The SEC took the position that a corporation committed fraud when an officer denied the existence of merger negotiations, when, unknown to that officer, merger negotiations were under way. To prevent this from happening, each public company should designate the people (such as the CEO, the CFO, and the head of investor relations) authorized to comment on market rumors and ensure that they are kept apprised of all material developments. In addition, these individuals and their staff must be schooled concerning their duties to speak and to correct or update prior statements.

Managers should not make any statement about the firm or its business unless they in good faith believe the statement to be true. For example, a prediction about the future can be a misstatement if the person making the prediction either does not believe it at the time or has no reasonable basis for believing it.[47]

Any financial projections or other types of forward-looking information should be accompanied by a discussion of the underlying assumptions as well as a statement making it clear that the information is forward-looking and that actual results may vary. The company should also discuss the factors that could cause the actual results to differ from those projected.

Again, the tone is set at the top. As Federal Reserve Board chairman Alan Greenspan testified in July 2002, "It has been my experience on numerous corporate boards that CEOs who insist that their auditors render objective accounts get them, and CEOs who discourage corner-cutting by subordinates are rarely exposed to it."[48]

No Selective Disclosure

Managers of public companies cannot disclose material information to only certain favored analysts or shareholders. Regulation Fair Disclosure (FD) prohibits *selective disclosure*, whereby issuers of publicly traded securities disclose material nonpublic information, such as advance warnings of earning results, to securities analysts or selected institutional investors before making full disclosure of the same information to the general public. Selective disclosure can also result in liability for insider trading.

The SEC has cautioned that an officer who engages in a private discussion with an analyst seeking guidance about earnings estimates "takes on a high degree of risk under Regulation FD."[49] On the other hand, an issuer is not prohibited from disclosing a nonmaterial piece of information to an analyst, even if, unknown to the issuer, the piece of information helps the analyst complete a "mosaic" of information that, taken together, is material.

Ban Insider Trading

Every public *and* private company should also prohibit insider trading.[50] In a textbook example of insider trading, ImClone founder and CEO Samuel Waksal told his daughter to sell 40,000 shares of ImClone stock after he learned that the Food and Drug Administration had rejected ImClone's application for its promising new cancer drug Erbitux but before the rejection was made public. Judge Pauley ignored Dr. Waksal's pleas for leniency, stating that Dr. Waksal had "abused [his] position of trust as chief executive officer of a major corporation and undermined the public's confidence in the integrity of the financial markets," then shown "a complete disregard for the firm administration of justice" when he "tried to lie [his] way out of it."[51]

A manager should carefully guard the information given in confidence by his or her employer or client. Managers must also instill these values in their subordinates. Everyone, from the person who empties the trash or runs the copy machine to the person who occupies the largest office in the executive suite, must be told to follow these rules or risk dismissal. This edict should be made clear in the corporation's code of ethics and in its personnel manual. Companies without adequate procedures in place to prevent illegal insider trading face potential liability for their insiders' illegal trades.

No Tipping

Insiders may not give tips to others in exchange for money or even just to enhance their reputation as "someone in the know." For example, if the controller tells her tennis partner that her employer will be announcing quarterly earnings that were below analyst expectations and the tennis partner trades before the earnings are announced, then the controller has committed a violation and can be held liable for up to three times the gain realized by the tennis partner or the loss avoided. This is the case even if the controller does not receive any of the proceeds from the trade by her partner. Tippees—persons who receive information from a corporate insider—may also be subject to liability if they know or should have known that the tipper's disclosure of the confidential information constituted a fiduciary breach.[52]

No Misappropriation

The insider-trading policy should make it clear that a person can be found guilty of illegal insider trading even if he or she has no relationship with or duty to the company whose securities are being traded or to the person from whom the securities were bought or sold. Under the *misappropriation theory*, any person who breaches a duty of trust or confidence to the source of nonpublic information by trading on the information is guilty of illegal insider trading.

For example, the U.S. Supreme Court upheld the conviction of attorney James O'Hagan, who had purchased Pillsbury Company stock and options prior to the public announcement of a tender offer for Pillsbury's stock by Grand Met PLC.[53] O'Hagan possessed material nonpublic information about Grand Met's intentions, which he had obtained as a partner of the law firm representing Grand Met in connection with its acquisition of Pillsbury. Although O'Hagan owed no fiduciary duty to Pillsbury or the Pillsbury shareholders from whom he acquired the Pillsbury stock and options, he did have a fiduciary obligation to Grand Met, which he violated when he secretly bought Pillsbury securities.

Preclear Trades and Encourage Insiders to Adopt Written Trading Plans

In most cases, corporate insiders decide to sell shares of their employer's stock not to take advantage of inside information but to diversify their holdings, to buy a house, or to send a child to private school or college. Public companies should require managers with access to material nonpublic information to preclear their trades with the general counsel or another designated person and to file any required ownership reports with the Securities and Exchange Commission in a timely manner. They should also be encouraged to adopt written trading plans declaring their long-term intentions in advance.

The SEC has created a safe harbor whereby insiders can plan their trades at a time when they are not aware of any material nonpublic information (such as shortly after the filing of the annual report on Form 10-K), then have them executed later without putting themselves or their employer at risk.[54] A trade is not considered to be based on material nonpublic information if the person trading can demonstrate that all three of the following conditions were true before the person became aware of the information:

- He or she entered into a binding contract to purchase or sell, gave instructions for the trade, or adopted a written plan to trade.

- The contract, instruction, or plan specified the amount of securities to be traded and the price, included a written formula or algorithm for determining the amount and price, or did not permit the person to exercise any subsequent influence over how, when, and whether to trade.

- The trade was pursuant to the contract, instruction, or plan.

Although the rule does not require trading instructions to be in writing, it is prudent to memorialize them in writing and to certify their date with a notary seal or other reliable date-stamping device. Martha Stewart claimed that her broker sold her ImClone shares based on a standing order to sell if the stock price dropped below $60 per share, but because that order was not in writing, she had no clear evidence to rebut the government's charges that she instructed her broker to sell the shares only after hearing that ImClone founder Sam Waksal was selling a big block of shares.

Figure 3-3 provides a decision tree for analyzing potential liability for insider trading. Although the law in this area is evolving and is

FIGURE 3-3

Decision tree analysis of insider trading laws

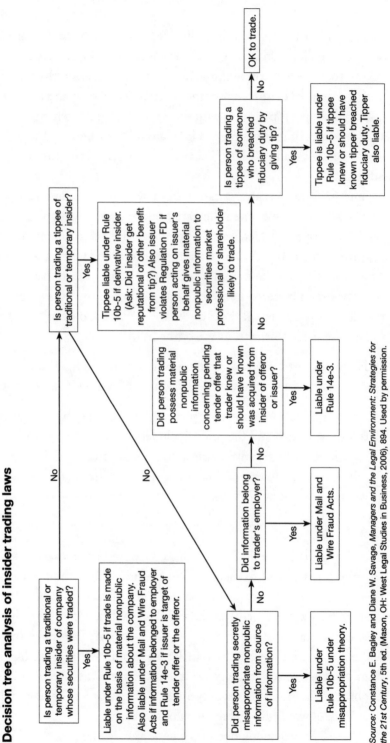

Source: Constance E. Bagley and Diane W. Savage, *Managers and the Legal Environment: Strategies for the 21st Century,* 5th ed. (Mason, OH: West Legal Studies in Business, 2006), 894. Used by permission.

not applied formulaically, figure 3-3 highlights some of the clear danger areas.

Compete Hard but Fairly

Meeting in the Black Forest in Germany to ensure secrecy, executives from six wholesale vitamin manufacturers, based in Switzerland, Germany, France and Japan, agreed to replace cutthroat competition with a gentlemen's agreement on price. They met quarterly to exchange information about pricing, sales volume, and market share on a country, regional, and worldwide basis, then they gathered annually to set a "budget" for global sales volumes and pricing for the following year.[55]

They agreed on the dates on which price increases would be announced and on the firms to announce them. The group was intentionally kept small and only trusted participants were invited to join. The plan seemed foolproof—the budget spreadsheets disguised the identity of the coconspirators, and the executives were careful not to be seen together in public. The participants destroyed (or thought that they had destroyed) all documents immediately after the meetings.

Unknown to the Swiss, German, and Japanese participants, one of the firms, Rhône-Poulenc SA of France, had gotten wind of a U.S. government investigation of wholesale vitamin prices. Rhône-Poulenc decided to take advantage of the U.S. Justice Department's long-standing leniency policy, which offers full criminal immunity to a firm that reports illegal conduct at a very early stage in the investigation, and ratted out the other firms in exchange for a promise of no criminal prosecution. In 1999, the five erstwhile partners in crime (Hoffman-La Roche of Switzerland, BASF AG of Germany, and Eisai Company, Daiichi Pharmaceuticals Company, and Takeda Chemical Industries of Japan) paid $862 million in U.S. fines, with Hoffman-La Roche alone paying $500 million. In November 2001, the European Union imposed record fines of 855.2 million euros against the same companies.[56]

High-ranking Swiss and German officers at Hoffman-La Roche and BASF were sentenced to prison and fined a total of $625,000.

The five companies, together with Rhône-Poulenc (which was not prosecuted because it provided key evidence against the other members of the cartel), agreed in November 1999 to pay $1.05 billion to settle the private class-action litigation brought in federal court on behalf of direct purchasers of vitamins and vitamin premix.[57] They paid an additional $335 million to settle lawsuits brought on behalf of indirect purchasers.[58]

No Horizontal Price-Fixing or Market Division

Every company has a stake in maintaining the integrity of the competitive markets.

Both price-fixing and market division by firms competing at the same level of distribution are flat-out illegal. In legal parlance, they are illegal per se. Such arrangements are prohibited even if they are intended to enable small competitors to compete with larger firms.[59] Employees should be cautioned: "Don't do it. Chances are you will get caught."

Experts have found that the danger of horizontal price-fixing is heightened in industries with overcapacity, undifferentiated products, large, price-sensitive customers, frequent job-order pricing, and frequent contact among competitors. Price-fixing also tends to occur in companies with a collusive culture, high rewards for profits, decentralized pricing decisions, widespread trade association participation, reactive legal staff, and loose, general ethical rules.[60]

Many of the industry characteristics are beyond an individual firm's control, but top management can manage the corporate culture by projecting "consistent and sincere company commitment" to compliance, backed up with a specific code of conduct, an appropriate evaluation and reward system, internal audits and policing, and proactive legal education[61]—in short, by using all the techniques presented in this chapter.

Competitors may have legitimate reasons to meet—to set industry standards, for example—but managers working for direct competitors should never meet to discuss their products, prices, sales practices, customers, or suppliers without first consulting an experienced antitrust attorney. If a manager attending a trade show hears competitors discussing price or other terms of sale, the manager should leave the room. When possible, he or she should exit in a manner that is memorable, for example, by spilling a drink on the way out. The highly visible departure might protect the manager and the firm should a case of collusion surface later on. It is also prudent to inform the general counsel's office of the incident.

No Minimum Resale Price Maintenance

Manufacturers of premium or luxury goods often seek to preserve the perceived value of the brand by charging a higher price than that charged by their competitors. Although a manufacturer can legally *suggest* a retail price, it is illegal for a manufacturer to *require* a distributor or retailer to agree to charge a *minimum* price. For example, if a manufacturer agrees to sell its designer jeans to a retail store only if the store agrees to charge the manufacturer's suggested retail price, then both parties have violated the ban on unreasonable restraints on trade.

In contrast, vertical *maximum* price-fixing, whereby a manufacturer sets a maximum sale price, perhaps to prevent price gouging in times of shortage, is not illegal per se, but it may be upheld under the rule of reason if the advantages to consumers outweigh the disadvantages.[62] According to the U.S. Supreme Court, low prices "benefit consumers regardless of how those prices are set, and so long as they are above predatory levels, they do not threaten competition."[63]

Only Reasonable Nonprice Restraints on Members of the Supply Chain

Often manufacturers try to strengthen the ability of their distributors to compete against other brands by imposing vertical nonprice restrictions, such as exclusive distributorships, territorial or customer restrictions, location clauses, areas of primary responsibility, and the like. These vertical restraints are upheld under the rule of reason if the net advantages to consumers outweigh the disadvantages. On the other hand, any arrangement that has a substantial net anticompetitive effect is deemed an unreasonable restraint of trade and hence is unlawful.

The marketer should always ask whether there is a valid business justification for the restraint. For example, major automobile manufacturers use geographic restraints to promote better customer service by preventing nearby distributors from free-riding on the full-service distributor's sales staff by selling cars at a cheaper price to customers who took advantage of the full-service distributor's facilities when deciding which car to buy.

In general, the shorter the time duration of a restraint, the more likely it is to pass muster. For example, it is easier for an automobile manufacturer to defend a contract to buy all its tires from one supplier for one year than it would be to defend a three-year deal. When at all in doubt, the marketer should consult experienced antitrust counsel before proceeding.

No Unlawful Monopolization

Attaining a monopoly as a result of superior business foresight, skill, or acumen is perfectly legal. In the words of Judge Learned Hand, "The successful competitor, having been urged to compete, must not be turned upon when he wins."[64] Using lawfully obtained patents, copyrights, or trade secrets to erect barriers to entry is also legal. However, engaging in exclusionary or anticompetitive conduct that has no business justification other than driving competitors out of business or eliminating consumer choice is not legal. Anticompetitive acts include predatory prices, the allocation of markets and territories, some refusals to deal, price-fixing, fraudulently obtaining a patent, and engaging in sham litigation against a competitor.

Firms must be particularly careful of what they say and how they say it when they have a substantial share of the market. Intel Corporation began training its executives and sales staff in antitrust law compliance back in 1987. When the company was later sued by the FTC, its compliance program allowed it to avoid large exposure and receive only minor sanctions. As of 2000, Intel included antitrust training as part of its annual sales conference.[65]

In contrast, Microsoft Corporation e-mails that called for "cutting off Netscape's air supply" and "knifing the baby," coupled with certain exclusionary conduct, helped demonstrate its monopolistic intent. Microsoft narrowly avoided a court-ordered break-up and has paid billions to settle government and private lawsuits for illegal anticompetitive behavior.[66]

No Illegal Bundling

Marketers often find it advantageous to bundle products together. For example, Microsoft has a practice of incorporating various new functionalities, such as its Internet Explorer Web browser and its media player software, in its dominant Windows operating system. Bundling (or, in legal parlance, tying) of separate products is generally permitted as long as the seller of the bundle does not have market power in any of the bundled products.

Products are physically tied when a consumer cannot buy one product without buying the other. For example, if a firm with market power in cameras bundled its cameras with its own brand of film in a single box, then that would be an illegal physical tie.

Charging a price for a bundle of separate products that is significantly less than the cost of the individual products in the bundle may constitute an illegal economic tie. For example, if a company with market power in word processing software sold the software with a spreadsheet program at a combined price less than the cost of buying the two types of software separately, then the bundle could be attacked as an economic tie. Consumers who buy the bundle because they want the word processing software cannot justify the extra cost of buying another brand of spreadsheet program, even if they prefer it to the bundled program.

Keep the Competitive Juices Flowing
Without Crossing the Line

Antitrust compliance is definitely not an armchair sport. Regular consultation with experienced counsel is essential, especially for managers of firms with significant market share, who must always remind employees that some forms of conduct that are legal for firms without market power constitute unlawful monopolization when engaged in by major industry players.

Of course, no company, regardless of its market position, can afford to lose its edge in today's highly competitive global marketplace. Former CEO of IBM Lou Gerstner blames IBM's thirteen-year antitrust battle with the U.S. Justice Department and the specter it raised of a federally mandated breakup for draining "the fighting spirit . . . from the company gene pool."[67] While the suit was going on, "terms like 'market,' 'marketplace,' 'market share,' 'competitor,' 'competition,' 'dominate,' 'lead,' 'win,' and 'beat' were systematically excised from written materials and banned at internal meetings."[68]

Bill Gates defended Microsoft's hard-hitting practices as being necessary to keep Microsoft from becoming another IBM.[69] On the other hand, being taught by their lawyers not to use the term "leverage" in memos or e-mail messages hardly seems to have crushed Intel's fighting spirit. The key is to make it clear to employees that they can compete hard but their conduct must be fair.

Actions that don't seem fair usually are not. Before engaging in any exclusionary conduct, managers should ask themselves whether there is a valid business justification for it. If there is not, then the manager in charge should not proceed without first obtaining the advice of experienced antitrust counsel.

Short-term gains through unethical or illegal behavior are almost always outweighed by longer-term losses, particularly in the area of antitrust with its treble-damages awards and prison sentences. Even if a manager believes that the benefits of violating the antitrust laws will exceed the likely penalties,[70] top management and the board of directors have the legal responsibility to reject this type of reasoning and require compliance with law.[71] Indeed, experts have concluded, "The most critical factor in preventing collusion is that managements unambiguously foster the kind of professional pride that is repulsed by any form of illegal profits."[72]

Convert Constraints into Opportunities

While U.S. auto makers fought early efforts by the Environmental Protection Agency to impose gasoline-mileage standards, their Japanese competitors worked with regulators to devise workable standards for reducing pollution and turned their ability to build more energy-efficient automobiles into a source of competitive advantage.[73] Similarly, a bank that viewed the requirements of the Community Reinvestment Act as an opportunity to do more for the community successfully developed creative, innovative, and profitable products to appeal to theretofore underserved lower-income customers.[74] Vonage, a voice-over-Internet protocol telephony firm, used the regulatory power of the Federal Communications Commission to avoid a patchwork quilt of onerous state regulations. Finally, PepsiCo responded to Food and Drug Administration regulations requiring trans fat labeling commencing in 2006 by voluntarily removing trans fats from many of its Frito Lay products in 2004, then used the absence of trans fats in its potato chips and other snacks as a marketing edge.

Managers who take a proactive approach to regulation are more likely to convert constraints into opportunities. By considering the underlying public policies behind various forms of business regulation and treating compliance as an investment, not an expense, legally astute managers are more likely to discover innovative ways to change their products or processes in ways that not only ensure compliance with law but also provide greater value for customers.

Play It Safe in the Gray Areas

Experienced managers understand that they will frequently be called on to make business decisions in the face of legal uncertainty. A manager may need an attorney to explain the options, but unless the attorney advises that an action is illegal, the manager, not the attorney, should decide whether the benefits of the deal outweigh the risk.

Figure 3-4 presents a framework managers can use to evaluate legal and business risk and reward before acting.

In the course of developing a business plan, legally astute managers consider the legality and propriety of the proposed course of action. If the course of action is neither illegal nor unethical, then the manager should take the following action:

- Identify and assess the likely effect of the proposed action on others.

- Ask whether there would be strict liability for any harm caused.

- Consider the nature of the relationship between the persons likely to be affected by the action (fiduciary or third party acting at arm's length, employer/employee, or principal/agent).

- Determine what standard of care applies.

- Ask whether the action would satisfy this standard of care.

Next the manager should consider what could go wrong and evaluate the potential defenses and the likely sanctions by asking the following questions:

- Would the preventative measures taken satisfy the duty of care?

- Are there any other legitimate defenses?

- What would the legal, financial, reputational, and other consequences be if the firm or the manager were convicted of a crime or found liable for a civil wrong?

- Would the sanctions and consequences vary by jurisdiction or depending on other procedural matters, such as the choice of applicable law?

Managers should explore any possible risk mitigation strategies. If it is possible to take steps to mitigate the risks without incurring undue cost (in time, money, reputation, or opportunity), then it is usually prudent to take the steps. If it is not possible to mitigate the risks of the proposed action, then the manager should reevaluate the

FIGURE 3-4

Prospective evaluation of risk and reward

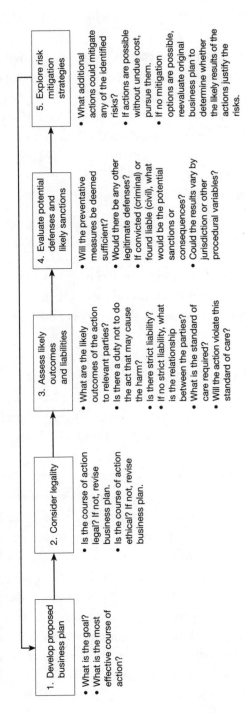

1. Develop proposed business plan
- What is the goal?
- What is the most effective course of action?

2. Consider legality
- Is the course of action legal? If not, revise business plan.
- Is the course of action ethical? If not, revise business plan.

3. Assess likely outcomes and liabilities
- What are the likely outcomes of the action to relevant parties?
- Is there a duty not to do the act that may cause the harm?
- Is there strict liability?
- If no strict liability, what is the relationship between the parties?
- What is the standard of care required?
- Will the action violate this standard of care?

4. Evaluate potential defenses and likely sanctions
- Will the preventative measures be deemed sufficient?
- Would there be any other legitimate defenses?
- If convicted (criminal) or found liable (civil), what would be the potential sanctions or consequences?
- Could the results vary by jurisdiction or other procedural variables?

5. Explore risk mitigation strategies
- What additional actions could mitigate any of the identified risks?
- If actions are possible without undue cost, pursue them.
- If no mitigation options are possible, reevaluate original business plan to determine whether the likely results of the actions justify the risks.

original business plan and decide whether the likely results outweigh the risks.

Managers should not engage in red-flag activities, such as self-dealing, having conversations with competitors concerning price or other terms of sale, repurchasing stock at a premium, or issuing options at a discount, without first consulting with counsel. Because courts continue to expand the types of situations in which companies are legally required to use due care to avoid harming others, legally astute managers take reasonable steps to protect others from fore-seeable harm even if there is no current legal duty to do so.

Educate All Employees and Distribute Written Policies

Managers should work with counsel to ensure that employees under-stand the laws and regulations that affect them. Exhorting employees to be ethical is not enough. An employee convicted of price-fixing explained:

> I thought I had morals. I still think I do. I didn't understand the laws . . . not morals. What might to me be an ethical prac-tice might have been interpreted differently by a legal scholar. The golden rule might be consistent with both views.[75]

For example, antitrust compliance is often not on the human resources staff's radar screen. As a result, marketers need to work with counsel to develop continuing education programs to alert cor-porate employees to potential antitrust problems. The training should clearly identify the activities or conditions that most often trigger antitrust liability, such as discussions with competitors, dis-cussions with buyers about their future prices, and activities that may increase concentration in any market that is already highly concen-trated. Managers should caution employees, especially sales reps, that any unauthorized communications by a company's employees with competitors regarding price or terms of sale or any direct involvement in such activities may subject the individual employee to disciplinary action, including termination of employment. Sales representatives and other employees should be encouraged, through an appropriate reward system, to inform the marketing manager or legal staff whenever any of the above "red flags" appear.

Unfortunately, marketers often do not involve the lawyers until there is a problem. Even when a company offers legal training, the lawyers often meet only with top-level managers on the assumption that they will spread the word throughout the organization. But "the word rarely reaches the people in an organization who are the most vulnerable and who need to hear it most."[76]

In contrast, one of the few companies that was not convicted in a price-fixing scandal that implicated more than 75 percent of the folding-box industry had directed its education program to the "danger line of the organization."[77] Its attorneys met one-on-one with several hundred point-of-sales representatives and grilled them about their expense reports and other files.

The legal staff also conducted a simulated grand jury inquiry at the general manager and vice president level, during which the president of the company was called as a witness to defend his actions in light of certain mock documents prepared by his vice presidents. The president of the company described the mock trial as "one of the most important ways we've sought to keep the organization sensitive to legal issues."[78] He went on to say, "We've had attorneys giving their fire and brimstone talks to large groups for 10 to 15 years, and we have simply concluded that isn't strong enough medicine for this ailment."[79]

Managers should caution employees to avoid using inflammatory language, especially in e-mail messages, which are fully discoverable in an investigation or lawsuit. It may sound like just semantics, but there is a big difference between saying, "We want to kill the competition" and saying, "We want to create such a great product that everyone will want to buy it."[80]

As discussed more fully in chapter 7, every company should develop and distribute written policies banning harassment and other employee misconduct. Every company should also promulgate a policy on the creation and destruction of documents (see chapter 8). Managers should use appropriate training tools to ensure that employees understand the discoverability of documents, including e-mail, and the absolute prohibition on the destruction of documents in the face of a lawsuit or government investigation.

Be Prepared to Deal with Compliance Failures

Even companies with the best of compliance programs and the most committed management team may find themselves subject to a governmental investigation or a criminal probe. They are what Max Bazerman and Michael Watkins call "predictable surprises."[81] The first thing a manager should do after becoming aware that an investigation is imminent or ongoing is to consult an experienced criminal lawyer who specializes in white-collar crime. Ideally, the company's general counsel should have previously identified qualified criminal lawyers to represent the company.

If a manager is personally under suspicion or was in any way involved in the activity under scrutiny, then the manager should hire his or her own personal counsel and refrain from speaking with company counsel until he or she has first discussed the matter with personal counsel. As explained in chapter 9, company counsel's client is the company, not any individual officer, director, or employee. As a result, the company may elect to waive attorney-client privilege and disclose to prosecutors or other third parties any communications between company counsel and company employees or directors.

It is important to instruct employees not to lie. When in doubt, they should invoke the privilege against self-incrimination. Lying to a government investigator is obstruction of justice and punishable by up to twenty years in prison. It is often far easier to prove that a person lied than that their actions were otherwise criminal.

As discussed earlier, most courts hold that a corporation or other employer can be held criminally liable for crimes committed by an employee acting within the scope of employment even if the employee acted contrary to a corporate policy or express instructions.[82] Nonetheless, in an exercise of its prosecutorial discretion, the U.S. Justice Department has indicated that it will not prosecute a corporation for criminal acts committed by its employees if the following criteria are met:

- The acts were not committed at the instruction or with the knowledge of the board of directors or members of top management.

- The company had an effective compliance program in place and diligently tried to prevent the criminal behavior.

- The company consistently reports the criminal misconduct of its employees to the authorities.

- The company cooperates fully in the investigation and prosecution of the individuals involved.[83]

Even if the company is prosecuted, the Federal Sentencing Guidelines offer companies reduced fines when they cooperate with the authorities and discipline wrongdoers.

Consider the case of Darling International, Inc., an animal feed manufacturer accused of polluting the Blue Earth River in Minnesota.[84] Under financial pressure in 1990–1991, the company boosted production, thereby overloading its manufacturing plant's wastewater system. Beginning in the autumn of 1991, the company began illegally dumping millions of gallons of contaminated water, which killed aquatic life in the river. By the spring of 1992, the wastewater system manager, on orders from the plant manager, began diluting wastewater test samples with tap water to try to fool pollution-control authorities. When the authorities found illegal pollution levels in the river, Darling International blamed it on a one-time spill.

The federal government began a grand jury investigation in 1993. But that investigation languished until Darling International began its own internal investigation in 1996. Under pressure from company counsel conducting this investigation, the wastewater system manager confessed to the entire dumping and cover-up scheme.

Unknown to the wastewater system manager, Darling International passed this information directly to the government prosecutor. The company also submitted the manager's name along with the names of three other employees whom the company intended to fire and hold responsible for the scheme. The four Darling International employees maintained that they were not the only ones aware of the company's illegal dumping.

The U.S. attorney prosecuting the case indicated that Darling International's disclosure provided the first corroboration of serious crimes and pushed the investigation "light-years ahead." He thought the outcome was fair because Darling International paid a significant fine and four individuals were held responsible for their actions. Not surprisingly, the four employees, who lost their jobs and faced criminal charges, had a different perspective. In their view, Darling International got "to pay their measly fine and wash their hands of the rest of us." Indeed, the employees who cooperated with the investigation bore the brunt of the punishment.

Although it may be appropriate to let a true "rogue" employee (such as Barings's Nick Leeson) take the rap, William S. Laufer describes "the dark side of the incentives fueling both prosecutorial and sentencing guidelines."[85] According to Laufer, corporate scapegoating raises fundamental questions of fairness. It is most likely to result in "self-deception, denial of responsibility, and lack of repentance" when top management is complicit or middle management tacitly encourages employees to engage in wrongdoing in spite of a comprehensive compliance program; when senior executives and managers condone the commission of the offense or consciously disregard knowledge of the illegality; when the person being blamed is far subordinate to those cooperating with the government; and when the firm "purchases" the trappings of compliance to impress regulators.[86]

Again, fairness and ethical behavior start at the top. Fairness concerns are minimized when the firm's leadership is committed to organizational integrity.[87]

Executive Summary

Table 3-1 summarizes the nine key steps managers can take to ensure compliance with the law, to reduce exposure to legal liability, and to more prudently manage legal and business risk.

TABLE 3-1

Nine-step program for strategic compliance management

Step 1: Start with ethics and start at the top.

- Institute comprehensive ethics program.
- Set tone at the top.

Step 2: Understand duties and recognize risks.

- Learn all the relevant laws to avoid torts and crimes.
- Appreciate responsibility for own acts and possible vicarious liability for acts of employees.
- Use due care to avoid harming others.
- Know terms of charter and relevant contracts.
- Fulfill fiduciary duties and duties of loyalty and care.

Step 3: Implement appropriate controls and processes.

- Implement effective internal controls.
- Institute good corporate governance practices.
- Design a compliance program to fit the business risk profile.
- Create proper incentives.
- Perform due diligence to uncover potential liabilities.
- Benchmark to expose potential trouble spots.

Step 4: Prevent securities fraud.

- Disclose fully and carefully.
- No selective disclosure.
- Ban insider trading.
- Preclear trades and encourage insiders to adopt written trading plans.

Step 5: Compete hard but fairly.

- No horizontal price-fixing or market division.
- No minimum resale price maintenance.
- Only reasonable nonprice restraints on members of supply chain.
- No unlawful monopolization.
- No illegal bundling.
- Keep the competitive juices flowing without crossing the line.

Step 6: Look for opportunities to convert constraints into opportunities.

- Consider what changes in business practices or operations might not only ensure compliance with the law but also reduce costs or increase product value to consumer at the same time.
- Treat compliance efforts as investments, not costs.

Step 7: Play it safe.

- Evaluate risk/reward in advance and eliminate unnecessary risk.
- Don't engage in red-flag activities without first consulting with counsel.
- If there is even an appearance of self-interest, excuse self from relevant decisions.
- Act reasonably to protect others from harm.

(continued)

TABLE 3-1 (*continued*)

Nine-step program for strategic compliance management

Step 8: Educate all employees and distribute written policies.

- Institute outgoing employee education.
- Distribute policies on insider trading, harassment, discrimination, document retention, and the like.

Step 9: Be prepared to deal with compliance failures.

- Deal with compliance failures promptly.
- Learn from mistakes.

4

Using Contracts to Define and
Strengthen Relationships

I N 1985, JOHN SCULLY, the CEO of Apple Computer, signed a
four-page agreement that gave Microsoft Corporation the right
to use "the visual displays in Windows 1.0 and the named applications programs [which embodied certain aspects of the Macintosh
graphical user interface, or GUI] in current and future software
products"[1] in exchange for Microsoft's agreement to write applications software for the Mac. The Mac GUI used overlapping windows, pull-down menus that could be manipulated with a mouse
rather than typed computer commands, and other novel technologies that made it much easier for less experienced users to operate a
computer. When Microsoft released Windows 2.03, which more
closely resembled the "look and feel" of the Macintosh GUI than
Windows 1.0, Apple sued Microsoft for infringing its copyrights on
the Mac GUI. Microsoft asserted that the 1985 agreement entitled
it to use any and all of the aspects of the Mac GUI embodied in
Windows 1.0 in all future versions of its operating system. Apple
countered that the 1985 agreement was only "a license of the interface of Windows Version 1.0 as a whole, not a license of broken out
'elements' which Microsoft could use to create a different interface,
more similar to that of the Macintosh."[2]

The term "visual display" was not defined in the agreement, and the court declined to give it "a specific, technical meaning."[3] The court reasoned, "Had it been the parties' intent to limit the license to the Windows 1.0 interface, they would have known how to say so."[4]

Of the 189 aspects of the Mac GUI that Apple claimed Microsoft had infringed, the court concluded that 179 were covered by the 1985 agreement. Aside from Apple's use of a trash can for deleted files, the court ultimately concluded that none of the remaining aspects of the Mac GUI was protectible under the copyright laws. Imagine what the relative market caps of Apple Computer and Microsoft might be today if the 1985 agreement had clearly limited the scope of Microsoft's license.

This was not the first time Bill Gates succeeded in negotiating highly favorable contract terms. When IBM first approached Gates in 1980 to write an operating system for the personal computer IBM was designing, Gates negotiated a contract that allowed Microsoft to retain the rights to MS-DOS. In the words of a prominent software executive, "I.B.M. thought they had Gates by the balls. He's just a hacker, they thought. A harmless nerd. What they actually had by the balls was an organism which has been bred for the accumulation of great power and maximum profit, the child of a lawyer, who knew the language of contracts and who just ripped those I.B.M. guys apart."[5]

The purpose of this chapter is to set forth a savvier, more forward-thinking approach to contracts that current and future business leaders can use to define and strengthen business relationships. Relationships are fundamental to every business. Even a sole proprietor without employees develops relationships with customers, suppliers, and competitors in the course of buying and selling goods and services. Indeed, one of the primary functions of management is to initiate, develop, organize, and maintain relationships that provide an enterprise with valuable resources, market access, and growth opportunities. These relationships can affect both the total amount of value that can be created in a given industry (the size of the pie) and the share of industry value that any given firm can capture (splitting up the pie).[6] Legally astute managers can use properly negotiated and structured contracts to define and strengthen business relationships, to build and allocate value, and to manage risk.[7]

For example, ten years before McDonald's opened its first restaurant in Moscow, it began working with Russia's most capable potato and beef farmers to transfer the know-how required to produce and store consistently high-quality potatoes and beef. By entering into exclusive supply contracts, McDonald's kept its newly improved suppliers from selling potatoes or beef to Burger King and other competitors.[8]

This chapter introduces the elements required to form a binding contract and the restrictions on entering into certain contractual relationships. Given the importance of ensuring that contracts accurately reflect the parties' intentions, the chapter provides practical insights and suggestions for negotiating and drafting effective contracts. It explains how managers can use contracts to define and strengthen business relationships; increase predictability; allocate the risks and rewards of business relationships; create and preserve options; and help parties work cooperatively to increase total economic value. Finally, it discusses how managers can protect themselves when contractual relationships go wrong.

Elements of a Valid Contract

A contract is the legal instrument most often chosen to define and govern the parties' rights and obligations.[9] By requiring a breaching party to pay damages calculated to give the nonbreaching party the benefit of the bargain, contract law encourages parties to honor their agreements.[10]

Not every promise is enforceable in a court of law. Formation of a valid contract requires four basic elements. First, there must be an agreement between the parties formed by an offer and acceptance. Second, the parties' promises must be supported by something of value, known as consideration. Consideration can be money, an object, a promise to do something one is not already legally required to do, a service, or relinquishing the right to do something one is otherwise legally entitled to do. Third, both parties must have the capacity to enter into a contract. For example, minors do not have the capacity to enter into contracts except for necessaries, such as food and shelter. Fourth, the contract must have a legal purpose.

Who Has Contracting Authority?

An employer is bound by a contract entered into by an employee with the actual or apparent authority to enter into it. An employee has actual authority when the employer expressly or implicitly authorizes the employee to enter into the contract.

Even if an employee does not have actual authority, he or she can still bind the employer if the employer engages in conduct (such as leaving the employee alone or giving the employee the title "manager") that would reasonably lead a third party to believe that the employee has authority. This is known as apparent authority. Some companies post signs or insert language into their documents stating that no employee other than a duly authorized officer of the company has the authority to modify the company's standard purchase orders or other contracts.

Anyone entering into a written or oral contract on behalf of a corporation or other business entity should always make clear the capacity in which he or she is acting. Otherwise, the person signing will be personally liable for performance of the agreement.

When in Rome

Whenever managers negotiate cross-border transactions, they should consult counsel who have experience with the laws of each country involved. Because legal duties can vary significantly from country to country, cross-border contracts should include a provision stating which country's law will apply (a choice-of-law provision) and in which jurisdiction a dispute must be brought (a choice-of-forum provision). The United Nations Convention on the International Sale of Goods (CISG) governs most contracts for the sale of goods between buyers and sellers from more than one country, unless the parties expressly agree not to follow the CISG rules. Managers should keep in mind that CISG has an overriding requirement that merchants act in good faith, which would, for example, preclude a buyer from refusing to accept goods delivered late if the delay in fact caused the buyer no harm.

International contracts often call for the arbitration of disputes. To encourage both parties to resolve any disputes amicably and out of court, contracts sometimes provide that any litigation or arbitration will occur in the country of the party who did not file the lawsuit or commence the arbitration proceedings.

Legally Permissible Relationships or Dangerous Liaisons?

Before entering into a relationship, managers should first consider whether it is legally permissible to do so and whether the law imposes any constraints on the relationship. For example, two direct competitors faced with cutthroat competition might prefer to mutually agree to divide up the market by customer category or geographic region or to agree on the minimum prices that they will charge. Yet, as Michael D. Andreas, the former executive vice president of Archer Daniels Midland, learned when he was fined $350,000 and sentenced to three years in prison for his role in fixing prices for citric acid and lysine, horizontal price-fixing is a clear violation of the antitrust laws.

Courts will not enforce contracts with an illegal purpose, such as a promise to pay a bribe. Courts will also not enforce unconscionable contracts, contracts that are so oppressive or fundamentally unfair as to shock the conscience of the court. This concept is applied most often to consumer contracts when the consumer may have little or no bargaining power.

In addition, courts will not enforce contracts purporting to waive certain rights. These include the right to file bankruptcy, the right of a nonexempt employee to be paid the minimum wage and overtime, and the right of an employee to receive workers' compensation or damages for a violation of the employment discrimination laws.

Certain government agencies may exercise an administrative prerogative to reclassify relationships in accord with public policy. For example, an employer and a worker might agree that the worker will be an independent contractor who will pay all of his or her own income and Social Security taxes and be ineligible to participate in employee benefit plans. Nonetheless, if the Internal Revenue Service or a court recharacterizes the relationship as one of employer/employee, then the employer is obligated to pay its share of the worker's Social Security taxes, to withhold income taxes from the worker's paycheck, and to provide the worker benefits under the employer's pension, stock purchase, or other employee plans.

Microsoft Corporation and the "temporary workers" it hired to do software programming and prepare documentation had agreed in writing that their relationship was one of independent contractor to employer. Nonetheless, the Internal Revenue Service required Microsoft to pay the workers' share of Social Security and unemployment taxes and to withhold their income taxes.[11] In addition, Microsoft ended up paying roughly $100 million to compensate the workers for the value they lost by not being able to participate in the Microsoft employee plans.

Many states require licenses for the conduct of particular kinds of business, ranging from real estate and securities broker licenses to chauffeur licenses and contractor licenses. If a party fails to have a required license, then the other party does not have to pay for the work even if the unlicensed party performed the work perfectly and the other party knew that the person doing the work was unlicensed. It is therefore important for managers to check with counsel to ensure that their employer holds whatever valid licenses are required.

Contracts Can Help Define and Strengthen Business Relationships

The process of negotiating a contract can help the parties get to know each other better, clarify their objectives and expectations, and thereby strengthen their relationship. Although some argue that contracting can signal distrust and encourage opportunistic behavior,[12] researchers have found that "clearly articulated contractual terms, remedies and processes of dispute resolution" can complement trust-building behavior, such as flexibility, bilateralism, and repeated exchanges.[13]

If negotiated and structured properly, formal contracts can illuminate common objectives and avert potential disputes. They are not necessarily a sign of mistrust. As one lawyer put it, "I am sick of being told, 'we can trust old Max,' when the problem is not one of honesty but one of reaching an agreement that both sides understand."[14]

On the other hand, if poorly managed, the process of reducing an agreement to writing can create mistrust or generate ill will. Danny Ertel of Vantage Partners cautions negotiators to avoid focusing on just closing the deal without regard for how the deal will be implemented: "To be successful, negotiators must recognize that signing a contract is just the beginning of the process of creating value."[15]

Real business issues should be identified early, and the business parties should meet promptly to "discuss them in as amicable a manner as possible."[16] Negotiators should avoid surprising the other side in public with potentially damaging or explosive information.

Rather than using the tactic of surprise or information asymmetries to try to get the other side to commit to something they might not commit to otherwise, negotiators should seek realistic commitments and ask tough questions about each party's ability to deliver.[17] It is important to remember that the goal is to create value by crafting a workable deal, not to position the company for a lawsuit.

Lawyers should be told to resist the temptation to include redundant or unnecessary language from other deals. Instead, they should insist on only provisions that are truly necessary for their client.[18] To do so effectively, the lawyers and managers need to work together so that the drafting attorney understands the company's business objectives.

The parties negotiating a contract should make every effort to be as clear as possible about their expectations. Slipping in a provision the manager knows would be unacceptable to the other side if it were pointed out is simply an invitation for a lawsuit. Instead of phrasing provisions that are unlikely to be well received in complicated jargon and burying them in lengthy drafts circulated to the entire working group, managers should instruct their lawyers to explain the provisions in understandable terms to the counterparty and their counsel and attempt to reach an agreement before circulating the drafts to the entire working group.[19] It is far preferable to hash out any ambiguities at the negotiation stage while the parties are on good terms and in the mood to make a deal. Positions tend to polarize once the agreement is signed and a dispute arises.

Similarly, it is inappropriate to bury offensive terms in a pre-printed form contract in the hope that the other party will not spot them. Courts sometimes refuse to enforce such terms, especially when they appear in consumer contracts, conflict with the position taken in the negotiations, or are contrary to the spirit of the deal.

HP Services has successfully negotiated a number of larger out-sourcing contracts. According to Steve Huhm, HP Services' vice president of strategic outsourcing, "Negotiating these kinds of deals requires being honest, open, and credible. Integrity is critical to our credibility."[20]

When negotiating a complex transaction, such as an acquisition, managers often find it helpful to have their counsel meet to resolve as many issues as possible while maintaining a list of open items. Periodically, the managers with decision-making authority then meet with their counsel present to go over the open items. After resolving whatever issues they can, the decision makers then meet separately with their lawyers and return to the bargaining table with a package offer that resolves the open items. This process provides a way for parties to trade issues that may be less important to them for issues that they value more. It also helps prevent the other side from using "salami tactics," which involve asking for a series of concessions with the suggestion that each concession is all that's needed to close the deal.

Meeting of the Minds and Mistakes of Fact and Judgment

Contracts require the parties to have a meeting of the minds, that is, to genuinely assent to the terms. If the terms of a contract are subject to differing interpretations, some courts construe the ambiguity against the party who drafted the agreement. More often, courts apply the following rule: The party who would be adversely affected by a particular interpretation can void, or undo, a contract when (1) both interpretations are reasonable and (2) the parties either both knew or both did not know of the different interpretations. If only one party knew or had reason to know of the other's interpretation, the court finds for the party who did not know or did not have reason to know of the difference.

A *mistake of fact* can result in a determination that there was no meeting of the minds and therefore no valid contract. In a case involving Mark Suwyn, an executive vice president of International Paper Company (the world's largest paper company), a federal court refused to enjoin Suwyn from joining Louisiana-Pacific, a producer of wood products.[21] Suwyn had signed a broad covenant not to compete with International Paper after allegedly being assured by International Paper's chairman and chief executive officer John Georges that the covenant was aimed at preventing Suwyn from going to one of the big paper companies. Suwyn had attached to the signed agreement a note indicating that it was meant to prevent him from joining a major paper company such as Georgia-Pacific, Champion, or Weyerhauser. Because Louisiana-Pacific did not make paper and was not on the list, Suwyn argued that he was free to join the company. Georges responded that the noncompete agreement was broad and included wood products, such as plywood and lumber, which both companies produced. The judge ruled that Suwyn and Georges had such different meanings in mind that there had been no real agreement on the noncompete pact. As a result, there was no contract.

It is important for managers to do their best to promptly correct any misunderstanding about contract language or fact. If too much time passes before the other party is notified, undoing the contract might create more problems than letting it stand.

Parties cannot invalidate a deal just because the manager negotiating the transaction made an erroneous assessment about the value or some other characteristic of the deal—a *mistake of judgment*. As long as both parties were talking about the same item and acting at arm's length, the fact that one party had superior knowledge that caused him or her to value it differently does not usually result in an invalid agreement.

To illustrate, CTA Inc. entered into a contract to provide technical support services to the government. The CTA bid had included labor rates for its workers that were substantially lower than the market rates. After CTA was awarded the contract, it claimed that it had made a mistake of fact in preparing the numbers for the labor rates. The court rejected this argument after finding that CTA had made an error in business judgment, not a mistake of fact.[22]

The lesson here is clear. Before submitting a contract bid or signing a contract, managers need to review the document carefully and should not expect a court to correct any mistakes.

On the other hand, if a deal looks too good to be true, if one party is paying or receiving much more than they would have expected, then the manager negotiating the deal should ask whether both parties are seeing the same thing. Otherwise, the contract may be little more than a ticket to a lawsuit in which the disadvantaged party argues that there was no meeting of the minds because of a mistake of fact.

Don't Dissemble and Don't Omit Critical Facts

Relationships built on lies or half-truths are unlikely to endure. Contracts that purport to shore up those relationships often collapse when the truth comes to light.

Managers should remind their employees, especially employees involved in sales, that any contract tainted with fraud can be voided by the defrauded party. Fraud usually involves a misstatement of fact—a lie. Under certain circumstances, however, a fraud claim can be based on an omission, a failure to speak when under a duty to do so. If there is a fiduciary relationship between the parties, that is, a relationship of trust and confidence, then the fiduciary must not only refrain from lying but must also fully disclose all relevant facts to the other party. For example, if an officer of a corporation sought board approval for a personal purchase of undeveloped land owned by the corporation, then the officer would be liable for fraud if he or she failed to tell the board that oil had just been discovered on the adjacent property. Similarly, a partner who knows that a building contains asbestos cannot sell it to a fellow partner without disclosing the asbestos.

Occasionally a court imposes a duty to disclose on parties acting at arm's length. For example, American Film Technologies convinced Brass and other plaintiffs to buy warrants that could be used to acquire common stock, but the company failed to reveal that the underlying stock was restricted and could not be freely traded for a period of two years. On discovering the omission, the plaintiffs sued for fraud. Because AFT had superior knowledge about the restrictions on its securities, the court held that AFT had a duty to reveal the restrictions. Its failure to do so amounted to fraudulent concealment.[23]

Over time, courts and state legislatures have expanded the instances where disclosure is required. A duty to disclose is more likely to be imposed when there is inequality of bargaining power and unequal access to information. For example, in 1965, the New Jersey Supreme Court adopted a rule requiring commercial builders of houses to disclose to potential buyers any structural or other defects in the houses.[24] In 1995, the same court went a step further and required a commercial builder to disclose that a house was built near property that had previously been used as a toxic waste dump.[25] The court justified the extension as being necessary to meet society's growing expectations of good faith and disclosure. Even if disclosure is not legally required, it is usually good business practice.

Don't Make Promises You Can't Keep

Managers should never make promises they do not intend to keep. Any person who makes a promise knowing that he or she does not intend to keep it can be held liable for promissory fraud, giving the other party the right to compensatory and even punitive damages. For example, the U.S. Supreme Court ruled that a company committed securities fraud when it promised to grant stock options knowing that it had no intention of honoring the promise.[26]

Managers should also be careful what they promise during the course of negotiations. If a manager makes promises on which the other party reasonably and foreseeably relies to his or her detriment, then even if the negotiations do not ripen into a contract, a court may invoke the doctrine of promissory estoppel to require the promisor to pay the promisee reliance damages, the out-of-pocket costs the promisee incurred as a result of relying on the promise.

Act in Good Faith and Deal Fairly with Others

Every contract contains an implied covenant of good faith and fair dealing that prohibits any party from doing anything that will deprive another party of the benefits of the bargain. If a manager is pursuing a course of action that would either embarrass the manager or the company if it became public or feel inappropriate if the manager were dealing with a friend or relative, then there's a good chance that the manager is violating this implied covenant.

Claims that a party has complied with the literal terms of the contract may not be sufficient to satisfy the duty of good faith and fair dealing. For example, Walt Disney Company entered into an agreement with Marsu B.V. regarding a cartoon character, Marsupilami, owned by Marsu. Under the terms of the agreement, Disney was to create half-hour animated films to show on television and to coordinate a merchandising campaign to create broad exposure for Marsupilami. Although Disney did some merchandising, the company used junior employees on the project and failed to coordinate the merchandising campaign with the television broadcast. A memo written by a Disney executive introduced as evidence of the company's attitude toward the campaign stated, "[W]e have neither the time nor the resources to do Marsu right" and "[W]e have lots of other Disney priorities, more important both financially and strategically." The appeals court affirmed the district court's determination that Disney breached the implied covenant of good faith and fair dealing.[27]

As a general matter, managers should not agree to use "best efforts" to do something because courts construe such a provision as a promise to do anything within the person's power, regardless of cost or inconvenience, to cause the event to occur. Before agreeing to use even just "reasonable efforts," the managers negotiating the deal should ensure that they have a common understanding of what that entails.

Put Agreements in Writing

Although most oral contracts are fully enforceable, the statute of frauds requires any contract relating to the purchase, sale, or lease of real property to be evidenced by some signed writing. Other contracts that must be in writing include promises to pay the debt of another person, agreements that by their terms cannot be performed within one year, prenuptial agreements, and contracts for the sale of goods worth $500 or more.

If an agent acts on behalf of another (the principal) in signing an agreement of the type that must be in writing, then the authority of the agent to act on behalf of the principal must also be in writing. For example, if a real estate agent signs a lease on behalf of the owner of a piece of real property, then the owner can invalidate the lease unless the agent's authority to act on the owner's behalf was also set forth in writing. As a result, managers buying, selling, or leasing real property should make sure that both they and their counterparts have written authority to act.

The prudent manager puts any and all agreements that might fall within the statute of frauds in writing. Even if a particular agreement is not covered by the statute of frauds, it is usually good business practice to put the terms of any significant agreement in writing. Memories of even the most well-intentioned parties fade over time. As Judge Frank Easterbrook explained, "Prudent people protect themselves against the limitations of memory (and the temptation to shade the truth) by limiting their dealings to those memorialized in writing."[28]

If parties elect to sign a written contract, they should make every effort to include all material terms. If an agreement that is complete and clear and unambiguous on its face is silent about a contingency that the parties must have foreseen when the contract was entered into, then, under the parole evidence rule, courts will not add an additional provision.

In one such case, Financial Performance Corporation issued warrants to two investors to acquire up to 1,698,904 shares of Financial Performance's common stock for 10 cents per share. Although Financial Performance had previously issued a warrant to a different investor that contained a provision adjusting the number of shares issuable in the event of a reverse stock split, the warrants for the 1,698,904 shares were silent on the issue. Thereafter, Financial Performance effected a one-for-five reverse stock split of its common stock, whereby each stockholder owned one-fifth of the original number of shares with the value of each share increased fivefold. When the two investors decided to exercise their warrants, they claimed that they were entitled to buy all the stock specified in the warrants at 10 cents per share without an adjustment to reflect the reverse stock split. In other words, they asserted that they were entitled to acquire $5x$ percent of the stock for $169,890 instead of the x percent they were entitled to buy before the reverse stock split.

Even though one would not expect a mechanical change in the capital structure, such as a reverse stock split, to materially affect the rights of the equity holders, the New York Court of Appeals (the highest court in New York) refused to imply a provision for adjustment in the event of a reverse stock split.[29] Because the agreement was unambiguous on its face, the court refused to "make a new contract for the parties under the guise of interpreting the writing."[30]

The holders of the warrants took advantage of a drafting error to reap a windfall. Although their legal stance failed to meet the Golden Rule ("Do unto others as you would have them do unto you"), the decision underscores the importance of carefully reviewing contracts before signing them.

Managers sometimes erroneously believe that just because a provision in a contract is "boilerplate" (such as a merger clause stating that the contract represents the entire agreement of the parties and supersedes all prior discussions or agreements), it is therefore not enforceable. Yet as Judge Easterbrook explained, "Phrases become boilerplate when many parties find that the language serves their needs. That's a reason to enforce the provisions, not to disregard them."[31]

If You Don't Understand It, Don't Sign It

No one should sign a contract without first reading it, and no one should sign a contract that he or she does not understand. Every manager, director, or employee with contract-making authority should be informed that they will be held responsible for the contracts they sign and cannot expect the courts to correct any drafting errors.

If the terms are unfamiliar or unclear, the person being asked to sign the agreement should first ask a lawyer to explain them in plain English, then ask why the agreement cannot be drafted in clear language. Contrary to popular belief, contracts need not be written in abstruse, convoluted language. The wording should be understandable by the managers expected to sign and implement the contract.

The Securities and Exchange Commission requires companies to use plain English in prospectuses, and there is no reason why managers should accept anything less. If a lawyer is incapable of drafting clear contracts, the manager should seriously consider finding a lawyer who can.

Consider the 1980 agreement to sell Trans Union to Jay Pritzker for $55 per share. The Delaware Supreme Court concluded that the directors of Trans Union (including the CEO) were grossly negligent for approving the sale after only a two-hour board meeting, and without first informing themselves of the company's intrinsic value, even though Pritzker was paying a premium of approximately 50 percent over Trans Union's trading price.[32] Pritzker made his unexpected offer on a Saturday, with an expiration deadline less than thirty-nine hours later. The board did not obtain a fairness opinion from its investment banker Salomon Brothers, and no one in the company even attempted to calculate its fair value.

At trial, several Trans Union board members testified that they had approved the agreement only on the condition that Trans Union remain free to accept a higher bid if one was forthcoming. Salomon Brothers was retained to find a higher offer and spent three months trying to do so. General Electric Credit Corporation was prepared to offer a dollar per share more but balked after it reviewed the contract between Trans Union and Pritzker.

Contrary to the directors' beliefs about Trans Union's right to accept a better offer, the contract (which none of the directors or the officer signing it ever read) did not give Trans Union that right. Instead, it stated only that the parties acknowledged that under certain circumstances the board of directors of Trans Union might have conflicting fiduciary duties. When General Electric Credit sought assurances from Pritzker about Trans Union's freedom to accept a higher bid, Pritzker replied that the agreement said what it said. As a result, General Electric Credit never made a higher bid.

In fact, Trans Union was not free to accept other offers. Therefore Salomon's inability to secure a better offer was deemed insufficient as evidence that no higher offer would have emerged if the Trans Union board had conducted an auction or better informed itself of the company's value. As a result, the directors were held personally liable for the difference between the "intrinsic value" of Trans Union and the price paid by Pritzker. The case ultimately settled for about $24.5 million, which represented the extra proceeds the Trans Union shareholders would have received if GECC had gone through with its $56-a-share bid.

Before signing an agreement, managers should also carefully consider whether there may be a conflict between the acts required by the contract and the manager's fiduciary duties to the corporation and its shareholders. In general, the board of directors should not agree to recommend a particular deal to the shareholders because it is always possible that a better offer will come along. The board should reserve the right to recommend the best deal and to abandon an inferior transaction, even if doing so requires paying a sizable break-up fee to the other party. (A break-up fee is an agreed-on amount payable to a merger partner if, through no fault of the partner, the merger is not consummated.)

For example, in 1999, the drug company Warner-Lambert (WL) entered into a $75.6 billion merger agreement with American Home Products (AHP) that provided for a $1.8 billion break-up fee. After the WL/AHP deal was announced, Pfizer made an unsolicited $82.4 billion offer to buy WL. WL walked away from its deal with AHP and agreed to be acquired by Pfizer for more than $90 billion. Pfizer initially challenged the break-up fee but ultimately agreed to pay AHP the $1.8 billion.[33] Courts have generally upheld break-up fees that were not more than 2 to 3 percent of the total deal.[34] Failure to preserve the flexibility to accept a better deal may itself be a breach of the directors' fiduciary duty.[35]

Preliminary Agreements and Intent to Be Bound

Sometimes it is not clear when negotiations have ripened into a contract. At some point, the parties usually manifest an intention, either orally or in writing, to enter into a contract. Intent to be bound can create an enforceable contract even if a more definitive agreement is contemplated.

Parties can make a preliminary agreement nonbinding by stating their intention not to be bound. However, courts honor such an intent only if it is expressed in the clearest language. Merely titling an agreement a "letter of intent" or using the phrase "formal agreement to follow" might not be enough to prove that the parties did not intend to be bound. Even when a signed letter of intent states that it is not meant to be binding, many courts let a jury decide whether there was intent to be bound and therefore a contract. Accordingly, managers should avoid signing a letter of intent, memorandum of agreement, or agreement in principle unless they intend to be bound by its proposed terms.

If a letter of intent is necessary to obtain financing or to begin due diligence, then the manager not intending to be bound if negotiations of the definitive agreement break down should consider doing the following. First, insert clear language into the letter stating that it is not binding, that there is no contract unless and until the parties execute a definitive written contract, and that the letter creates no obligation to negotiate in good faith and cannot be reasonably relied upon by either party. Second, label the document "tentative proposal" or "status letter." Third, do not sign the document.[36]

The great bulk of litigation concerning the enforceability of preliminary agreements has involved the problem of intent, as in the infamous case of *Pennzoil v. Texaco*.[37]

In late December of 1983, the Getty Trust (owner of 40 percent of Getty Oil Company) and the Getty Museum (owner of about 12 percent) entered into a five-page "memorandum of agreement" with Pennzoil calling for the sale of a controlling interest in Getty Oil to Pennzoil at a price of $110 per share. Shortly thereafter, the Getty board of directors countered with an offer valued at $112.50 per share, which Pennzoil accepted. Congratulations were exchanged, and most of the Getty directors then left town to return home.

A press release dated January 4, 1984, stated that Getty Oil and Pennzoil had "agreed in principle" to a merger and that the "transaction is subject to execution of a definitive merger agreement, approval by the stockholders of Getty Oil and completion of various governmental filing and waiting period requirements."

That same day, Geoff Boisi, Getty Oil Company's investment banker, phoned Texaco seeking a higher bid. Texaco responded by offering to buy 100 percent of Getty Oil at a price of $125 cash per share. The Getty Oil board accepted this offer on January 6. Texaco agreed to indemnify the Getty entities and board of directors for any claims arising out of Texaco's contract to buy Getty Oil. After Texaco issued a press release announcing that Texaco and Getty Oil would merge, Pennzoil sued Texaco for tortious interference with contract.

During the four-and-a-half-month trial, Pennzoil made this an issue of honor and the value of a man's word, asserting that a handshake could and often did seal a bargain. For its part, Texaco pointed to the fact that it had not made an offer until it was invited to do so by Getty. John McKinley, chairman of Texaco, repeatedly asked if Getty Oil were free to deal and was assured by Gordon Getty and by the Getty Museum that there was no contract with Pennzoil. Yet the word "contract" never appeared in the jury instructions.

The jury returned a $10.53 billion verdict in favor of Pennzoil, $7.53 billion in compensatory damages and $3 billion in punitive damages. (The punitive damages were eventually reduced to $1 billion.) The Texas appeals courts upheld the verdict, and Texaco ultimately paid Pennzoil $3 billion cash to settle the case.[38]

It is tempting to dismiss the Pennzoil-Texaco case as an example of a corrupt judicial system run amok. At the time, Texas judges were elected, and it was common for Texas lawyers to make substantial campaign contributions. In fact, Pennzoil's lawyer, Joe Jamail, was not only a personal friend of the judge but had made a $10,000 contribution to his campaign for election to the bench.[39] Even if Texaco's lawyers had been right as a matter of New York law that there was no contract between Getty and Pennzoil, they should have told the board that the case was unwinnable in Texas.[40]

Texaco's problems were compounded by the indemnities it gave the Getty entities. Although it is customary for a public company acquiring another public company to agree to indemnify the seller, in this case Texaco's indemnity shifted to Texaco the blame that should have been on the Getty entities and their investment banker and lawyers. Only Getty and its agents were really in a position to know whether they had intended to be bound by the agreement with Pennzoil. Although Gordon Getty, Marty Lipton, and others representing Getty and the Getty Trust and Museum verbally assured Texaco that they were free to deal, Texaco did not require any of the Getty entities to represent and warrant their freedom to deal in the acquisition agreement. Indeed, the representations and warranties in the acquisition agreement between the Getty Museum and Texaco concerning the Getty Museum's right to sell its shares to Texaco expressly stated that the museum was making no representation with respect to "the Pennzoil Agreement."[41] It is not known whether the executives at Texaco negotiating the deal focused on this language or were even aware of it. At a minimum, Texaco should have required the museum to word its exemption differently by saying "the agreement, if any, with Pennzoil."

Because the Getty entities were not on the hook if Pennzoil did have a contract, the deal with Texaco gave them the benefit of the higher price while shifting to Texaco all the risks associated with the prior dealings with Pennzoil. One must ask whether the Getty entities would have expressed the same degree of confidence in their freedom to deal if they had been required to formally represent and warrant that the sale to Texaco did not violate any preexisting contracts and to back up the statement with a promise to indemnify Texaco if they were mistaken.

The point here is simple. If one party is relying on statements made by the other party when entering into a contract, the statements should be memorialized in the contract as representations and warranties. That way the party who relied on them will have a contractual right to damages if they prove inaccurate or untrue.

Contracts Permit Managers to Allocate Risk and Reward

As we saw in the Getty Oil case, a contract can require one party to assume the risk of the uncertain or the unknown and to indemnify the other party if the risk materializes. Companies often use contracts to allocate the risks and rewards of their relationships. Managers should take special care to recognize these risk/reward arrangements, which can arise unintentionally when negotiating other issues, such as price.

If one party accepts a risk while negotiating a contract, then this allocation of risk becomes part of the bargain even if it is doubtful that the risk will materialize. As a result, that party must bear the consequences if the risk comes to pass. For example, suppose Gerald wants to sell Cameron a building. Gerald says he is uncertain whether there are any underground gasoline storage tanks in the adjacent lot. Cameron does not want to pay for a report by an environmental expert. She says she doesn't think the lot contains any underground tanks and that she is willing to take the risk of being wrong if Gerald will lower the selling price. They sign a contract to this effect. Cameron subsequently discovers that underground tanks on the adjacent property have leaked hazardous waste onto the property. The parties have allocated the risk of a mistake about the presence of tanks, and the contract is valid. Cameron has no rights against Gerald.

If the parties have not expressly allocated a risk, sometimes a court will place the risk on the party who had access to the most information. In other cases, it might impose the risk on the party better able to bear it. In others, it will let the risk fall on the party last owing performance.

Negotiate Comprehensive Acquisition Agreements

The Trans Union, Warner-Lambert, and Pennzoil cases all underscore the importance of clear and complete acquisition agreements. By entering into an acquisition contract, the buyer can achieve the following:

- Lock in the negotiated purchase price.

- Keep the seller from selling the business to someone else while the buyer does its due diligence and arranges financing.

- Use covenants specifying how the business will be conducted from the date of signing to the closing date so that the buyer receives at closing a business that has not been saddled with new onerous long-term contracts or burdened by losses caused by transactions outside the ordinary course of business.

- Memorialize the representations and warranties made by the seller concerning the company, its property, financial condition, and prospects and give the buyer a right not to close the deal and/or a right to receive money damages or indemnification if a representation or warranty proves to be untrue or inaccurate.

- Specify which conditions must be satisfied before the buyer is obligated to close (such as obtaining financing, government approvals, or approval by shareholders of the buyer).

- Identify events that would excuse the buyer from its obligation to close (such as enactment of a government regulation that has a material adverse impact on the business).[42]

The seller can use an acquisition contract to achieve the following:

- Lock in the buyer's obligation to buy the business at the negotiated price.

- Preserve the flexibility to sell the company to someone else if the directors deem it to be their fiduciary duty to do so (a "fiduciary out"), often in exchange for payment of a break-up fee.

- Limit its representations and warranties by a knowledge qualifier (for example, "To the best of seller's knowledge, there are no hazardous wastes located on any of the Company's properties") or disclaim certain representations and warranties altogether.

- Identify conditions to closing (such as approval by selling shareholders).

- Limit the seller's liability for breaches of representations and warranties and covenants.

If the buyer wants to ensure that the company's products and operations do not infringe the rights of others, the buyer should demand an unconditional representation and warranty to that effect. If the seller wants to be liable only for knowingly misrepresenting the facts, the seller should try to negotiate a knowledge qualifier. The same give-and-take negotiation can be extended to environmental liabilities, unfunded pension plans, product defects, employment disputes, litigation (both pending and threatened), and undisclosed liabilities.

If the business is unseasoned, the parties might consider negotiating an earnout arrangement, whereby the purchase price is adjusted depending on the future performance of the business. Because the buyer will usually be operating the business, the parties should be as explicit as possible about their expectations of how the business will be run. For example, the agreement should specify whether the buyer owes the seller a duty to operate the business to maximize the payout to the seller.[43]

Buy Insurance—But Pay Attention to the Terms

The clearest example of private risk allocation is an insurance contract. Risk management officers frequently bargain hard for price concessions from insurance companies but do not focus on the defined terms and the legal ramifications of nonprice terms of the insurance contract.

Aggressive negotiation of the definitional and legal terms can be very important. In the case of the destruction of the twin towers of the World Trade Center on September 11, 2001, the definition of "occurrence" ultimately determined whether the lessees would recover $3.5 billion—if the loss was considered a single occurrence—or $7 billion—if the destruction of each tower was deemed a separate occurrence.[44] Although a jury ultimately ruled that there were two occurrences, the result was by no means assured beforehand.

Use Releases and Limitations of Liability

Another way to allocate risk is through the use of releases and contractual limitations of liability. By enforcing such contractual arrangements, the courts permit parties to allocate risk to the party best able to prevent it, to bear it, or to distribute it by spreading it over a large number of consumers.[45]

Releases are most likely to withstand scrutiny when they meet all of the following conditions:

- Involve activities (such as sports) that are not subject to extensive government regulation and are not a matter of public necessity or interest.

- Are written in clear language set forth in large type.

- Clearly describe the risks associated with the activity.

- Do not attempt to shift to the releasing party a risk that only the party to be released can control.

- Do not reallocate the risks in an objectively unreasonable or unexpected manner.

A risk allocation that shifts the risk to the party who cannot avoid it is particularly suspect. For example, a New Jersey court refused to enforce a storage agreement that purported to limit the storage company's liability to $50 even though the goods were totally within the storage company's control and the storage company was negligent in permitting water to flood the storage space.[46]

Contracts Create and Preserve Options

Options give the option holder the right, but not the obligation, to defer an action or a decision until additional information becomes available or uncertainties are otherwise resolved.[47] For example, a private equity firm might buy index put options to hedge its long position in technology stocks. If technology stocks drop in value, causing a drop in the index, then the private equity firm will exercise its put option to mitigate the loss on its technology portfolio. If the technology market goes up in value, then the firm will let its put options expire unexercised. Similarly, a property manager leasing office space in a time of excess capacity should consider acquiring a written option to renew the lease at a later date at today's favorable rents.

Consider a situation in which a minority shareholder is willing to sell its shares to the majority holder only if no sale of the company is imminent. In addition to requiring the controlling shareholder to represent that no negotiations are going on, the minority holder can also try to negotiate, perhaps in exchange for a lower purchase price, a right to share in the proceeds of any sale of the company occurring within, say, eighteen months of the sale of stock by the minority holder.

Contracts Enable Parties to Expand the Size of the Pie by Aligning Incentives

Often, two parties can create more value if they cooperate and work together than if they act unilaterally. In other words, contracts can convert a zero-sum game into a variable-sum game.

V. G. Narayanan and Ananth Raman explain the importance of using properly structured contracts to reward partners for acting in the supply chain's best interests: "By changing how, rather than how much, they pay partners, companies can improve supply chain performance"[48] and increase profits for each member of the supply chain.

For example, rather than enter into a simple supply contract for the purchase of goods at a stated price, the parties might find it more advantageous to enter into a revenue-sharing arrangement. Newspaper dealers, for instance, usually share with the publisher the revenues generated by the sale of newspapers and magazines and simply return the unsold copies. A properly structured revenue-sharing or markdown-money contract can lead to higher profits for both the newspaper publishers and the news vendor.[49]

Sometimes technology makes such cooperative arrangements possible. Initially, the Hollywood studios, such as Sony Pictures and Universal Studios, charged video rental chains $60 per copy to buy videocassette tapes of films for rental.[50] A store like Blockbuster had to rent a tape roughly twenty times to recoup its investment, so its managers were reluctant to buy more than a couple of copies of any one film. The rental stores would run out of copies of popular films, and their customers would leave empty-handed or at best disgruntled when they had to settle for a less desired selection. Yet it cost the studios only $3 to put another copy on a retailer's shelf, so neither the studios nor the rental chains were well served by the flat fee of $60 per copy. The studios wanted to sell more tapes but the retailers wanted to buy fewer tapes and rent them out more often.

A third party, Rentrak, developed a system for monitoring scanner data to determine how many times a given copy was rented in the late 1990s. Rentrak also had the ability to perform audits and do surprise checks to ensure that the rental chains were accurately reporting their revenues to the studios.

Once a mechanism existed to verify rental revenues, the studios and the rental chains were able to negotiate an arrangement whereby the studios sold tapes to retailers for $3 per copy plus a percentage (usually about 50 percent) of the retailer's revenues derived from rentals of a copy. This arrangement enabled the rental chains to reduce their overstock cost so that it approximated the studio's supply cost. In less than a year, the advantages of the revenue-sharing arrangement were clear. The studios sold many more copies than before; rental revenues from videotapes increased by 15 percent; more customers went home happy with the tape they wanted; and both the rental chains and the movie studios earned 5 percent more profits than they had before.

By aligning incentives, contracts can also reduce temptations to cheat. For example, when venture capitalists are negotiating the rights of their preferred stock with the founders, they often try to ensure that the preferred and common shareholders are "on the same side of the table," that is, that their interests are aligned, when it comes time to decide whether to sell the company.[51]

What to Do When Circumstances Change

Even the best drafted contracts may not anticipate every future occurrence. Sometimes a party may be able to excuse its failure to perform on the grounds that performance was impossible or became commercially impracticable. For example, a landlord's obligation to provide office space is excused if the building burns down (assuming destruction of the building was not addressed in the lease). In the case of commercial impracticability, performance is still technically possible, but an event or circumstances unforeseen by the parties has caused the cost of performance to be so commercially unjust to one party that it would be inequitable to force the party to perform.

The courts have not articulated a clear bright-line rule to determine just how unprofitable performance must be and just how unforeseeable the supervening event must be to excuse nonperformance based on commercial impracticability. As a result, managers should consider which events might make performance far more expensive and expressly allocate the risks of those events to one party. For example, long-term supply contracts often contain provisions tying the price to an index (such as the Consumer Price Index) that is chosen because it approximates the rate of inflation for goods of that type.

Sometimes, the parties use a catch-all provision—called a *force majeure* clause—that specifies which types of events beyond the control of either party will excuse or postpone performance or limit the damages for nonperformance. Each provision must be tailored to the deal at hand, but a typical force majeure clause covers unexpected and disastrous "acts of God" (such as earthquakes and floods) as well as war, riots, strikes, inclement weather, and government interference. Force majeure clauses should apply equally to all parties to the contract. Sometimes clauses will excuse performance that has become more expensive because a third party, such as a supplier or subcontractor, failed to perform its obligations to one of the contracting parties.

When circumstances change and make performance of a contract more difficult, the concerned manager should seek assurances from the other party that it still intends to perform despite the new difficulties. Parties to a contract for the sale of goods have a clear right to demand adequate assurances from the other party if there is reason to be concerned that the party may breach the contract. If adequate assurances are not given, then the party from whom assurances were sought is deemed to be in breach of contract. The New York Court of Appeals extended this principle to long-term commercial contracts between corporate entities to provide an incentive and tool for parties to resolve their own differences by engaging in open, serious renegotiation of dramatic developments and changes in unusual contractual expectations and circumstances.[52]

It is rarely to a manager's advantage to sit by passively while changed circumstances make it ever more likely that the other party will not be able to perform its part of the bargain. Instead, it is often better either to renegotiate the deal so that it makes sense for both sides or to sever the relationship in exchange for some payment. Otherwise, the parties can end up embroiled in very expensive and protracted litigation in which the nonperforming party is likely to allege impossibility or commercial impracticability. Even if the court ultimately dismisses those defenses, the judge may still refuse to enforce the original deal and instead require both sides to renegotiate.

This is exactly what happened in a series of cases brought by twenty-seven utilities seeking to require Westinghouse to honor contracts to deliver 70 million pounds of uranium at a price of $6.50 per pound for use in nuclear reactors. After the price of uranium increased to $26 per pound, Westinghouse refused to supply the uranium. Westinghouse claimed that the price increase was due to an illegal cartel of uranium producers and had made its performance commercially impracticable. Martin Wickselman, one of the judges hearing the cases, ordered the CEOs of the companies involved to appear before him and explain why they couldn't work out a settlement, saying:

> I am tired of pussyfooting and, more than that, I am tired of talking to lawyers when other, more powerful men, who have the ultimate power of decision, have not been here. The fiscal well-being, possibly the survival of one of the world's corporate giants, is in jeopardy. Any decision I hand down will hurt someone . . . because certain captains of industry could not together work out their problems so that the hurt might have been held to a minimum.[53]

The federal judge deciding seventeen of these cases ultimately ruled that the doctrine of commercial impracticability did not apply, but he too refused to order Westinghouse to fulfill its contracts according to their original terms. He pushed the parties to settle, characterizing the disputes as "really business problems [that] should be settled as business problems by businessmen."[54] Ultimately, the cases were settled, which kept Westinghouse out of bankruptcy and resulted in a resolution that all parties were able to characterize as a victory.

Remedies for Breach

If one party breaches a contract, the other party is entitled to monetary damages or, under limited circumstances, to a court order requiring performance (specific performance). Before walking away from a deal or deviating from its terms, managers should consult with counsel to discuss the possible ramifications. They should also consider trying to renegotiate the deal or to reach another business arrangement, alternatives discussed in chapter 8.

It is important to remind employees that even if the other party breaches a contract, the nonbreaching party has a duty to use reasonable efforts to mitigate, or lessen, the amount of damages that flow from the breach. If, for example, a supplier fails to deliver goods on time, the buyer must use reasonable efforts to obtain the goods elsewhere at as low a price as possible.

A contract may include a provision—a liquidated damages clause—that specifies the amount of money to be paid if one of them should later breach the agreement. This is another example of less is more. Courts do not enforce penalties, that is, excessive amounts that are intended to punish the breaching party. The managers negotiating the deal should honestly try to anticipate the damages that would actually result from breach and use that as the amount of liquidated damages.

Bankruptcy Changes Everything

Properly employed, the law of bankruptcy can not only provide a release of claims going forward but can also offer a way to renegotiate or terminate burdensome wage agreements, above-market leases, and certain other unfavorable contracts.[55] On the other hand, if a contract or unexpired lease is a valuable asset, then the bankrupt debtor has a right to assume it so that it can be preserved for the reorganizing business or sold at a profit. Even if a contract or lease contains provisions barring assignment or purporting to terminate the agreement in the event of bankruptcy, the bankrupt debtor can still sell or assign it as long as the new buyer or assignee's future performance is adequately assured.

Similarly, even if a contract gives a party a unilateral right to terminate it if the other party is in bankruptcy, a contract cannot be terminated unless the bankruptcy court orders relief from the automatic stay. Willful violations of the automatic stay may also constitute contempt of court and warrant punitive damages.[56] As a result, if a manager realizes that another party has filed or plans to file for bankruptcy, then the manager should consult with counsel before taking any steps to enforce or to terminate a contract with that party.

Executive Summary

Contracts can define and strengthen business partnerships, but in the end partnerships are only as strong as the relationships underlying them.[57] Although having legally enforceable rights does reduce the temptation to cheat,[58] suing for breach of contract is time-consuming and expensive. As a result, managers should always do their best to structure deals that make economic sense for both parties and remain attentive to any indications that the relationship is faltering. When all else fails, the responsible manager must be prepared to act, a subject I return to in chapter 8.

5

Capturing the Value of Intellectual Capital

INTELLECTUAL PROPERTY (IP) protection transforms ideas into revenue-generating assets and sources of competitive advantage. According to the *New York Times*, "Intellectual property has been transformed from a sleepy area of law and business to one of the driving engines of a high-technology economy."[1] Companies can use patents, copyrights, trade secrets, and trademarks to differentiate their products, command premium prices, erect barriers to entry, sustain first-mover advantage, create a culture of innovation, reduce costs, and generate revenues.

Although any given intellectual property right, taken alone, is not enough to sustain first-mover advantage over the long term, securing patents and copyrights and protecting trade secrets help create a corporate culture of innovation. By rewarding creativity, managers can build on the initial boost provided by the early inventions to establish a stream of innovation that not only improves on the original technologies but also embraces new ways of creating value for customers.

Some managers assume that intellectual property issues are important only to high-technology companies with large scientific and engineering staffs. In fact, virtually all businesses have knowledge and information that are important to competitive success.

Does the company have a name or a logo? Product literature? Customized software? A new way of doing things? A customer list? When properly protected, these items may be among a firm's most valuable assets.[2]

By the same token, all businesses should take precautions to avoid violating the intellectual property rights of others. After seven years of litigation, Avanti Corporation was convicted and ordered to pay $195 million plus interest to Cadence Design Systems for stealing its source code. Avanti founder Stephen Wuu was sentenced to two years in prison and led away in handcuffs. Two cofounders and an engineer received jail terms, and Avanti's CEO and its head of business operations were fined and placed on probation. The chief prosecutor, Santa Clara County deputy district attorney Julius Finkelstein, defended the decision to bring criminal charges, saying, "Why is stealing trade secrets different from any other theft?"[3] Even unintentional violations can result in time-consuming and costly litigation.

A company can either use its IP itself or license it to others. Microsoft's copyrights, patents, and trade secrets make the unauthorized copying of its products illegal. Trademark law protects the "Microsoft" and "Windows" brands. Together this portfolio of rights makes it possible for Microsoft to maintain margins in excess of 90 percent.

Licensing is big business worldwide. Patent behemoth IBM, which proudly claims the largest patent portfolio in the world, earned $1.5 billion in licensing fees and patent royalties in 2001, up from approximately $500 million in 1994 when IBM announced its first serious push to sell its technology to outsiders.[4]

In contrast, Xerox Corporation failed to capture the value of many of the highly creative inventions developed at its Palo Alto Research Center (Xerox PARC), including the computer mouse and graphical user interfaces, which were both first commercialized by Apple Computer when it created the Macintosh personal computer. Because Xerox had failed to patent or otherwise protect these inventions, Apple Computer was free to use them for free.

Managers can use IP rights both offensively and defensively. On the offense, a company can force a competitor to pay royalties or even shut down an offending operation. Polaroid successfully used its seven patents on its instant camera and film technology to force Kodak out of the instant camera business. Kodak paid Polaroid $910 million in damages and was left with $200 million worth of useless manufacturing equipment and losses of $600 million.[5]

On the defense, IP rights can become bargaining chips to negotiate a settlement when another firm claims infringement. For example, Amgen and Chiron settled their interleukin-2 patent infringement case by giving each other cross-licenses.

This chapter first highlights the importance of capturing the value of intellectual capital developed by employees and independent contractors. It then discusses four basic types of intellectual property protection—patents, copyrights, trade secrets, and trademarks—and outlines the factors managers should take into account when deciding which forms of protection are appropriate. The chapter concludes with a discussion of the pros and cons of licensing IP to others.

Who Owns the Idea?

Managers should take steps to clarify ownership of the intellectual property created in their companies. Employees and independent contractors should be required to sign assignments of inventions and nondisclosure agreements giving the employer the right to commercialize and thereby capture the value of any works, ideas and inventions prepared, conceived of, or reduced to practice by its workers during the period of employment. Absent an agreement, all independent contractors and employees (except those falling in the narrow category of employees "hired to invent") personally own the patentable inventions they create.

Similarly, absent a written agreement to the contrary, the author of an original work of authorship is generally the owner of the copyright. The main exception is works made for hire created by employees acting within the scope of their employment, which automatically belong to the employer. Before commissioning any original work of authorship, the party paying the author should clearly delineate who will own the copyright for the work.

For example, suppose a company hires a Web site designer and agrees to pay the designer $50,000 to create elaborate Web pages for advertising and informative purposes. The commissioning company might assume that because it paid for the work, it owns all rights to the work, but the assumption may not be correct. If the designer is an employee of the commissioning firm and designs the site in the ordinary course of his or her employment, then the employer automatically owns the copyright. If the designer is an independent contractor, however, then the designer owns the copyright and is entitled to sell the same page layouts or computer code to someone else.[6]

It is not always clear who is an employee hired to invent or when works are created by employees acting within the scope of their employment. Rather than leaving the matter open to dispute, companies should negotiate for the copyright to any commissioned work and require both employees and independent contractors to sign written assignments of copyrights. If an independent contractor refuses to transfer the copyright, then the commissioning firm may want to require the developer at least not to sell or license the invention or work to direct competitors.

Patents

Patents can be used to protect "anything under the sun that is *made* by man."[7] In exchange for receiving the right to exclude others from using, making, selling or importing the invention for a limited period of time, the inventor makes public a detailed description of the invention with instructions on how best to build it. Once the patent expires, the invention becomes part of the public domain and can be made or sold by anyone. Patents are granted on a country-by-country basis, but the Patent Cooperation Treaty offers a centralized filing procedure.

Utility Patents

Utility patents protect novel, useful, and nonobvious processes, machines, manufactured articles, and compositions of matter (such as drugs). Computer software, genetically engineered living organisms, and genes isolated from their natural state are all patentable. Although a mathematical algorithm taken alone is not patentable, a process that employs an algorithm to make a calculation that has a practical application is patentable. For example, an inventor successfully patented a computerized system for calculating net asset value for a "fund of funds," which is a type of mutual fund that invests in other mutual funds.[8]

Companies in a variety of industries have successfully patented business method inventions, particularly in connection with the Internet and electronic commerce. Dell Computer, for example, holds multiple patents for its supply chain management systems. Managers should ask themselves whether their company has developed any novel techniques for manufacturing or distributing their products and consult with patent counsel to decide whether it makes sense to try to patent them.

Design and Plant Patents

Design patents will protect any novel, original, and ornamental (rather than useful) design for an article, such as the appearance or shape of a computer terminal cabinet or a perfume bottle. Inventors can use plant patents to protect any distinct and new variety of plant that is asexually reproduced (that is, not reproduced by means of seeds).

Genetically engineered plants cannot be protected by a plant patent (because they are reproduced by means of seeds), but they can be protected by a utility patent.[9] For example, the U.S. Supreme Court ruled that Pioneer Hi-Bred could prevent a farm supply dealership from selling patented corn seeds to farmers without Hi-Bred's permission.[10]

Paying Employees to Be Inventive

A number of firms have stepped up efforts to build their patent portfolios, both to reap licensing fees and to use as bargaining chips. For example, Microsoft had obtained almost 2,000 software patents by the end of 2001, a sharp increase from the 113 U.S. patents it had procured by the end of 1995.[11]

In an effort to increase its patent applications 50 to 150 percent by October 2004, Hewlett-Packard offered employees $175 for each patent idea submitted on an invention disclosure form and $1,750 for each formal patent application. HP gives commemorative plaques to inventors, and IBM has a Hall of Honor celebrating its most prolific inventors. Some firms offer stock options for each patent filed or issued, and 3Com Corporation gives each business unit a share of the licensing fees their patents produce.

HP lawyer Marc Shuyler told a group of scientists and researchers, "We get patents not to protect our own products, but because it gives us power to exclude in areas where others might want to participate."[12] HP assumes that its competitors are likewise filing for patents in a variety of different areas, and Shuyler commented that "We don't want to be the last ones on the block."[13]

Prior Art and Competing Claims for a Patent

An invention is not considered novel if others have previously revealed or disclosed it or, as lawyers put it, if it is anticipated by the prior art, that is, inventions already in existence. For example, Compton's New Media was issued a very broad patent for using a computer to integrate pictures and text. Concerned that the patent would shut them out of the emerging market for multimedia, several computer firms presented evidence to the U.S. Patent and Trademark Office (PTO) of prior art, which prompted the PTO to invalidate the patent.

Managers must be diligent in securing patent protection. No patent protection is available in the United States if the inventor fails to file a patent application within one year of the date the invention was first described in a printed publication anywhere in the world or was first publicly used or sold in the United States. Public use includes any use of the invention by a third person who is not required by law or contract to keep it confidential. For example, Netscape Communications, Microsoft, and America Online successfully invalidated three U.S. patents for a remote database access system after proving that the inventor had demonstrated the invention to two computing personnel at the University of California, without first requiring them to sign a confidentiality agreement, more than one year before filing the U.S. patent application.

Other countries are even more strict and deny patent protection if the invention is publicly disclosed or sold in that country (or, in the case of Japan, disclosed to a Japanese national anywhere in the world) before a patent application is filed. As a result, managers must ensure that scientists and others do not disclose inventions at conferences or to any third party that is not bound by a nondisclosure agreement unless one of the following conditions has been met:

- A patent application for the invention has been filed.

- The manager has decided, with advice from patent counsel, not to seek patent protection outside the United States and is prepared to file the U.S. patent application within one year of the disclosure.

- The manager has decided, with advice from counsel, not to seek patent protection anywhere.

Patent applications are usually made public eighteen months after they are filed. Once the patent application is made public, any confidential information disclosed in the application becomes publicly known and therefore cannot be protected as a trade secret even if the patent application is ultimately denied. Managers must take this into account when deciding whether to file for patent protection.

If two inventors independently develop essentially the same patentable invention, the U.S. patent system awards the patent to the first to invent. Every other country awards the patent to the first person to file a patent application covering the invention. Thus, documenting the dates of invention and reducing the invention to practice can be critical for securing patent rights in the United States. Scientists, engineers, and other inventors must keep detailed records of their progress. Often this information is kept in lab books. These records must be signed and dated by both the inventor and another witness not involved in the development process. An attorney can provide more detailed advice on setting up an effective invention record-keeping program tailored to a particular firm. Inventors may resent the paperwork, but managers must explain that these records can be the difference between securing a valuable patent and losing it to a competitor.

When Does It Make Sense to Pursue a Patent?

Patents often convey prestige and can be used to help promote the image of a technologically innovative company. The familiar phrase "patent pending" may convey an image of technical superiority that may be useful in marketing. A strong patent portfolio may also make it easier to raise money from outside investors who are looking for a proprietary technology that creates a barrier to others who might otherwise enter the market. As noted earlier, having a portfolio of patents that can be cross-licensed gives a company something to trade in a patent dispute.

Even if a company is successful in obtaining one or more patents, it is important for managers to remember that patents will rarely be enough to create an impenetrable barrier to entry by other firms. It may give the patent holder a head start, but usually that early lead is sustainable only if the company keeps a stream of new inventions flowing through the pipeline.

In addition, as Clayton Christensen warned in *The Innovator's Dilemma*, managers cannot afford to let their preoccupation with protecting their current technologies distract them from recognizing disruptive technologies that create a new product market altogether and leave the incumbents with 100 percent of an ever-shrinking market.[14] Polaroid failed in part because its obsession with winning its instant camera patent dispute with Kodak blindsided it to the risks and opportunities associated with digital cameras.

Before spending the $10,000 or more and the twelve to eighteen months it takes to procure a patent, the manager should evaluate the technologies key to the firm's success. Technologies outside this core area are often not worth the expense of patenting. Managers should also consider the expected life of the invention at issue. If a piece of software code, for example, is likely to be obsolete within eighteen months, then it may make no sense to try to patent it.

Competitors frequently review patents with an eye to designing around them, that is, coming up with a functionally similar invention that does not legally infringe the patent's claims. If larger companies can design around a patent and use their superior sales and marketing resources to capture the market, then a patent may be of little value.

A competitor's ability to design around a patent depends in large part on the scope of the claims in the patent itself. This is the most legally technical part of the patent application, and it is critical to have the claims drafted by experienced patent counsel who are familiar with both the technology and the industry involved.

In one practice, known as *bracketing*, companies systematically review patent issuances and seek to obtain patents on improvements to the issued patents. With its patent on the improvement, the company may seek either to exact a royalty-free cross-license from the company that holds the initial patent or to block use of the improvement altogether. In some instances, it may be worthwhile to pursue additional patents to block potential bracketers.

Sometimes a company erects a *patent thicket* consisting of multiple patents for various aspects of a technology to deter competitors from even attempting to design around the patents. Because patent applications are not made public for at least eighteen months from the date of filing, some inventors, Mark Lemelson in particular, have become notorious for filing "submarine patents," which they keep amending to include new features. Once a company releases a product that appears to infringe on the claims in the application for the submarine patent, the filer of the submarine patent application encourages the PTO to issue that patent as soon as possible. As soon as the PTO issues the submarine patent, its holder sues other companies for infringing a patent of which they were totally unaware.

Even if a company does not plan to file for patent protection, it is still usually prudent to undertake a patent search to reduce the risk of inadvertent patent infringement. Because a company that willfully violates the patent of another may be required to pay treble damages, managers should discourage scientists and other employees from doing their own patent searches. Instead, managers should ensure that there are procedures in place for referring patent issues to experienced counsel who can often conduct patent searches and protect their findings under attorney-client privilege.

If a search uncovers a competitor's patent for an invention that achieves superior results, then pursuing the technology may make little sense. However, if the patent for that superior technology is owned by a company that is not a direct competitor, then a licensing arrangement, whereby the company gets the right to use the invention for a noncompeting product, can frequently be worked out. Competitors' patent filings can also provide clues about future product and development directions.

If a firm decides not to commercialize an invention or to protect it as a trade secret, then it is often advisable to make the invention public. That way even if another firm independently comes up with the same invention, it cannot patent the invention because it would fail the requirement of novelty.

Don't Infringe the Patents of Others

Patent infringement can cost a company hundreds of millions of dollars. After a trial in which a Texas jury found that Hyundai Electronics had infringed patents owned by Texas Instruments, Hyundai agreed to a patent license that earned Texas Instruments approximately $1 billion over its ten-year term. Courts can triple damage awards for intentional infringement and can also award attorneys' fees.

It can be difficult for smaller companies to recover for patent infringement because the cost of litigation can be prohibitive. In fact, some well-funded corporations may purposely lengthen and complicate the discovery process in order to strain the resources of their smaller challengers. Nonetheless, intellectual property rights can provide a David with an effective means to strike down a Goliath.[15]

For example, Stac Electronics sued Microsoft for patent infringement of its data compression technology, which Stac claimed was incorporated into MS-DOS 6. Aware of the danger that Microsoft could make the litigation process as expensive as possible, Stac significantly narrowed its claims and limited its requests for discovery. As a result, the case went to trial only one year after the complaint was filed. In 1994, a jury awarded Stac a $120 million judgment against Microsoft for infringing two of its patents.[16]

After a four-year legal battle, Intel agreed in 2002 to pay Intergraph $300 million to settle claims that its Pentium microprocessors infringed on patents related to Intergraph's Clipper computer workstation chip. Intel also agreed to pay another $100 million if the court overseeing a separate suit determines that Itanium, Intel's high-end server chip, infringes on Intergraph's patents.[17]

Public Policy Concerns

Patents are creatures of statute, and their scope is subject to changes by legislators to meet society's changing needs. As a result, managers should be sensitive to the public policy considerations involved. This is particularly true for providers of pharmaceuticals and other products affecting public health and safety. Sometimes discretion is the better part of valor. A company that insists on premium pricing, regardless of a country's ability to pay, runs the risk of generating adverse publicity and ill-will—or of having the government eliminate patent protection altogether.

Critics have faulted companies selling drugs to treat HIV and AIDS for charging prices that are prohibitive to millions in Africa and other third-world areas. The World Trade Organization agreed during talks in Doha, Qatar, in late 2001 that the right of countries "to protect public health" during public health emergencies trumped the patent rights of pharmaceutical companies.[18]

Several biotech companies have sued farmers for patent infringement after they used seeds from genetically modified plants to plant the next season's crops. This has sparked claims of "bioserfdom" as farmers were prohibited from planting seeds generated by the genetically modified plants they had purchased. It also focused additional unwanted attention on the hazards of genetically modified food.

Patent litigation cost American companies more than $4 billion in 2000, leading some analysts to assert that "it is lawyers and business executives skilled at writing patent applications—not innovations—who are being rewarded the most."[19] Economist Josh Lerner has faulted policy makers for equating "stronger intellectual property rights with more innovation in a very simplistic way"[20] and calls for a "more nuanced approach."[21]

In testimony before the House Judiciary Committee in 2001, Andrew Steinberg, vice president of the Travelocity.com Internet travel site, lamented that the proliferation of business process patents was stifling innovation and wasting money on legal fees that could be spent developing products.[22] In response to Steinberg's complaints about having to pay Priceline.com a royalty to sell name-your-own-price airline tickets over the Internet, Priceline founder Jay Walker retorted, "The only people who really dislike intellectual property are the people who don't have any."[23]

Copyrights

Computer software, best-selling novels, award-winning films, and music are all copyrightable works. So are restaurant menus, designer linens, plush toy animals, and cereal boxes. To be copyrightable, a work must be original and fall within one of the following categories:

- Literary works

- Musical works

- Dramatic works

- Pantomimes and choreographic works

- Pictorial, graphic, and sculptural works

- Motion pictures and other audiovisual works

- Sound recordings

Exclusive Rights

The copyright owner owns exclusive rights to the following actions:

Fig

Mar
Mic
poli
whe

M
byis
soft
"An
Alta
awar
ware
ator
com
soft
word

C
and
in th
and
tice
and

In
ica's
Vide
held
plan
"Spe
delet
inste

Pr
amor
They
tribu
ing r

- Reproducing the copyrighted work

- Preparing derivative works based on the copyrighted work

- Distributing copies of the copyrighted work to the public

- Performing the work publicly

- Displaying the copyrighted work publicly

These rights are transferable and can be conveyed in part or in full to others.

Copyright protection is not available for an idea, procedure, process, system, method of operation, concept, principle, or discovery. The Copyright Act prohibits unauthorized copying of the protected *expression* of a work, but the *ideas* embodied in the work remain freely usable by others. Facts are not copyrightable in the United States, nor are databases unless they feature an original selection or creative arrangement of facts. Nonetheless, companies selling databases in the United States can, by contract, prohibit purchasers from reselling the data.[24] Databases are protectible in the European Union.

Copyright protection is automatic. Neither registration nor the use of a copyright notice is required. However, it is usually helpful for a growing company or an established firm selling a new product to register the copyright so that statutory damages and attorney's fees are available. Otherwise, the company can recover only its actual damages, which a company with a limited track record or a new product with uncertain prospects often will have difficulty proving.

International Copyright Protection

In most countries, American copyrighted works receive the same protection that is afforded to the works created by a national in the foreign country. Before distributing a copyrightable work outside the United States, marketers should discuss with local counsel what, if any, copyright protection is available for the work in the relevant foreign jurisdictions and what steps are necessary to obtain copyright protection.

Fair Use Doctrine

Under the *fair use doctrine*, a person may infringe the copyright owner's exclusive rights without liability in the course of such activities as literary criticism, social comment, news reporting, education, scholarship, and research. In deciding what constitutes fair use, the courts balance the public benefit of the defendant's use against the effect on the copyright owner's interests. The factors they consider are the purpose of the use (including whether it was for profit); the nature of the work used (creative or factual); the amount of the work that is used; and the economic effect of the use on the copyright owner.

The Ninth Circuit rejected Napster's assertion that its users were engaged in fair use when they used Napster's file-sharing technology to copy and distribute copyrighted MP3 music files over the Internet.[25] Napster users "get something for free they would normally have to buy," thus satisfying the "commercial use" prong of the fair use test. The copied works are "creative in nature" as opposed to "factual in nature," thus defeating the second prong of the fair use defense. In looking to the third test of fair use, the "portion used," Napster's users engaged in "wholesale copying." Finally, with regard to the fourth fair use prong, "market effect," Napster harmed the market in at least two ways: first, it reduced audio CD sales among college students, and second, it raised the barriers to the music labels' entry into the market for the digital downloading of music.

Copyrights in Cyberspace

The Digital Millennium Copyright Act (DMCA)[26] provides copyright protection for books, music, videos, software, and other creative works transmitted in digital form over the Internet and generally prohibits firms from selling products designed to circumvent encryption and other control devices. Armed with the DMCA's legal protections and the criminal penalties it provides, copyright owners have stepped up their development of technology-based protection schemes designed to control the flow and use of copyrighted content.

Fighting Piracy

Managers must be resourceful about finding ways to combat privacy. Microsoft helped persuade the authorities in several countries to police piracy more aggressively by pointing out the tax revenues lost when pirated (and untaxed) products were sold.

Microsoft also tried educating its customers. After computer hobbyists began making free copies of Microsoft's BASIC operating software to run on their Altair 8800 computers, Bill Gates published "An Open Letter to Hobbyists" in the February 1976 issue of the Altair newsletter. Gates stated, "As the majority of hobbyists must be aware, most of you steal your software."[27] He then argued that software represented an individual's intellectual work for which the creator should be compensated, just as hardware developers were compensated for their work. To supplement that approach, Microsoft began encrypting some applications and requiring user passwords to install and activate its programs.

Choosing another tack, movie studios have changed their release and pricing strategies to thwart would-be pirates. Thus the third film in the *Matrix* series was released simultaneously in the United States and in the key international markets to counter the widespread practice of making bootlegged copies of new movies in the United States and showing them abroad before their foreign release date.

In 2003, the director of the Motion Picture Association of America's Mexico antipiracy program met with representatives from Videomax SA and art-house distributor Quality Films, two closely held Mexican film and video distributors. Together they hatched a plan to slash DVD prices by more than 50 percent and to market "Special Edition" double features with no director's commentary or deleted scenes. They hired street vendors to sell authentic DVDs instead of lower quality bootleg video compact disks.[28]

Products such as TiVo and Replay TV have caused consternation among television broadcast and cable companies and filmmakers. They fear that these devices will facilitate the illegal copying and distribution of their copyrighted content and will erode their advertising revenues by making it easy for viewers to skip over commercials.

This has led to a surge in paid product placement in television shows as a partial substitute for stand-alone advertisements.

Sometimes widespread piracy is an indication that customers are not being well served by a company's or industry's pricing, product features, or methods of distribution. A number of experts have criticized record companies for failing to meet consumers' demand for on-line distribution of music at reasonable prices. Despite decreasing manufacturing costs, most compact disks are still sold for roughly $14, a price many consider excessive for the one or two "good" songs on the average CD.

Rather than sue (and thereby alienate) their customers, record company executives might be better advised to come up with a value proposition that makes sense for music lovers. The proposition might include lowering the price of CDs (as Warner has done), offering more value for the money by providing detailed and artfully designed liner notes, or embracing the Internet and making it easier for customers to buy just the songs they want. The wild success of Apple Computer's iTunes service, which enables consumers to buy individual songs for 99 cents, shows the wisdom of reassessing the business model instead of fighting with customers.

This is not the first time that an industry has fought a new technology that ended up creating new and very lucrative lines of business. Had Universal and a number of other movie studios had their way, the fledgling videocassette recorder industry would have crumbled under the weight of the copyright infringement suits brought by the big studios. After the U.S. Supreme Court ruled that "time-shifting" of broadcast television programs (whereby a viewer records a program to view later) was a substantial noninfringing use of Sony's Betamax videocassette recorder,[29] the studios and other content providers decided, "If you can't beat 'em, join 'em," and began selling prerecorded movies and television programs. Today, Hollywood derives more than 50 percent of its profits from the sale of videotapes and DVDs.

In short, if there is widespread piracy, managers must consider the legal options (such as litigation, persuading local authorities to confiscate counterfeit goods, and lobbying for tougher penalties for counterfeiting), the technological options (such as the use of encryption), and the changes in the value proposition and business model that might convert pirates into paying customers.

Types of Copyright Infringement

There are three ways to infringe a copyright. *Direct copyright infringement* is the copying, modification, display, performance, or distribution of a work without the permission of the copyright owner. Scientists at Texaco directly infringed when they made photocopies for their own files of articles from scientific journals purchased by Texaco and circulated among its scientific staff.[30]

Contributory infringement occurs when a person who knows or should know that someone else is directly infringing makes it easier for that person to infringe. The RIAA effectively shut down Napster after persuading the U.S. Court of Appeals for the Ninth Circuit that Napster had materially contributed to the direct infringement by its users.

A person or company can be liable for *vicarious infringement* if it has the power to control the infringing conduct of another and receives a direct financial benefit from the conduct. For example, the owner of a swap meet who charged $5 per car and sold refreshments to participants was held vicariously liable for copyright infringement when participants sold bootlegged copies of music tapes.[31] Napster was also found liable for vicarious infringement because it had the right and ability to control its users' illegal copying and received a financial benefit from the direct infringement by its users, in the form of its ability to sell advertising or otherwise economically benefit from the millions of users accessing its site.[32]

Trade Secrets

The value of many types of information decreases with availability. An effective trade secret policy is essential to almost all forms of business today to protect valuable proprietary information ranging from customer lists to formulas and computer programs.

Trade secrets can take almost any form. Any information that a competitor would like to know because it provides a competitive advantage may be protectible as a trade secret, as long as reasonable steps are taken to keep it secret. Consider the formula for Coke, never registered as a patent but kept as a trade secret by generations of executives at the Coca-Cola Company.

Plans, formulas, devices, research and development results, sales data, pricing information, computer programs, marketing techniques, production methods, and human resource practices can all qualify as trade secrets. For example, a court concluded that departing employees of a roofing company misappropriated trade secrets when they took with them their collection of business cards representing 75 percent of the company's customers.[33] Because it is difficult to determine the decision makers with authority to purchase roofing services, these names were not readily ascertainable and gave the employer's sales rep a competitive edge. Moreover, the company tried to protect the information by allowing only restricted access and requiring employees to sign confidentiality agreements. As a result, the roofing company was able to prevent the former employees from using the business cards to contact and lure away its existing customers.

Protecting a Trade Secret

Managers must be proactive to ensure that trade secrets remain secret. The disclosure of a trade secret, whether intentional (for example, as part of a sale) or by mistake, destroys any legal protection.

Virtually every company should have a written trade secret program with a statement explaining its purpose. It should cover four areas in detail: notification, identification, security, and exit interviews. The program must then be properly implemented, explained to employees, and maintained. Because the specifics of any plan vary with the industry and the size of the company, managers should always consult experienced counsel.

Notification

Managers must ensure that all employees are made aware of the trade secret program. At a minimum, companies should post a written notice prohibiting the misappropriation of trade secrets. Ideally, the company's trade secret policy should be explained to each new employee during orientation, and each new employee should be required to sign a nondisclosure agreement (NDA).

The company should also require any consultant, vendor, joint venturer, or other party to whom a trade secret may be revealed to sign a confidentiality agreement that describes the protected information and limits the receiving party's rights to use it.[34] Otherwise, the receiving party might unwittingly release trade secrets into the public domain.

Sometimes an NDA may contain a "residuals" provision, which permits either party to use any information learned in the course of an engagement or discussions that is retained in the minds of the representatives of the nondisclosing party. Managers disclosing trade secrets should resist the inclusion of a residuals provision because it can create a very large loophole in the strictures on nondisclosure.

Identification

There is some controversy concerning the appropriate method of identifying trade secrets. Although some people take the view that everything within the workplace or pertaining to the business is a trade secret, a court is likely to consider that approach overly restrictive of commerce and therefore against public policy.

At the other extreme is a program that attempts to specify each trade secret of the company. For example, some firms attempt to label their confidential material by stamping it "CONFIDENTIAL" and by posting signs in areas containing sensitive materials. This approach may be too narrow, because any trade secrets that are not specified will not be protected. The best solution may be a program that specifies as much information as possible while also including a limited number of catchall categories, such as customer lists and sales data.

Security

Managers should take appropriate steps to ensure that trade secrets are not unintentionally disclosed during a public tour of a company's facilities. An offhand remark in the elevator overheard by a visitor or a formula left written on a whiteboard in plain view of a tour group is all that is needed. The best way to avoid this situation is to keep all trade secrets in areas restricted from public access. If such physical barriers are not possible, visitors' access should be controlled through a system that logs in all visitors, identifies them with badges, and keeps track of them while they are on the premises.

Files containing confidential information should be kept locked. Computers should be password-protected and desks should be left clean. Sensitive documents should be shredded prior to disposal in accordance with the company's document retention policy (discussed further in chapter 8).

Trade secrets may also be inadvertently disclosed by employees participating in trade groups, conferences, and conventions and through publication of articles in trade journals and other periodicals. To avoid this problem, supervisors should consistently and continuously remind employees and contractors of when and how to talk about the company's business activities.

Exit Interviews

When an employee who has had access to trade secrets leaves the company, a supervisor or human resources representative should conduct an exit interview to remind the employee of his or her duties to keep all trade secrets confidential. The exit interview puts the departing employee on notice that the company is serious about protecting its trade secrets and that any breach of confidentiality could result in legal proceedings.

The employer should inspect all materials, computers, and files being removed by the departing employee. In addition, the employer should inspect any home or laptop computers used by the employee and require the employee to certify that he or she has returned any and all files, disks, and other materials containing confidential information about the company.

Avoid the Misappropriation of Trade Secrets

Misappropriation is the unauthorized use or disclosure of the trade secret of another or the discovery of a trade secret through improper means, such as lying or other deceit. If an employee misappropriates another firm's trade secrets, then both the employee and the current employer may be held liable. It is therefore critical for employers to ensure that no confidential information, including trade secrets, belonging to another firm is used or disclosed by any employee, whether in the form of documents, electronic files, or information in the manager's head.

In particular, managers should ensure that the human resources department or a designated supervisor provides written notice to all employees that it has a policy against receiving, using, or purchasing any trade secrets belonging to third parties. Further, firms should require new employees to agree not to use or disclose trade secrets belonging to a prior employer, and they should sanction any employee who violates the policy. Failure to do so can prove very costly.

For example, Volkswagen AG of Germany paid General Motors Corporation (GM) $100 million in 1997 as part of its settlement of GM's allegations that its former purchasing chief stole trade secrets, including plans for future GM models and car-building techniques, when he left GM to join Volkswagen. The settlement also called for Volkswagen to purchase $1 billion of auto parts from GM over seven years, to sever all business ties to the former employee in question, and to return all documents belonging to GM.

Inevitable Disclosure Doctrine

Under the emerging doctrine of inevitable disclosure, an employer may be able to prevent a former employee from working for a competitor, even in the absence of a covenant not to compete, if the new position would result in the inevitable disclosure or use of the former employer's trade secrets. This doctrine was first recognized in a case involving William Redmond Jr., a senior PepsiCo manager who left PepsiCo to work as the vice president of field operations in Quaker's Gatorade subsidiary.[35] Redmond's high-level position gave him access to PepsiCo's strategic and operating plans for its sports drink AllSport. Redmond had signed a confidentiality agreement with PepsiCo but no covenant not to compete.

Because of the competition between AllSport and Gatorade, the court concluded that Redmond could not help but rely on PepsiCo's trade secrets as he plotted Gatorade's course. Specifically, Quaker would have a substantial advantage by knowing how PepsiCo planned to price, distribute, and market its sports drinks. The court likened the situation to that faced by a football team whose key player leaves to play for the other team and takes the playbook with him. The court enjoined Redmond from working at Quaker for six months.

Companies have increasingly invoked this doctrine to prevent former employees from working for competitors. When BellSouth tried to prevent its vice chairman from becoming the CEO of Sprint, a court-appointed arbitrator decided that he could join Sprint but prohibited him from participating in discussions about mergers and acquisitions for one year. The arbitrator also barred him from hiring BellSouth employees for one year or planning strategy for marketing combinations of landline and wireless services in areas served by BellSouth.[36]

If a new employee cannot fulfill all the duties of his or her job without violating a former employer's trade secrets, the supervisor may need to scale back the employee's activities and responsibilities. This measure can be accomplished by having the former employer and the new employer agree that the manager will not assume responsibility for certain product lines until the strategic and other confidential information known by the manager is stale. Before hiring new employees, the manager making the offer of employment should encourage the employee to address this issue up front and negotiate it as part of his or her severance arrangements, rather than wait for a costly lawsuit to be brought by the former employer.

Trademarks: What's in a Name?

A *trademark* is "any word, name, symbol, or device or any combination thereof adopted and used by a manufacturer or merchant to identify and distinguish its goods, including a unique product, from those manufactured or sold by others, and to indicate the source of the goods, even if that source is unknown."[37] Trademarks provide a powerful way to differentiate a company's products and to build brand equity. Trademarks are used in connection with tangible products. A *service mark* is used in connection with services. The law concerning service marks is almost identical to the law of trademarks, and the discussion that follows is applicable to both.

Although most trademarks are verbal or graphic, trademark law also protects distinctive shapes, odors, packaging, and sounds. For instance, trademark protection covers the unique shape of the Coca-Cola bottle and NBC's three chimes. Color may also qualify as a trademark: Mauna Loa Macadamia Nut Corporation has a trademark on the shade of blue used on its cans of nuts. The packaging or dressing of a product may also be protected as *trade dress*. For example, the U.S. Supreme Court held that a Mexican restaurant's menu and décor were protectible trade dress.[38]

As with patents, registered trademarks can enable young firms to go after much bigger rivals and win. The fledgling GoTo.com was successful in forcing Walt Disney Company to abandon use of a logo for its Go.com service that was similar to GoTo's trademarked logo.[39]

Trademark rights are determined predominantly by the perceptions and associations in the minds of the buying public. A trademark tells a consumer where a product comes from and who is responsible for its creation. A trademark also implies that all goods sold under the mark are of a consistent level of quality. Indeed, a company will lose trademark protection if it fails to monitor the quality of the goods bearing its trademark sold by its licensees.

Trademarks reduce consumers' cost of finding information about products by dividing the many available products into a few brand types. Without such reference points, a buyer would have to gather information about each individual item. Thus, a trademark represents the goodwill of a business, that is, an accumulation of satisfied customers who will continue buying from that business.

Table 5-1 shows just how valuable trademarks can be. It lists the ten most valuable brand names in the world in 2004, according to a survey by Interbrand Corporation, J.P. Morgan Chase & Company, and *BusinessWeek*.[40]

TABLE 5-1

Most valuable global brand names

Rank	Brand	Value (billions)	Company	Percentage change (from prior year)
1	Coca-Cola	$67.39	Coca-Cola Co.	–4%
2	Microsoft	$61.37	Microsoft Corp.	–6%
3	IBM	$53.79	International Business Machines Corp.	+4%
4	GE	$44.11	General Electric	+4%
5	Intel	$31.11	Intel Corp.	+1%
6	Disney	$27.11	Walt Disney Co.	–3%
7	McDonald's	$25.01	McDonald's	+1%
8	Nokia	$29.44	Nokia	–2%
9	Toyota	$22.67	Toyota	+9%
10	Marlboro	$22.12	Philip Morris	0%

Source: Interbrand Corp., J.P. Morgan Chase & Co., *BusinessWeek*, as reported in "The Top 100 Brands," *BusinessWeek*, 2 August 2004, 68–70.

Choosing a Trademark

Before investing time and money in a brand or other mark, brand managers should consult counsel and perform a trademark search to determine whether the proposed mark is available and protectible as a trademark. It is also important to check whether the proposed name can be registered as a domain name (or Internet address) with the Internet Corporation for Assigned Names and Numbers (ICANN).

No protection is given to generic terms, such as "spoon" or "software." Doing so would permit a producer to monopolize a term that all producers should be able to use equally to describe the same type of product. Generic terms are not protected even when they acquire *secondary meaning*, that is, a mental association by the buyer that links the mark with a single source of the product.

Descriptive marks, geographic terms, and personal names are not initially protectible, but they can become protectible if they acquire secondary meaning by becoming associated with a single source of the product. Establishment of secondary meaning depends on a number of factors, such as the amount of advertising, the type of market, the number of sales, and consumer recognition and response. For example, Microsoft's initial application to register "Windows" as a trademark for its operating system was denied by the Patent and Trademark Office. Five years later, the PTO granted the application after Microsoft submitted consumer survey data that showed that the public had come to associate the term "Windows" with the Microsoft operating system.

In contrast, a coined term having no prior meaning until used as a trademark in connection with a particular product, such as Kodak for camera products and Exxon for gasoline, is a very strong mark. However, because the mark does not indicate to the consumer the type of product involved, the company using the mark has to use extensive advertising and promotions to create an association in the minds of consumers between the mark and the product. A mark that suggests something about the product without directly describing it—such as "Chicken of the Sea" for tuna—is not as strong as a made-up word or other fanciful mark, but it has the advantage of creating an immediate association with a class of products in the minds of consumers.

Creating Rights in a Trademark

Trademark rights in the United States are initially obtained through use of the mark on goods that are sold or distributed in commerce or by filing an intent-to-use application with the Patent and Trademark Office. Although rights to a mark in the United States can be obtained through interstate use alone, it is almost always advisable to register a mark. The registration process can be complex and confusing, and marketers should consult legal counsel before proceeding.

Loss of Trademark Rights

Brand managers must be diligent to preserve the firm's trademarks and protect the brand. Failure to use or police a mark—known as *abandonment*—may result in the loss of rights and the brand equity associated with the mark.

Actual abandonment occurs when an owner discontinues use of the mark with the intent not to resume use. Abandonment is presumed if a mark is not used for two years.

Constructive abandonment results when a mark loses its connection with a particular brand of product and becomes an ordinary noun. Constructive abandonment can result from a mark lapsing into genericism through improper use, such as using "thermos" as a noun rather than a brand name. Many terms that were once enforceable trademarks have become generic and therefore unprotectible. For example, "escalator" was once the brand name of a moving staircase, and "cellophane" was a plastic wrap developed by DuPont.

Marketers can try to avoid this problem by always using the trademark as an adjective in conjunction with a generic noun. It is all right to say "Sanka decaffeinated coffee" or "a Kleenex tissue," but not "a cup of Sanka" or "a Kleenex." Once the buying public starts using the mark as a synonym for the product, rather than as a means of distinguishing its source, loss of the trademark is imminent. That is the reason Xerox Corporation spends more than $100,000 a year explaining that you don't "Xerox" a document, you "copy" it on a Xerox brand copier.[41]

Constructive abandonment can also result from the failure of an owner to adequately control the quality of the products produced by companies licensed to use its mark. Thus, brand managers should make sure that appropriate quality controls and approval procedures are in place to ensure that all branded products sold by the owner of the mark or its licensees are of a consistent quality.

Since 1905, when Coca-Cola Company registered its trademarks "Coke" and "Coca-Cola," the company has diligently policed the brand by suing "all who had the temerity to sell a soft drink under a name anything like Coca-Cola."[42] Coca-Cola sent teams of investigators to soda fountains, restaurants, and stores around the country, where they ordered "a Coke," then poured some of the contents into a container for chemical analysis at Coke's headquarters in Atlanta. If the analysis revealed anything other than genuine Coca-Cola syrup, Coca-Cola promptly obtained an injunction to ensure that any customer who orders a "Coke" receives genuine Coca-Cola, not Pepsi or another brand of cola.

Global Protection

Registering a trademark in the United States confers no rights in foreign countries. However, U.S. registration can provide an easy basis for obtaining corresponding trademarks in countries that participate in the Madrid Protocol, a multilateral trademark filing system. In most countries outside the United States, use of a mark confers no rights. Firms must register the mark to obtain protection.

First-Sale Doctrine and Gray Market Goods

Often the sellers of luxury or premium brands seek to limit the channels of distribution to preserve the cachet of the brand. Under the first-sale doctrine, the right of a producer to control the distribution of a copyrighted or trademarked product extends only to the first sale of the product. The first-sale doctrine applies even when the product is sold outside the United States with the expectation that it will not be resold in the United States.[43] As a result, a company selling premium products in the United States cannot use copyright or trademark law to prevent sales of their products to discounters on the gray market, that is, a market where products are sold outside the normal channel of distribution, often at a discounted price.[44]

Choosing the Best Type of Protection

In many cases, a single invention or work of authorship may be eligible for more than one type of protection. For example, a formula for a drink can be protected as a trade secret or by a patent. Patentable software can also be copyrighted, differentiated by a trademark, or protected as a trade secret.

In deciding whether to seek patent protection, managers should always consider other, less costly forms of protection, such as trade secrets and copyright. Trade secret protection may be adequate for some inventions, particularly those that involve a process employed in making a product rather than those embodied in the product itself. Adobe Systems, for example, protects aspects of its printer software as a trade secret.

Some forms of protection are mutually exclusive. Once the patent application is made public, trade secret protection becomes unavailable. Copyright registration requires a deposit of the copyrightable work, with certain exceptions. There is always a risk that protection will not be granted by the reviewing agency after the sensitive information has been revealed. To avoid this risk, sometimes trade secret protection is the safest course of action.

Unlike the more formal procedures for patent and copyright protection, there are no lengthy application and filing procedures for trade secret protection. No review or approval by a government agency is required. To create and protect a trade secret, one needs only to develop confidential information that provides a competitive advantage, then take reasonable steps to protect it.

Trade secrets are immediately protectible. When the information being protected has a short shelf-life, trade secret protection may be a more practical solution than copyright or patent protection. Unlike patents or copyrights, there is no fixed length of time for ownership of a trade secret. As long as the protected information remains confidential and is not developed independently by someone else, a trade secret continues to be protectible under the law.

A trade secret does not need to be as unique as a patentable invention or as original as a copyrightable work. It needs only to provide a competitive advantage. It may be merely an idea that has been kept secret, such as a way to organize common machines in an efficient manner, a marketing plan, or a formula for mixing the ingredients of a product.

Utilizing trade secret protection has two primary disadvantages. First, the confidentiality procedures must be continuously and rigidly followed in order to preserve trade secret status. The cost of a full-fledged program to protect trade secrets can be substantial. Second, trade secret protection provides no protection against reverse engineering or independent discovery. This uncertainty of protection may limit the productive uses of the trade secret. Consulting an experienced attorney is usually advisable to assess the best strategy in the face of these complicated trade-offs.

Table 5-2 summarizes the various types of intellectual property protection available; the benefits, duration, weaknesses, international validity, and required steps for each; and the remedies and penalties for infringement or misappropriation.

Licensing Intellectual Property: Pros and Cons

Licensing arrangements can create mutually beneficial relationships that provide significant strategic benefits for both parties—a classic case of expanding the economic pie. However, managers should take into account a variety of factors when deciding whether to license technology or other intellectual property.

Advantages and Disadvantages for the Licensor

One obvious reason to license technology is to generate revenue. Lou Gerstner, former CEO of IBM, discovered that IBM was not commercializing various types of technology it had developed in the 1970s and 1980s for fear of "cannibalizing IBM existing products, especially the mainframe, or working with other industry suppliers to commercialize new technology."[45] Licensing provided a way to capture the value of the discoveries that IBM did not have the ability to commercialize. It also distributed IBM's technology more broadly and increased its ability to influence the development of industry standards and protocols.[46] IBM then went a step further and began manufacturing technology components for sale to other companies

TABLE 5-2

Intellectual property protection: comparative advantages

	Patent	Copyright	Trade secret	Trademark or service mark
Benefits	Very strong protection. Provides exclusive right to exclude others from making, using, and selling an invention. Protects the idea itself.	Prevents copying of a wide array of artistic and literary expressions, including software. Very inexpensive.	Very broad protection for sensitive, competitive information. Very inexpensive.	Protects marks that customers use to identify the source of a product or service. Prevents others from using confusingly similar identifying marks.
Duration	Twenty years from date of filing utility or plant patent application; 14 years from date of filing design patent application.	If author is a known individual, life of author plus 70 years; for a work made for hire for a corporation or other employer, 95 years from date of first publication or 120 years from date of creation, whichever is shorter.	Indefinitely as long as the information remains valuable and reasonable steps are taken to keep it secret.	Indefinitely as long as the mark is not abandoned and steps are taken to police its use.
Weaknesses	Must meet high standards of novelty, utility, and nonobviousness. Often expensive and time consuming to pursue (especially when overseas patents are needed). Must disclose invention to public.	Protects only the particular way an idea is expressed, not the idea itself. Hard to detect and prevent copying in digital age.	No protection from inadvertent disclosure, independent creation by a competitor, or disclosure by someone without a duty to maintain confidentiality.	Limited scope—protects corporate image and identity but little else. Can be costly if multiple overseas registrations are needed.
Required steps	Detailed filing with U.S. Patent and Trademark Office that requires search for prior art and hefty fees.	None required; however, notice of filing can strengthen rights and filing is required before an action for infringement can be filed.	Take reasonable steps to keep information secret. Institute a trade secret protection program.	Only need to use mark in commerce; however, registration with U.S. Patent and Trademark Office is usually desirable to gain stronger protections.

TABLE 5-2 (continued)

Intellectual property protection: comparative advantages

	Patent	Copyright	Trade secret	Trademark or service mark
International validity of U.S. rights?	No, but the Patent Cooperation Treaty established a centralized international filing system.	Generally, yes.	No. Trade secret laws vary significantly by country, and some countries do not protect trade secrets.	No, but the Madrid Protocol established a centralized international filing system for creating and maintaining trademarks. A mark available in the U.S. may not be available overseas.
Remedies and penalties for misappropriation or infringement	Greater of all profits earned with the infringing product and a reasonable royalty (triple that amount and attorney's fees in cases of intentional infringement). Seizure of infringing products and exclusion of infringing products from import into United States.	If copyright is registered within three months of first publication or prior to the alleged infringement, statutory damages of up to $100,000 for willful infringement and attorney's fees. Injunctive relief, seizure of the infringing copies, and exclusion of infringing copies from import into the United States. Actual damages and the infringer's profits attributable to the infringement and, under certain circumstances, attorney's fees. Criminal fines and prison for copying of compact discs, videocassettes, or software worth more than $1,000 without permission of the copyright holder under	Injunction to prevent disclosure of trade secret or to prevent infringer from selling product created using misappropriated trade secrets. Damages to make the owner whole and to disgorge misappropriator's wrongful profits or to compensate the owner for the diminution in value of the trade secret as a result of breach of contract. Punitive damages and attorney's fees if misappropriation is willful and malicious. Criminal fines of up to $10 million and up to 15 years in prison for knowingly stealing or receiving a trade secret under the Economic Espionage Act.	Injunction to prevent use of confusingly familiar mark or dilution of famous mark (through blurring or tarnishment). Accounting for lost profits due to customer confusion. Other damages may also be available.

(continued)

TABLE 5-2 (*continued*)

Intellectual property protection: comparative advantages

Patent	Copyright	Trade secret	Trademark or service mark
	No Electronic Theft Act. Criminal penalties for circumventing technological antipiracy measures; manufacturing or selling technologies and devices that enable consumers to circumvent antipiracy measures; intentionally removing or tampering with copyright management information; and providing false copyright management information under the Digital Millennium Copyright Act.		

Source: Excerpted in part from Constance E. Bagley and Craig E. Dauchy, *The Entrepreneur's Guide to Business Law*, 2d ed. (Mason, OH: West Legal Studies in Business, 2003), 539–540. Used by permission.

in hopes of positioning IBM to benefit from the growth of businesses outside the computer industry that rely on components to power new networked digital devices.[47]

Licensing is often an inexpensive way to gain market presence, technology, or sources of supply. A licensor may be able to push many of the costs of developing a target market onto the licensee in exchange for a share of the profits from the venture. Likewise, the licensor may require a grantback of any future technology developed by the licensee. The licensor may also obtain the right to use the licensee's existing technology through a cross-license.

A license transaction may give the licensor an inexpensive source of supply of the licensed product. When the licensee is operating in a low-cost labor market, such product-purchase rights may be highly valued by the licensor.

As noted earlier, licenses can sometimes be used as bargaining chips. Cetus Corporation and Amgen, Inc., resolved patent litigation concerning Interleukin-2 by agreeing that certain of Amgen's patent rights would be assigned to Cetus and Cetus would grant Amgen a license to use certain Cetus patents.

Participants in a *patent pool* might agree to cross-license their patents to permit the emergence of an industry standard or a technological development no single firm has the right to pursue. Because the companies contributing patents to a patent pool are often direct competitors, it is critical for any manager considering such an arrangement to secure expert antitrust advice early on.

A licensor may choose not to license its technology for a variety of reasons. By far the greatest risk is that its licensee may become the licensor's future competitor, as many firms have discovered to their distress.

A licensor that relies exclusively on its licensee for the manufacture of the licensed product may find that it loses its own ability to manufacture the product efficiently. Moreover, it may be difficult for licensors to control the quality of the licensee's work. Licensors may be reluctant to undertake the service obligations that often arise in license transactions. A licensee may require a lot of training and assistance for the license transaction to be successful. The licensor may not be able ultimately to recoup such costs.

The managements of the licensor and licensee may differ on fundamental aspects of the license transaction, such as commitment, strategy, and marketing, thereby making success improbable. If language and cultural differences are added, the licensor may well decide that a proposed transaction is not worthwhile.

Advantages and Disadvantages for the Licensee

By taking a license, a licensee can obtain immediate access to new technology and thereby avoid the research and development costs that would be necessary to duplicate the technology. For example, drug powerhouses Merck and Pfizer augment their own preclinical research and development activities by entering into strategic licensing agreements, which enable them to detect and develop high-promise compounds invented by others.[48] A strategic license may enable the licensee to penetrate its target market sooner and get a head start on its competitors.

A licensee may be seeking a long-term relationship with its licensor, which will enable it to graduate to higher and higher levels of the licensor's technology (including future developments). A licensee may seek to share in the goodwill of its licensor through the license transaction. If the licensor has strong trademarks or is otherwise the beneficiary of substantial goodwill, the licensee may be able to benefit in its local market.

A licensee, too, may decide that its differences with the licensor make the transaction less than worthwhile. A licensee may have concerns about technology transfer problems. Just because a licensor can operate its technology at a certain level does not necessarily mean it can effectively teach the licensee to use it at the same level. Licensees are often bitterly disappointed by the technology they have paid so dearly to acquire. In addition, continuing royalty payments can become burdensome to a licensee, particularly if competitors who are not paying a comparable royalty enter the market. Finally, a licensee may conclude that giving the licensor a grantback right to use the technology it develops prevents it from realizing the full value of its own inventions.

Executive Summary

Managers can use patents, copyrights, and trade secrets to command premium prices, to exact royalties, to reduce costs, and to erect barriers to entry. Trademarks help create and preserve brand equity.

To help identify, capture, and protect intellectual property rights, managers should ask themselves the following questions:

- What is distinctive about our product or service?

- Do we have any "secret ingredients" in our supply chain or final product?

- Are there any names, colors, or sounds our customers have come to associate with our products?

- Do we have any original text or graphics, ranging from product labels and instructions to employee training handbooks, that help consumers identify and use our products?

- Do we require every employee to sign an assignment of inventions and a nondisclosure agreement?

- Are we sure that any new employees we hire are not violating covenants not to compete with their prior employers or e-mailing, copying, or using confidential information belonging to others?

6

Protecting Brand Equity

A STRONG CORPORATE BRAND creates advantage for the company and its customers alike. Brands help customers sort through the competing claims that bombard them daily as they seek products to satisfy their needs. The brand "builds a virtual relationship with the customer, communicates the meaning of the product, and introduces an element of trust into the relationship between seller and buyer."[1] As David Martin, U.S. president of Interbrand Corporation, explained, "When a brand earns our trust, we not only repeat our purchases, but we also tell all our friends about it."[2]

Customers' trust in a brand can represent enormous value for the corporation, as we saw in chapter 5. Brand equity—an intangible asset encompassing all the images, associations, relationships, and expectations that engender customer loyalty—can become the firm's greatest source of wealth.

It takes years of careful, consistent effort to build brand equity. Unfortunately, much of this strategic value can be lost if the company—or any of its employees—engages in activities that damage its credibility with customers and other key constituencies.

Volvo's ill-fated "Bear Foot" advertising campaign in 1990 almost destroyed thirty years of consistent brand messaging that equated Volvo with safety. The ad showed a Volvo suffering no damage after being driven over by a monster truck. It failed to disclose, however, that the internal structure of the Volvo had been reinforced and the pillars in competing cars had been weakened for the purpose of the commercial.[3]

According to five-time Clio award winner Mike Moser, "When people found out that the demonstration was rigged, the credibility of the brand was suddenly on shaky ground. People had bought into safety's being a core value of Volvo. . . . These same people didn't want to hear that Volvo didn't believe its own demonstration."[4]

The attorney general of Texas called the ads "a hoax and a sham"[5] and fined Volvo and its ad agency, Scali, McCabe, Sloves, $150, 000 each for deceptive advertising. Volvo withdrew the spots and ran corrective ads in nineteen Texas newspapers, *USA Today*, and the *Wall Street Journal*. One month later, Scali, McCabe, Sloves resigned from the Volvo account. The incident cost the agency $40 million in annual revenues and the jobs of thirty-five to fifty staffers.[6]

Chapter 5 explained how legally astute managers can use trademarks and other IP protection to create strong brands. This chapter explores how to avoid common pitfalls that can damage brand equity and deplete the corporate treasury. Specifically, it focuses on the steps marketers can take to earn customers' trust, manage product liability risk, and implement product safety and recall programs.

This chapter also discusses the importance of preserving consumers' right to privacy, and it shows the value of a simple apology when mistakes are made. Finally, it argues for responsible self-regulation as a way to avoid more stringent external standards.

Recognize the Importance of Trust

Relationships require trust, honesty, and dialogue. Mike Moser writes, "As with any relationship, if what you're communicating isn't really who you are, then your brand is in jeopardy."[7] Because brands are built on trust, "One lie can destroy that trust."[8] Or as Tony Broadout put it, "A brand is determined by all promises made, all promises kept."[9]

Increasingly, customers are expanding their idea of trustworthiness to cover the entire life cycle of a product, its packaging, and its relationship to the environment. Environmental watchdogs monitor whether companies take responsibility for product packaging, disposal and recycling, and consumers factor this information into their purchasing decisions.

Sometimes, firms betray consumer trust by just paying lip service to corporate responsibility. A number of businesses in the United States professing to offer recycling services for retired electronics were not recycling them responsibly. Up to 80 percent of electronics waste collected in America for recycling purposes ends up in developing countries where laborers tear the waste apart, often by hand, to extract traces of copper, small amounts of gold, and other valuable minerals.[10] The health and environmental risks are substantial. An average fourteen-inch monitor contains five to eight pounds of lead, which can seep into groundwater or disperse into the air if the monitor is crushed and burned. Semiconductor chips contain cadmium; PC exteriors contain chromium; batteries and switches contain mercury; and circuit boards contain brominated flame retardants.[11] As workers pick apart the waste and its toxic ingredients disperse into the soil and air, people in China are suffering high incidences of birth defects, infant mortality, tuberculosis and blood diseases, and severe respiratory problems.[12]

Recently, several United States computer companies started offering more responsible recycling services. Dell and Hewlett-Packard, the nation's two largest personal computer makers, both now offer responsible computer waste recycling programs.[13] Environmentalists favor Dell's program because it uses state of the art practices and helps to build the recycling infrastructure. Critics complain that the Hewlett-Packard system is "primitive" and that it interferes with the creation of a profitable recycling industry. Hewlett-Packard utilizes labor in the prison system through Unicor, an industrial prison system operator. Although Hewlett-Packard's methods are less advanced than those of Dell, the inmates who participate in the voluntary system have a 24 percent lower rate of recidivism than inmates who do not. Either option seems preferable to just dumping high-tech garbage in developing countries.

Companies that cultivate customer relationships based on trust can build powerful loyalties—and they may even save money in the process. For example, rather than require its policy holders to file written claims for automobile accidents and await payment, Progressive Insurance has roving insurance inspectors who can drive to an accident site and offer to cut a check on the spot. This has not only increased customer satisfaction but has also reduced the amount Progressive pays in claims.

On the other hand—as we've seen in countless examples in this book—the heat of competition induces some marketers and sales representatives to be overly aggressive in advertising and promoting their products or services. When companies fail to see the value of trustworthy behavior, the law steps in to protect the consumer.

The Federal Trade Commission (FTC) and its state counterparts are charged with preventing unfair and deceptive trade practices, including false advertising, deceptive price and quality claims, and false testimonials and mock-ups. The FTC and state regulators can impose civil damages and require corrective advertising campaigns. When that happens, errant companies discover that their failure to exercise self-restraint can be very costly.

Unfair Trade Practices, Deceptive Advertising, and Deceptive Pricing

During the 1980s and early 1990s, Prudential Insurance agents tricked policyholders into cashing in old whole-life policies with accrued cash-surrender value to purchase new, expensive ones with no surrender value. At the same time, they made false promises that dividends would build up quickly enough to pay for premiums, and they disguised insurance policies as retirement programs. The company paid more than $2.6 billion to settle claims brought by state insurance regulators and policyholders.[14]

Sometimes the behavior in question dates from the company's earliest history. In 1977, the FTC required the maker of Listerine to cease and desist from claiming that Listerine prevented colds and sore throats or lessened their severity. Testing performed by the FTC revealed that this claim, which the company had made for more than fifty years, was false. To counteract years of false claims, the FTC also required the company to disclose in the next $10 million of advertisements that, contrary to prior advertising, Listerine did not help prevent colds or sore throats or lessen their severity.[15]

Quality claims made without substantiation are also considered deceptive. For example, the marketers of Doan's Pills were held to have disseminated false and deceptive statements when they claimed greater effectiveness in relieving back pain than other over-the-counter pain relievers without any reasonable basis for substantiating the representations.[16]

In another case, the FTC enjoined Campbell Soup from continuing to use a commercial showing a mock-up of a bowl of soup that had marbles hidden in the bottom to make it appear thicker than it really was.

Furthermore, the Lanham Act gives competitors the right to sue for damages caused by another competitor's deceptive advertising. In one such instance, the Coca-Cola Company, maker of Minute Maid orange juice, successfully sued Tropicana Products, Inc., after Tropicana ran a television commercial in which athlete Bruce Jenner squeezed an orange while saying, "It's pure, pasteurized juice as it comes from the orange," then poured the juice into a Tropicana carton. Coca-Cola claimed that the commercial was false because it represented Tropicana as containing unprocessed, fresh-squeezed juice when in fact the juice is heated (pasteurized) and sometimes frozen before packaging. The court agreed and ordered Tropicana to discontinue the advertisement.[17]

Deceptive pricing practices include offers of free merchandise with a purchase—such as two-for-one deals—in which the advertiser recovers the cost of the free merchandise by charging more than the regular price for the merchandise bought. An advertiser violates the FTC *bait-and-switch advertising* rules if it refuses to show an advertised item, fails to have a reasonable quantity of the item in stock, fails to promise to deliver the item within a reasonable time, or discourages employees from selling the advertised item.

Warranties and Limitations of Liability

Marketers should ensure that sales personnel understand the characteristics, appropriate uses, and limitations of the company's products and the types of warranties they are authorized to offer buyers. Any statement regarding the goods being sold (or any sample or model) can create an express warranty under the Uniform Commercial Code (UCC).

The UCC implies a *warranty of merchantability*—that is, a warranty that the goods are of at least average quality and are adequate for the purposes for which they are usually used—unless the seller expressly and clearly disclaims the warranty. If a buyer discloses to the seller its intended use for goods and the seller recommends particular goods, then there is an *implied warranty of fitness for a particular purpose*, which is breached if the goods do not in fact satisfy the buyer's needs.

Sellers usually limit their liability for property damage caused by their products by including a limitation of liability clause in their contract with the buyer. Any clause that purports to limit liability for personal injury, however, is contrary to public policy and void. Even limitations of liability for property damage may be struck down if they contain ambiguous language, if the seller has superior knowledge about the product and its risks,[18] or if the buyer lacks bargaining power. Marketers should consult with counsel to decide whether it makes good legal *and* business sense to disclaim any implied warranties or to limit the manufacturer's liability for breaches of warranty or defects. A company that touts the reliability that its products may dilute that message if it disclaims responsibility for defects.

Manage Product Liability Risk

Research shows that product liability cases resulting in the imposition of punitive damages damage a firm's brand name or reputation, undermine its market position, generate litigation and negative publicity, and threaten firm survival.[19] Legally astute managers are proactive: They don't wait until there is a product liability problem to implement corrective measures. They stay informed of legal requirements and take pains to protect their customers and the environment.

As explained in chapter 2, the general rule holds manufacturers and each firm in the chain of distribution (including distributors, wholesalers, and retailers) strictly liable for any injury caused by a defective product sold in an unreasonably dangerous condition. The manufacturer may be held liable even if the distributor made final inspections, corrections, and adjustments of the product. Injured parties frequently sue manufacturers of component parts as well.

A company that purchases another company may be found liable for injuries caused by the acquiree's defective products. This liability applies even for products sold before the acquisition, and even if the acquiring firm did not expressly agree to assume that liability. For example, a corporation that acquired all of a truck manufacturer's assets was held liable for an injury caused by a defective truck sold long before the acquisition.[20] The court reasoned that the new company was essentially a continuation of the predecessor corporation and that it was in a better position than the consumer to bear and allocate the risk.

What Is a Product Defect?

A product can be defective because of a manufacturing defect, a design defect, or inadequate warnings, labeling, or instructions.

Manufacturing Defects

A *manufacturing defect* is a flaw in the product that occurs during production, such as a failure to meet the design specifications. A product with a manufacturing defect is not like the others rolling off the production line.

Design Defects

A *design defect* occurs when the product is manufactured according to specifications but its inadequate design or poor choice of materials makes it unreasonably dangerous to users. A 1981 jury concluded that the Ford Pinto was defectively designed because its fuel tank was too close to the rear axle, causing the tank to rupture when the car was struck from behind at relatively slow speeds. The plaintiffs introduced evidence showing that Ford's top management understood the risks posed by the placement of the gas tanks but decided not to recall the cars after calculating that a recall would cost more than defending potential lawsuits and paying damages.[21] As a result, Ford Motor Company paid more than $100 million in punitive damages to victims burned or killed when their Pinto gas tanks exploded.

Eighteen years later, a jury awarded the occupants of a Chevrolet Malibu $4.9 billion in punitive damages after the car exploded on impact.[22] Like Ford, GM engineers had prepared a memorandum in which they calculated that it would cost more to recall the cars ($8.95 per car) than to pay damages to crash victims ($2.40 per car). Even though the memo stated that "a human fatality is really beyond value, subjectively," the jury concluded that GM had been aware of problems with the fuel tank but chose not to redesign it in order to save money.

According to one of the jurors interviewed after the verdict, "It was a business decision that [GM] made to go ahead and fight lawsuits from fuel-set fires rather than fixing something that wouldn't have cost them much at all."[23] This case stands as a stark reminder of the consequences of failing to fulfill society's expectation that manufacturers will not trade human safety for dollars, especially when the defect is not readily apparent to the potential buyer.

In contrast, Regina Corporation equips its home spa appliances with an immersion detection circuit interrupter that protects users from electrical shock if they accidentally drop an appliance in water. Even though the circuit interrupter increases Regina's costs and consumers are unwilling to pay extra for it, Regina includes it to reduce its potential liability exposure.[24]

Inadequate Warnings, Labeling, or Instructions

To avoid charges of *failure to warn*, a product must be accompanied by instructions for its safe use and carry adequate warnings of the risks involved in its normal use. Manufacturers should also warn against foreseeable misuse. For example, tool manufacturers often warn against striking a screwdriver with a hammer.

Companies have a postsale duty to warn of any hazards of which they have become aware, even if the product was initially thought to be safe. Some jurisdictions also require management to inform consumers of technological advances or safety improvements.

Legislative Relief

In recent years, legislators have tended to reduce companies' strict liability for injuries caused by their products. In one example, Cessna and other light aircraft manufacturers threatened to stop selling planes in the United States unless they were given some protection from product liability claims. They persuaded Congress to adopt a statute of repose, which cuts off the right to assert a claim after a specified period of time from the date the product was delivered to the buyer.[25] The resulting General Aviation Revitalization Act of 1994 limited an aircraft manufacturer's liability for performance of an aircraft after the first eighteen years of the aircraft's life. Because the average light aircraft was thirty years old in 1994, the act significantly limited the product liability exposure of aircraft manufacturers.[26]

One commentator noted, however, that the pendulum may reverse if companies do not act responsibly:

> The law can be said always to be moving toward some point of equilibrium. Perhaps it is at that point now for products. However, should it become apparent in the future that corporations are abusing their current degree of protection or that more persons are being injured by hazardous substances than society can justify, then one may expect to see a return to the trend of increasing the liability of the suppliers of such substances.[27]

Implement a Product Safety Program

One way manufacturers can reduce their liability for punitive damages is to show evidence of an effective product safety program. Too often, companies delegate safety issues to the engineering or legal departments. Melvyn Menezes calls on marketers to play a larger role:

- Identify ways in which consumers might misuse the product and as a result encounter safety problems.

- Participate in the firm's trade-off decisions, such as safety versus other features and safety versus cost.

- Decide the level and type of communication needed.[28]

In fact, marketers, engineers, designers, operations staff, shop floor personnel, and lawyers all play important roles in ensuring product safety. The product safety program should start with the overarching goal of preventing accidents. It should include systems that regularly reveal and correct any defects in order to ensure that products are safe and legal. Production line employees and others should be empowered to make suggestions on how to improve product safety and thereby protect consumers.

The program should include appropriate internal loss-control procedures, adequate insurance protection, and advice from experienced product liability counsel. Critical also is some form of whistleblower protection for any employee who brings product safety issues to the attention of a supervisor or the board.

Top management should appoint a product safety officer or a committee to monitor product design in the engineering, manufacturing, and marketing groups. To preserve their independence, these safety officers should report to the CEO and the board of directors.

The safety officers should ensure that the company keeps internal records of all engineering and manufacturing decisions. These records should include design specifications, design failure tests, and safety reviews. The records should indicate a careful, considered design process that goes beyond the mere suggestions or ruminations of employees. If another company supplies parts or components, it is important for both companies to share data about product safety and accidents.

Manufacturing companies should conduct regular safety audits to identify and correct problems. Although it may be helpful to follow industry standards, sometimes a company must break new ground and go beyond the industry practices of the past. Similarly, mere compliance with government requirements may not be sufficient to release a manufacturer from liability if the company has superior product information and should have taken additional precautions. Marketers should consider the reasonably foreseeable risks of using the product, the ways to avoid the risks, and the consequences of ignoring the risks. As noted earlier, it is important to check the safety of products both in their intended use and in reasonably foreseeable misuse.

To ensure that their products are performing as intended over their usable lifetime, managers should continuously monitor field reports of injuries. Failure to react appropriately to such information can result in punitive damages. Concealment of a safety problem or inaction on the part of a supervisor may also subject him or her to criminal prosecution and a possible jail sentence.

Tell the Truth

If a product does not comply with applicable product safety rules or if it contains a defect that could create a "substantial risk of injury to the public," then the manufacturer must notify the Consumer Product Safety Commission. If the product cannot be made free of unreasonable risk, the CPSC may ban its manufacture, sale, or importation altogether. A recall, or at least a very clear warning, is necessary if the product can cause harm that the consumer does not know about.

Product managers are often reluctant to generate negative publicity about their product, so they try to negotiate press releases with the CPSC using language that minimizes the hazards. For example, the company may issue a press release that announces a "recall for repair" rather than a straight recall. Unfortunately, these vaguely worded press releases may not inform consumers of potential dangers.[29] As always, managers should resist the temptation to obfuscate the truth.

Sometimes a company that has been sued for an allegedly defective product requires the plaintiffs to keep the resolution confidential as a condition for settlement. Several state legislatures and courts have challenged this practice because it lessens the likelihood that the publicity generated by the settlement will alert others to the danger associated with the product or the wrongdoer settling the case.[30]

To Recall or Not to Recall?

Recalls to correct a defective product may be voluntary, or the government may, under consumer protection laws, order a company to remedy a potentially hazardous situation. Every manufacturer should have a recall plan in place that has the following elements:

- Specifies the company's philosophy on product safety.

- Designates the managers with recall responsibility.

- Provides decision rules for deciding whether a recall is necessary.

- Includes information procedures to identify the need for a recall, to trace the defective products (by batch, plant or otherwise), and to notify customers, channel intermediaries, and other interested parties of the recall.

- Sets out logistical arrangements for the identification, movement, storage, and repair or disposal of the recalled product.

- Includes procedures to evaluate the recall's effectiveness and to determine the conditions for product relaunch.[31]

Philip Kotler and Murali Mantrala provide a useful framework managers can use to decide whether to recall a product. They suggest that managers ask the following questions:

- Is there a flaw in the product?

- If so, is the flaw dangerous to customers or our reputation?

- If so, is the flaw removable and can the cost of removing the flaw be covered?

- If not, can the customer be educated to use the product safely?

- If not, withdraw the product.[32]

James Burke, former CEO of Johnson & Johnson, received kudos for his decision to remove Tylenol from store shelves after several capsules were found to be laced with cyanide. In a business where consumer trust is essential, prompt remedial action can help preserve the value of a brand.

The Ford/Firestone Fiasco

If prompt remedial action is not taken, the consumer's trust is abused. Critics accused Bridgestone's CEO, Yoichiro Kaizaki, of stonewalling the press and public after tires manufactured by its Firestone unit were linked to accidents resulting in more than 300 deaths in the United States and 48 in other countries.[33] Many of these accidents involved Firestone tires installed as original equipment on Ford Explorer sport utility vehicles (SUVs) and other light trucks. The tires allegedly had a defect that caused the tread to separate from the body of the tire.[34]

Apparently one reason it took the two companies so long to recognize the role of the Firestone tires in rollovers was inadequate sharing of information: only Firestone, which warranted the tires, received customer claims for tread separation, and only Ford received the claims for rollovers.

Firestone spent $450 million to recall 6.5 million tires in 2000 and set aside an additional $450 million to cover possible damage claims.[35] This was the industry's second largest recall ever, and it prompted a congressional investigation to determine how long the companies had been aware of the problems with the tires. Investigators claimed that Firestone documents showed that tests conducted in 1996 indicated that approximately 10 percent of the tires experienced tread-separation defects. Critics blamed confidential settlements of personal injury suits for hiding the potential hazards from buyers who for years purchased new Ford Explorers with the same tires that had caused problems before.[36]

When Bridgestone was required to appear before a congressional hearing, "it dispatched an executive who didn't speak English and looked bewildered and confused by the technical issues."[37] In what the *Los Angeles Times* characterized as "a tacit admission of how badly Kaisaki and his team handled the crisis in its early days,"[38] Kaizaki and two executive vice presidents on his team were forced out in early 2001 along with the CEO of the Bridgestone/Firestone subsidiary.

Rather than collaborating to figure out what was causing the accidents and working together to prevent any further problems, Ford and Firestone blamed each other for the injuries and deaths resulting from accidents of the Ford Explorer. Ford's president and chief executive officer testified before Congress, "First, this is a tire issue, not a vehicle issue."[39] A Firestone executive vice president countered, "We firmly believe that the tire is only part of the overall safety problem."[40]

Only in May 2001, after Firestone gave Ford its list of fourth-quarter 2000 warranty and damage claims, did Ford learn that the claims rates for Firestone's Wilderness AT tires were three times the industry norm. Ten days later, CEO Jacques Nasser announced that Ford would spend $3 billion to recall all 13 million of the Wilderness AT tires installed on Ford's SUVs and pickup trucks. Nasser indicated that Ford had lost confidence in the tires and "wanted to act in a precautionary sense."[41] Ford chairman William Clay Ford Jr., who is the great grandson of both Henry Ford and Harvey Firestone, described the recall decision as "painful" but necessary because "our bond with our customers is only as good as the trust between us."[42]

Unlike Ford and Firestone, companies typically present a united front as part of a legal strategy to avoid paying large sums to settle with plaintiffs. One prominent product liability lawyer commented, "It's a plaintiff lawyer's dream when codefendants are fighting among themselves."[43] Another plaintiff's lawyer commented, "Now I've got the Goliaths fighting each other, instead of David fighting Goliath."[44]

Firestone announced a series of measures designed to prevent future tire failures, among them the following:

- Setting up three top-level committees to review the company's quality controls, production processes, and tire design

- Having the quality control group report directly to the chief executive and the board chair

- Improving its tracking of safety problems with tires installed on vehicles shipped outside the United States

- Using data on tire-related deaths in its quality reviews

- Conducting a review of the materials and techniques used in making tires[45]

Firestone also agreed, in 2003, to install nylon caps or belt edge strips on a number of tire lines used on SUVs and other light trucks as part of a nationwide class-action settlement.

In the aftermath, several auto industry officials told the *Wall Street Journal* that they were "increasingly resigned to the likelihood that public outrage over the Firestone recall will lead to new regulations that the industry has long lobbied against."[46] One official lamented, "A misstep by one leads to a punishment for all."[47]

The Rat Stops Here: Take Personal Responsibility for Public Safety

Any high-ranking officer who becomes aware of a hazardous condition should follow up personally to ensure that it is remedied. Consider John Park, the chief executive officer of Acme Markets, and his reaction when the Food and Drug Administration (FDA) discovered rats in one of the company's warehouses. Acme was a national retail food chain that employed 36,000 people and operated 874 retail outlets. When the FDA first alerted Park to the presence of rodents, Park ordered a subordinate to take care of the problem. Park was later told that the rats had been eliminated.

The FDA did a second inspection. Although the situation had improved, the FDA inspectors still found evidence of rodent infestation. When there were still rats after the third inspection, the U.S. Attorney charged Park with a criminal violation of the Food, Drug and Cosmetic Act. The Supreme Court upheld his conviction for introducing adulterated articles into interstate commerce.[48]

Park might not have been expected to personally examine the warehouse after the first FDA inspection, but once the FDA notified him that the problem persisted, he should have personally confirmed eradication of the rodents. He could no longer reasonably rely on his subordinate's assurance that the rats were gone, because the second FDA inspection put him on notice that the subordinate's assurance after the first inspection was false.

Respect Consumer Privacy

Information technology allows firms to know their customers as never before. Armed with extensive data about individual customers, companies can provide greater value by tailoring their products and services to meet specific needs. For example, CapitalOne created "the most robust customer database in the industry" and "developed proprietary actuarial models that forecast the customer's needs, preferences, and profitability by targeting and monitoring key consumer data."[49] This effort made it possible for Capital One to weed out the unprofitable customer segments while successfully targeting high-value customers who do not pay their entire bill each month yet have low default rates.

Proper use of customer data enables firms to differentiate their products to meet the needs of ever-smaller consumer groups. But misuse of the same valuable information results in consumer mistrust, invasions of privacy, credit card fraud, and identity theft. Failure to adequately protect consumer privacy also violates an increasing number of federal and state privacy laws. For example, California law requires any firm, regardless of where it is located, to take reasonable steps to protect any personal information (including names, addresses, and Social Security numbers) relating to California residents.[50]

PricewaterhouseCoopers found that less than 20 percent of the companies it audits for privacy policy adherence were in compliance. Approximately 30 percent could pass the audit if they addressed a few problems, but approximately 50 percent would fail outright.[51] As Eli Lilly and Company and others have found out the hard way, marketers need to do better.

From March 2000 through June 2001, Eli Lilly and Company offered, through its Prozac.com Web site, a service called "Medi-

Messenger," which enabled its subscribers to receive individualized e-mail reminders from Lilly concerning their Prozac antidepressant medication or other matters. Lilly promised to take all steps appropriate under the circumstances to maintain and protect the privacy and confidentiality of subscribers' personal information.

Then disaster struck. On June 27, 2001, Lilly sent a form e-mail that inadvertently disclosed every subscriber's e-mail address to every other subscriber by including all the addresses in the "To" entry of the message. The FTC sued Lilly for false or misleading representations regarding its consumer privacy policies. The FTC claimed that Lilly had not, in fact, taken appropriate steps to protect subscribers' privacy. This lapse, according to the FTC, constituted unfair or deceptive acts or practices. Lilly's failure to implement appropriate measures also violated certain of its own written policies. In particular, Lilly failed to do the following:

- Provide appropriate training for its employees regarding consumer privacy and information security.

- Provide appropriate oversight and assistance for the employee who sent out the e-mail, who had no prior experience in creating, testing, or implementing the computer program used.

- Implement appropriate checks and controls on the process, such as reviewing the computer program with experienced personnel and pretesting the program internally before sending out the e-mail.

In January 2002, the FTC and Lilly agreed on a consent order that prohibited Lilly from misrepresenting the extent to which it maintains and protects the privacy or confidentiality of any personally identifiable information collected from or about consumers.[52] It also required Lilly to implement a four-stage information security program to establish and maintain reasonable safeguards for consumers' personal information and to protect such information against unauthorized access, use, or disclosure. In particular, Lilly agreed to take the following steps:

- Designate appropriate personnel to coordinate and oversee the information security program.

- Identify reasonably foreseeable internal and external risks to the security, confidentiality, and integrity of personal information, including any such risks posed by lack of training, and address these risks in each relevant area of its operations, including (1) management and training of personnel; (2) information systems for the processing, storage, transmission, or disposal of personal information; and (3) prevention and response to attacks, intrusions, unauthorized access, or other information systems failures.

- Conduct annual written reviews to monitor and document compliance with the program, evaluate the program's effectiveness, and recommend changes to it.

- Adjust the program in light of any findings and recommendations resulting from reviews or ongoing monitoring, and in light of any material change to Lilly's operations that affect the program.

As the Lilly example shows, managers are well advised to review their company's privacy policies with counsel and other internal experts. Rather than wait until there is a problem, they should work with their information technology staff to implement procedures of the sort the FTC required after the Prozac.com debacle.

Consider Apologizing for Mistakes

When a customer is injured by a product or otherwise wronged, corporate executives should think about offering something as simple and human as an apology. Properly proffered corporate apologies can help defuse an unhappy customer's anger.

Consider Sheryl Cole's reaction after America West Airlines apologized in July 2002 for throwing her off a flight after she joked about the company's recent drunken pilot episode. Joette Schmidt, America West's vice-president for customer service, appeared on the *Today Show* and declared, "I'm here primarily to apologize to Mrs. Cole. We overreacted." Cole, who had spent the first minute of the segment tearing into America West, was caught off guard. "I appreciate the apology," Cole responded. "I'm sympathetic to America West right now. I know they're going through a tough time."[53]

In a case that has become the poster child for tort reform, an elderly woman named Stella Liebeck received third-degree burns on her legs when she spilled a cup of McDonald's coffee on her lap. Contrary to many press reports, she was not driving the car at the time of the mishap. The car was parked, and she spilled the coffee while trying to remove the lid to put in cream and sugar.

There had already been some 700 other instances of people scalded by McDonald's coffee, which was served some twenty degrees hotter than that of its competitors. Indeed, McDonald's own expert testified that its coffee was not fit for human consumption at the temperature served. Noting that McDonald's sold millions of cups of coffee a day, managers testified at trial that they had dismissed the prior incidents as meaning nothing.

When Liebeck asked McDonald's to reimburse her for the $2,600 she had spent on out-of-pocket medical expenses, McDonald's lawyers gave her a take-it-or-leave-it offer of $800. A jury awarded Liebeck $2.7 million, which represented the profits McDonald's made on an average day from its coffee sales. The judge reduced the award to $400,000. Although this case is often cited as an example of a tort system run amok, the *Wall Street Journal* faulted McDonald's for not only failing to respond to prior scalding incidents but also for mishandling the injured woman's complaints by not apologizing.[54]

Even though insurers and hospital lawyers have historically discouraged physicians from apologizing for fear of fueling lawsuits, prestigious hospitals (such as Johns Hopkins) and major insurers (such as General Electric's Medical Protective unit) now encourage doctors to be candid about their errors and to apologize to injured parties. In fact, the managing attorney for claims and litigation at Johns Hopkins attributed the hospital's 30 percent reduction in expense payments for malpractice in 2003 at least in part to the new policy Johns Hopkins adopted in 2001.[55]

Andrew Meyer, a prominent Boston plaintiff's lawyer who represents victims of malpractice, explained: "The hardest case for me to bring is the case where the defense has admitted error" and apologized to the injured patient. "If you have no conflict, you have no story, no debate. And it doesn't play well."[56]

Regulate Yourself, or the Government Will Do It for You

Managers should embrace the opportunity to self-regulate or at least to work closely with a regulatory agency to establish industry standards for products and services that meet the concerns of both the agency and the company. The infomercial industry offers a good example of self-regulation. Faced with the threat of government regulation, the industry established its own watchdog agency. In doing so, it was able to avert government involvement and the possibility of more restrictive regulation.

In contrast, the failure of direct marketers to exercise restraint in telephoning consumers at home during dinnertime led to the national Do Not Call List. Ironically, officers of the Direct Marketing Association privately added their names to the list while publicly opposing it. Simple application of the Golden Rule would have led marketers to refrain from making calls they themselves found intrusive and annoying. The same holds true for the federal laws banning unsolicited faxes and e-mail (so-called spam).

The Consumer Product Safety Commission (CPSC) has the authority to set mandatory consumer product safety standards to protect the public against unreasonable risks of injury from consumer products only if it first determines that voluntary standards are inadequate. But once the CPSC adopts a standard, it is unlawful to manufacture, offer for sale, distribute, or import into the United States any consumer product that does not conform to the applicable standard. Violators are subject to civil and criminal penalties, injunctive enforcement and seizure, private suits for damages, and private suits for injunctive relief. Again, it pays to be proactive.

The European Union has enacted sweeping privacy legislation that prohibits firms from collecting personal information from consumers without their consent. Congress has passed far less protective legislation designed to safeguard the confidentiality of financial and medical records and to prevent identity theft. The ability of U.S. companies to avoid far more restrictive and costly federal or state privacy legislation will depend in large part on their success in regulating their own behavior.

Executive Summary

Managers have a responsibility to make sure that current and potential customers are treated fairly and in a manner that does not subject them to injury, either economic or physical. Moreover, products and their packaging should be designed, manufactured, and marketed with public safety in mind. They should have as little adverse effect on the environment as possible under current technology.

Managers should work with counsel to ensure that employees are aware of and in compliance with all federal and state consumer protection and product-safety requirements. Mere conformance with these rules is considered a minimum requirement, however, and it does not automatically release a company from liability.

Marketers should make sure that specific procedures are in place to monitor and respond to field reports of injuries caused by the use and misuse of their products. Their diligence will reduce the chance of a criminal indictment or a crippling damages award while also protecting the value of the brand.

7

Unleashing the Power
of Human Capital

ELIZABETH P. SMITH, the first female corporate vice president at Texaco, experienced firsthand the opportunities and challenges of creating a diverse work force in the rough-and-tumble world of Big Oil. Smith served under four Texaco CEOs: John McKinley, James Kinnear, Al deCrane, and Peter Bijur. Shortly after Smith was appointed vice president of investor relations and shareholder services in 1992, Kinnear asked her to join him on a trip to the Middle East. Several fellow executives claimed that it would be impossible to get Smith a visa unless Kinnear was prepared to "marry her or adopt her." Kinnear replied, "Since I do not plan to do either, let's just apply for a visa, shall we."[1] The visa was issued, and Kinnear and Smith set out to visit a key oil minister.

But at the palace, Smith was directed to a side door while Kinnear was ushered into the front. When she tried to open the side door, Smith discovered that it was locked. Realizing this, Kinnear stopped at the front door. He asked his host to inform the oil minister that Mr. Kinnear, CEO and chair of Texaco, and Ms. Smith, VP of Investor Relations and Shareholder Services, awaited him downstairs. Within minutes, both Kinnear and Smith were ushered upstairs through the front door. Kinnear then proceeded to explain Smith's role at Texaco and why it was important for her to attend the meeting. By the end of the day, the oil minister asked her to stand next to him in the group photo.[2] This was one of many examples Smith gave of the senior-level support she received as she pioneered her way in the male-dominated industry.

Roughly five years after Smith's Mideast trip, a group of Texaco employees filed a Title VII class action suit alleging that qualified African Americans were denied promotions and subjected to racial slurs at Texaco. They offered as evidence a recording of racist comments made by a senior executive and secretly taped by a disgruntled employee. Public reaction ranged from the threat of boycotts to a massive selloff of Texaco stock by public pension plans. The company lost $1 billion in market capitalization in a single day.

Employee morale hit lows not seen since the $10.5 billion verdict against Texaco in the lawsuit by Pennzoil over the acquisition of Getty Oil. Liz Smith, who had suffered through the Pennzoil ordeal, received calls from friends asking how she could work at a "place like that." She commented, "It's one thing to be called stupid; it's another to be called a bigot."[3]

One week after the disclosure of the tapes, Texaco settled the lawsuit at a total cost of $176 million, including cash payments, salary raises, and the cost of designing and implementing new diversity programs. Most of the executives involved were suspended and eventually fired.

Texaco's newly installed chief executive officer and chairman, Peter Bijur, expressed sincere sorrow and disappointment that such events had happened. He denounced all racially motivated behavior, met with Jesse Jackson and other African American leaders to prevent a consumer boycott, and launched an internal investigation into Texaco's diversity and equal opportunity policies and practices.

Bijur's predecessor, Al deCrane, had circulated memos about Texaco's policies against discrimination, but Bijur went a step further. He summoned his direct reports and told them to inform all managers that there would be zero tolerance of racial epithets, taunts, or joking on the job. When one officer asked whether Bijur thought this was realistic, given the somewhat rowdy atmosphere on oil rigs and the like, Bijur responded, "Tell the local managers that if they can't enforce this policy, then you will replace them." He went on to say, "And if you can't find managers who can enforce this policy, I'll replace you."[4] Further, he instituted a policy requiring an African American and a female to be present at each HR meeting to prevent a repeat of the odious comments that triggered the lawsuit.[5]

As part of the settlement, Texaco created the Texaco Task Force on Equality and Fairness in June 1997 to oversee and evaluate the firm's diversity efforts. Five years later, the Task Force's final report praised the company's "strong commitment to creating and maintaining a workplace that operates on the fundamental principle of respect for the individual, where employees are treated fairly without regard to race, religion, color, national origin, age, sex, sexual orientation, veteran status or position within the company."[6] Texaco's diversity efforts are discussed more fully later in this chapter.

People: The Key to Success

Relatively few companies experience as painful and public an incentive to improve their human resources practices as Texaco did. But most recognize that hiring, cultivating, and retaining talented and motivated workers are critical to their success. Indeed, Peter F. Drucker describes "developing talent [as] business's most important task—the *sine qua non* of competition in a knowledge economy."[7]

Yet the cost of complying with the multitude of employment laws and regulations has caused some companies (especially smaller ones) to replace the old mantra "People are our greatest asset" with "People are our greatest liability."[8] Drucker concedes that *employees* may be our greatest liability, but he maintains that "*people* are our greatest opportunity."[9]

This chapter describes the policies, practices, and agreements that legally astute managers can use to build a winning team. Companies can generate employee loyalty, minimize misunderstandings, decrease the likelihood of work-related disputes or union organizing efforts, and protect themselves against wrongful discharge or discrimination lawsuits by taking the simple steps described.[10]

The chapter begins with tips on hiring talented people for maximum commitment while maintaining flexibility for the organization.

The chapter covers the specifics of antidiscrimination law and the best practices in companies that embrace diversity. It offers advice on preventing harassment in the workplace and beyond. Finally, it discusses how senior management can help create work environments where people feel eager to give their best.

Building a Winning Team

A manager's first team-building task is to exercise care in selecting employees. Especially in fast-growth situations, companies sometimes make the mistake of hiring individuals quickly to satisfy an immediate need, rather than seeking qualified, compatible people no matter how long the process may take. Many employment disputes stem from lack of care in hiring. To the extent possible, companies should screen applicants thoroughly through careful interviews, references, and background checks.[11]

Managers should ensure that applicants and employees are treated in a fair and nondiscriminatory manner at every stage. The recruiting materials should accurately describe job requirements and omit non-job-related criteria. The company must then hire or promote the candidate who best fits the criteria for the job, without regard to age, race, or any other protected classification.

Hire at-Will, but Fire Only for Cause

U.S. employers can preserve their flexibility to manage work force levels by hiring employees at-will. *At-will* means that an employee is not guaranteed employment for a fixed period of time. Rather, both the employee and the employer remain free to terminate the relationship at any time for any reason, with or without cause. In contrast, every other major industrialized nation requires either good cause before an employer can terminate an employee or advance notice with severance pay.

Lawyers usually advise employers to protect at-will status by avoiding behaviors that could imply an employment contract. If there is an implied contract, an employer who fires an employee without good cause may be held liable for wrongful termination. Courts in the United States may interpret the parties' conduct as creating an implied contract under any of the following conditions:

- The individual is a long-term employee.

- The employee has received raises, bonuses, and promotions throughout his or her career.

- The employee has been told that he or she was doing a good job.

- The company has stated that it does not terminate employees at his or her level except for good cause.

- The employee has never been formally criticized or warned about his or her conduct.

Even if employees are engaged at-will, most states prohibit an employer from discharging them for reasons that violate public policy. In other words, an at-will employee may be terminated for *no* reason, but not for a *bad* reason. A wrongly terminated employee may be able to recover both contract and tort damages, including damages for pain and suffering. In egregious cases, punitive damages may be available as well. Most states protect employees against termination for the following:

- Refusing to commit an unlawful act, such as perjury or price-fixing

- Alleging that the company has violated a law

- Taking time from work to serve on a jury or for military leave

- Filing a workers' compensation claim

- Joining a union

Federal law also protects workers from retaliation due to union organizing and certain types of whistleblowing.

Nor can at-will employees be deprived of benefits they have rightfully earned. In one case, the court held that an employer wrongfully terminated a twenty-five-year employee without good cause just to deprive him of $46,000 in commissions.[12] Similarly, a company that fired an employee just before her stock was due to vest might be found to have violated the implied covenant of good faith and fair dealing. This is one reason why many companies vest stock monthly after some initial period (usually six months to one year).

Be Flexible but Fair

Hiring at-will keeps an employer's options open and protects the company against crushing labor costs when markets shift. But a company that treats its employees cavalierly in trying times may miss the chance to earn their trust. Here again, the legal decisions may be too important to leave to the lawyers. Jeffrey Pfeffer cautions that "an employer that signals through word and deed that its employees are dispensable is not likely to generate much loyalty, commitment, or willingness to expend extra effort for the organization's benefit."[13] Pfeffer eschews the standard wisdom of removing from employee handbooks all references to job security, longevity, and probationary periods of employment because it hinders the development of high-commitment work practices. He warns:

> [I]f management is more concerned about the legal technicali-
> ties of the language in employee handbooks and policy manu-
> als than about their efforts on motivation and commitment; if
> management, through this process, comes to see employees
> as potential legal adversaries, then that management will
> probably engage in behavior that creates a self-fulfilling
> prophecy of distrust, conflict, and litigation. Its policies will
> signal a lack of trust and mutual commitment, which will
> almost certainly be returned in kind.[14]

Pfeffer cites a RAND Corporation study's finding that the typical plaintiff in a wrongful termination lawsuit receives the equivalent of one-half year's severance pay. The study concluded, "By inducing terminated employees to accept such a severance, employers could save $84,000 in defense fees."[15] Pfeffer faults managers for "turn[ing] their employee relations over to attorneys who think in terms of cases won or lost, not in terms of resources expended and certainly not in terms of the effect of employee relations practices on the organization's competitive success."[16] He proposes another approach:

> Organizations do not have to discharge employees at will without trying to pay compensation and without due process. There is no reason to pursue these cases all the way to trial and spend the several hundreds of thousands of dollars this often takes, and then to appeal decisions and drag the process out more.[17]

When Necessary, Fire—but Be Careful

Employers do not need to resign themselves to carrying unproductive, uncooperative, or unneeded employees forever. When it becomes necessary to terminate an employee, managers should do so—but use due care. Even if an employee is at-will, the supervisor should review the personnel file to see whether the record justifies termination for cause. If not, then the supervisor should be prepared to explain why this person, not someone else who was perhaps younger or of a different race, was let go. The supervisor should also consider whether there is a basis for finding an implied contract not to discharge the employee without good cause.

Under no circumstances should the supervisor lie about the reasons for termination. Evidence of a lie can itself be enough to show that the employer's stated reason was a pretext intended to disguise illegal discrimination or other wrongful conduct.[18]

A supervisor or HR representative should review the employment agreement to make sure that all amounts due to the employee are paid. Some states require employers to pay everything the employee is owed on the last day of work. An exit interview is often useful for airing the departing employee's grievances, for collecting all company property, and for explaining exit compensation and benefits issues. A supervisor should remind the departing employee of the obligation to keep the employer's proprietary information and trade secrets confidential.

When a high-level or disgruntled employee is terminated, it is often desirable to enter into a written separation agreement. Generally, severance should not be paid without obtaining a signed release of all claims other than workers' compensation and other nonwaivable claims. The separation agreement should bar the employee from reapplying to the company. Otherwise, the employer could find itself in a retaliation suit if it decides not to rehire the employee.

It can be particularly difficult for departing employees to leave unvested stock options behind. Experts suggest that "stock option plans are really a great way to settle; it doesn't cost employers that much, and it means a lot to employees."[19]

For employees aged forty or older, a release of age discrimination claims is effective only if it complies with the strict requirements of the Age Discrimination in Employment Act. As a result, managers negotiating severance agreements should review all ADEA waivers with experienced counsel or with human resources personnel acting on the advice of counsel.

Document the Relationship

As Jeffrey Pfeffer pointed out, legal technicalities should not take precedence over good employee relations. Nevertheless, once the hiring decision is made, the company should formalize the relationship in a document signed by both the employee and the employer.[20] For people hired to work outside the United States, companies should require a detailed employment agreement tailored to local laws. Employment practices vary widely by country, so it is important to consult legal counsel before hiring either U.S. citizens or foreign nationals to work abroad.

Although a lengthy employee handbook is neither legally required nor always advisable, every new hire should receive notice of the company's principal policies. Table 7-1 lists the sorts of written policies that companies should distribute to all employees, and the types of agreements they should sign. If a worker is hired as an independent contractor, the parties should sign an agreement that includes the project description and milestones, fees, a recitation of the inde-

TABLE 7-1

Key employment policies and agreements

Policies	Agreements	Comments
An at-will employment policy or an employment security policy that provides for progressive discipline, specifies grounds for termination, and establishes a formal grievance procedure that guarantees employees an opportunity to be heard.	If applicable, an independent contractor agreement.	All policies should be in writing and distributed in writing to all new hires and existing employees.
A policy prohibiting unlawful harassment, discrimination, and retaliation, with an effective mechanism for employees to report and seek redress for any such conduct.	Mandatory arbitration agreements to resolve employment disputes.	If an arbitration agreement is part of the hiring process, then the job offer itself will be adequate consideration for a binding contract. If, however, an existing employee is requested to sign an arbitration agreement, then it is important for the employer to provide some new value, such as a one-time cash bonus, as consideration for the employee's agreement to arbitrate.
Policies governing eligibility for and use of leaves of absences.		
A whistleblower protection policy, including a process for employees to report accounting irregularities to management, supervisors, or the board without reprisals.		
Explicit, written policies on the proper and improper use of e-mail and instant messaging.		
An electronic systems policy to avert improper or illegal use of the company's computer and electronic systems, clarifying that the systems are the company's property, and that employees have no reasonable expectation of privacy in communications sent or received on those systems.	Assignments of inventions.	
	Nondisclosure agreements.	
Privacy policies and procedures to safeguard protected health information, including a firewall around the employee medical plans, to ensure that private health information is used only for purposes of plan administration and not for any other employment-related decisions, such as termination of employment (required by the Health Insurance Portability and Accountability Act of 1996 [HIPAA]).	Noncompete covenants.	Consult counsel: enforceability of postemployment noncompete covenants varies by state.

(continued)

TABLE 7-1 *(continued)*

Key employment policies and agreements

Policies	Agreements	Comments
A proprietary information and inventions policy, as discussed in chapter 5.	Nonsolicitation covenants, under which a former employee agrees not to solicit the former employer's employees or customers.	Consult counsel: enforceability of nonsolicitation covenants varies by state.
An insider trading policy prohibiting employees from giving tips or trading any securities of the employer or any other company based on material nonpublic information learned while on the job and requiring persons who are likely to obtain material nonpublic information to preclear all trades, as discussed in chapter 3.		
A document retention policy and a policy on the dissemination and storage of privileged communications with counsel, as discussed in chapter 8.		
A policy reserving the company's unilateral right to revise its policies and benefits as it deems appropriate.		

pendent contractor relationship, an assignment of inventions and provisions for the protection of proprietary information, indemnification provisions, and language regarding the contractor's right to control the manner and means of performing the work and to work for others.[21]

Before using new technology, such as global positioning systems and other location detection technology in company cellphones, vehicles, or badges, managers should consider whether it conflicts with employees' legitimate and protected privacy interests. Although monitoring technology has legitimate uses, such as increasing efficiency by facilitating real-time rerouting of employees who are on the road, it should not be used to track movements during nonworking hours, impede union organizing drives, or weed out whistleblowers.[22]

Managers should resist the temptation to try to save money on Social Security and other employer taxes by misclassifying employees as independent contractors. Employers who misclassify their workers may be fined and required to pay the misclassified employee's income taxes.

Employee status is more likely to be found for workers who are lower paid and less skilled, lack bargaining power, have a high degree of economic dependence on their employer, and are subject to regular supervision. Even a shareholder-director or a partner might still be considered an employee, depending on the relationship.[23]

Apply Policies Consistently and Address Performance Issues Promptly

Once the company adopts policies, supervisors need to ensure that they are always applied consistently. The only thing worse than having no written policies is failing to honor the policies a company does have. For example, if a company has a progressive discipline system, it must follow it to the letter, or the company may be found liable for wrongful termination.

When evaluating an employee's performance, the supervisor should be timely, honest, specific, and tactful. Evaluation criteria should be objective and job related. A copy of all performance evaluations should be signed by the employee and kept in his or her personnel file.

Performance problems should be documented and communicated to the employee as they arise. All warnings should be put in writing along with a description of the action necessary to correct the difficulties and the consequences of continued unsatisfactory performance. No one likes conveying criticism to someone they see every day, but failure to do so can undermine the employer's ability to terminate or discipline an underperforming employee at a later date. An employee who is fired after receiving average or unobjectionable employee evaluations for years is far more likely to win a suit for wrongful termination or employment discrimination than one who has been duly warned to improve subpar performance.

If an employee complains about a failure to promote or about harassment or discrimination of any kind, the employer must promptly and thoroughly investigate the circumstances surrounding the claim. The company should choose an appropriate investigator—preferably one whom the employee trusts. A supervisor should document the results of the investigation and report the results to the employee. If harassment or discrimination has occurred, immediate and effective action must be taken to remedy the situation and to prevent it from occurring again.

Listen to and Protect Whistleblowers

Whistleblowers are the canaries in the mineshafts of business. The misdeeds at Enron and WorldCom and the late-trading scandals that have rocked the mutual fund industry were all revealed by whistleblowers who first tried to work within the company to correct the wrongdoing before going public.[24]

An effective whistleblower protection program is an essential part of a prudent risk management program. Implemented properly, it provides an important early warning system for top management and ultimately the board of directors.

The Sarbanes-Oxley Act requires public companies to put policies in place so that employees can report accounting irregularities to top management, supervisors, or the board of directors without reprisals. The act also makes it a crime, punishable by up to ten years in prison, for a publicly traded company to retaliate against employees who provide information about fraud on shareholders to a federal agency, members of Congress, or a party in a judicial proceeding, such as a plaintiff suing the employee's company for securities fraud.

Several federal statutes award a share of the fines and other proceeds to a whistleblower who successfully brings a suit for fraud against the U.S. government. In one such instance, TAP Pharmaceutical Products paid a record fine of $875 million in 2002 to settle charges of criminal conspiracy to bilk federal and state medical programs out of $145 million during the 1990s.[25] Doug Durand, the TAP vice president for sales, received $77 million (14 percent of the total fine) for his role in bringing the massive fraud to light. Durand had secretly gathered damning information about the kickbacks and free big-screen TVs TAP sales representatives were giving to urologists who promoted TAP's new prostate cancer drug, Lupron. The sales reps also gave urologists free samples of Lupron, for which the urologists billed Medicare at inflated prices, pocketing the cash.

Before talking with a federal prosecutor Durand had tried to work within the TAP system. He offered sales reps who kept accurate records an extra year's salary, but senior management killed the idea. Colleagues told Durand that he just didn't understand TAP's number-driven culture, and Durand found himself increasingly marginalized. TAP had no inside counsel. According to Durand, "legal counsel was considered a sales prevention department."[26] Durand finally got spooked when one regional manager responded to another manager's concerns about getting caught bribing the urologists by joking, "How do you think Doug would look in stripes?"[27] Afraid to be the fall guy, Durand fed two hundred pages of incriminating information to an aggressive federal prosecutor who ultimately brought the charges against TAP.

Be Careful with Outsourcing

Some companies attempt to save the time and expense of managing the work force by outsourcing the human resources function. Even if a worker is hired and paid by an employment agency, the company may still be treated as a coemployer if it has the right to control the work performed and to set the compensation. Coemployers can be held liable for employment law violations and can be required to offer their workers the same benefits offered their other employees. Even if a company is not legally a coemployer, it is still important to develop, motivate, and satisfy all workers whose performance can affect the firm's results.[28]

Embracing Diversity and Preventing Discrimination

Managing diversity means more than hiring workers with racial and other characteristics that reflect the society at large. David A. Thomas and Robin J. Ely explain that the benefits of a diverse workplace "go beyond financial measures to encompass learning, creativity, flexibility, organizational and individual growth, and the ability of a company to adjust rapidly and successfully to market changes."[29]

Realizing these benefits requires managers to acknowledge differences and incorporate employees' different perceptions into the main work of the organization. To accomplish this, Thomas and Ely urge managers as follows:

- Make it safe for employees to be themselves.

- Expect high standards of performance by everyone.

- Make workers feel valued.

- Clearly articulate the firm's mission.

- Create a relatively egalitarian and nonbureaucratic structure.[30]

Title VII and subsequent federal laws acknowledged the value of diversity by banning workplace discrimination on the basis of race, color, religion, sex, national origin, age or disability. The U.S. Supreme Court reaffirmed the importance of diversity in education when it upheld race as a legitimate factor to consider when admitting students to the Michigan Law School.[31]

Racial discrimination suits can be brought by whites as well as minorities, and sex discrimination suits can be brought by men as well as women. Moreover, employers may not retaliate against employees who complain about discrimination or harassment.

Table 7-2 summarizes the major federal statutes barring various kinds of employment discrimination. The U.S. antidiscrimination laws apply to all employees working in the United States (regardless of their nationality or the nationality of their employer) and to all U.S. citizens working outside of the United States if the employer is either based in the United States or is controlled by a U.S. employer. In addition, many states and cities have passed their own fair employment acts.

The Texaco Example: Reversing a Pattern of Discrimination

Discrimination saps employee morale, as we saw in the Texaco example that opened this chapter. But when companies decide to repair past problems and embrace diversity, they can discover hidden talents and energy in their work force.

After settling its class action racial discrimination suit in 1997, Texaco instituted a companywide diversity and sensitivity program, which was monitored by the Texaco Task Force on Equality and Fairness. The centerpiece was mandatory diversity training for every employee, a learning experience that usually took place in a two-day session. The first day focused on having employees identify their own negative assumptions and learning how their behavior influenced others. On the second day, employees learned about the business case for diversity, "as a counter to some employees' misperception that diversity equates to hiring less qualified women and minorities."[32] Texaco eventually implemented an online version specifically tailored for overseas employees.

Critics called the sessions insulting, futile, even poisonous,[33] but proponents pointed out that 95 percent of participants rated the classes a four or five on a five-point scale.[34] "I didn't think I needed this, and I was wrong" was a typical comment from participants.[35]

Over time, the Task Force recommended improving the diversity-training program by using context-based examples of incidents that could actually occur in day-to-day operations.[36] The Task Force also

TABLE 7-2

Major pieces of federal civil rights legislation

Statute	Major provisions
Civil Rights Act of 1866 (Section 1981)	Prohibits racial discrimination by employers of any size in the making and enforcement of contracts, including employment contracts.
Equal Pay Act of 1963	Mandates equal pay for equal work without regard to gender.
Title VII of the Civil Rights Act of 1964 (Title VII)	Prohibits discrimination in employment on the basis of race, color, religion, national origin, or sex. Later amended to provide that discrimination on the basis of sex includes discrimination on the basis of pregnancy, childbirth, or related medical conditions.
Age Discrimination in Employment Act of 1967 (ADEA)	Protects persons forty years and older from discrimination on the basis of age. The ADEA was amended in 1990 by the Older Workers' Benefit Protection Act, which prohibits age discrimination in providing employee benefits and establishes minimum standards for waiver of one's rights under the ADEA.
Vocational Rehabilitation Act of 1973	Prohibits discrimination against the physically and mentally disabled. Imposes affirmative-action obligations on employers having contracts with the federal government in excess of $2,500.
Veterans Reemployment Act of 1974	Gives employees who served in the military at any time the right to be reinstated in employment without loss of benefits and the right not to be discharged without cause for one year following such reinstatement.
Immigration Reform and Control Act of 1986 (IRCA)	Prohibits discrimination against applicants or employees based on national origin or citizenship status.

underscored the importance of acknowledging "the reality of race and gender bias in American society" and offering managers specific strategies for creating a visibly diverse workplace.[37]

The settlement required Texaco to include "diversity performance" in management's objectives and compensation. To do this,

Employers subject to statute	Comments
All public and private employers	The bar against racial discrimination applies not only to hiring, promotion, and termination but also to working conditions, such as racial harassment, and to breaches of contract occurring during the term of the contract.
All public and private employers with twenty or more employees (including federal, state, and local governments)	
All public and private employers with fifteen or more employees (including federal, state, and local governments)	An employer may lawfully apply different standards of compensation, or different terms or conditions of employment, pursuant to a bona fide seniority or merit system. The employer has a defense in a disparate-impact case if the challenged practice is a matter of business necessity. There is also a defense when discrimination based on sex, national origin, or religion is a bona fide occupational qualification (BFOQ).
Employers with at least twenty employees, employment agencies, and labor unions	Prohibits both intentional discrimination (disparate treatment) and specific employer practices that on their face do not discriminate based on age if they have a statistically significant impact on workers over forty (disparate impact). The employer has a defense in a disparate-impact case if it bases its decision on a reasonable factor other than age.
Employers receiving federal financial assistance of any amount	Enforced by the U.S. Department of Labor. This legislation was the precursor to and guided the development of the Americans with Disabilities Act.
All public and private employers	
All private employers with four or more employees	If employer has fifteen or more employees, plaintiff must file national-origin discrimination claims under Title VII.

(continued)

Texaco began tying managers' bonuses to their success in meeting targets for hiring and promoting minorities and women and to the results of employee surveys about the company's "respect for the individual."[38] The Task Force commented, "The Texaco experience has demonstrated that objective measures of diversity performance

TABLE 7-2 (continued)

Major pieces of federal civil rights legislation

Statute	Major provisions
Americans with Disabilities Act of 1990 (ADA)	Prohibits discrimination in employment on the basis of a person's mental or physical disability. Also requires businesses to provide "reasonable accommodation" to the disabled so the disabled employee can perform his or her job, unless doing so would cause the employer "undue hardship" on business operations. Reasonable accommodations include: (1) making work facilities accessible; (2) restructuring jobs or modifying work schedules; (3) acquiring or modifying equipment or devices; (4) modifying examinations, training materials, or policies; and (5) providing qualified readers or interpreters or other similar accommodations for individuals with disabilities. Absent special circumstances, an employer is not required to provide an accommodation that would conflict with a bona fide established seniority system (embodied in a collective bargaining agreement or a written policy) unless the employer has a practice of making exemptions from the policy for other reasons or of making frequent changes to the policy.
Civil Rights Act of 1991	Legislatively overruled several parts of certain Supreme Court rulings that were unfavorable to the rights of plaintiffs in employment discrimination cases. Also extended coverage of the major civil rights statutes to the staffs of the president and the senate.
Family and Medical Leave Act of 1993	Entitles eligible employees up to twelve weeks of unpaid leave per year (1) in connection with a serious health condition that renders the employee unable to do his or her job; or (2) to take time off from work to handle domestic responsibilities, such as the birth or adoption of a child or the care of a child, parent, or spouse. Employees are entitled to reinstatement following the expiration of the leave, unless the employee is a key employee (among the top 10 percent based on salary) and substantial and grievous injury will result from reinstatement. As soon as the employer determines that reinstatement would cause such injury, the employer must notify the employee that the company intends to deny job restoration and give the employee a reasonable time to return to work.

can be used as a useful management tool without becoming quotas or goals that are rigid or inflexible."[39]

A number of other initiatives continued, in some fashion, after the merger that created ChevronTexaco in 2001. For example, the company expanded its internal recruitment efforts for senior job openings and its presence at certain educational institutions known

Employers subject to statute	Comments
All private employers with fifteen or more employees	A *disability* is defined under the ADA as (1) a mental or physical impairment that substantially limits one or more of an individual's major life activities (such as walking, seeing, hearing, and procreating); (2) a record of such an impairment; or (3) being regarded as having such an impairment. If the physical or mental impairment is corrected by medication or other measures (such as eyeglasses for someone with myopia), then the person will not be deemed to be disabled. An employer is not required to hire a disabled employee for a position if, even after reasonable accommodation, the work would pose a direct threat to the safety of the employee or others. An employer considering disciplining an employee for missing work should ensure that the absences are not related to a disability requiring reasonable accommodation.
Varies	
Private employers with fifty or more employees at work sites within seventy-five miles of each other	To be eligible, an employee must have worked for the employer for at least twelve months and for at least 1,250 hours per year. Under some circumstances, leave may be taken intermittently, in increments of as little as one hour at a time, until the twelve weeks is exhausted. Part-time employees are excluded from the act's coverage and are not counted in calculating the fifty employees necessary for an employer to be covered by the act. An employee cannot contract out of his or her right to leave under the FMLA. However, the employer may require the employee, or an employee may choose, to substitute any or all accrued paid leave for the leave time that is provided for under the act.

for their ties to minority communities. Prior to the merger, the percentages of minority and female employees and new hires increased steadily. Postmerger data suggested that, by 2002, minority and female employees were being hired and promoted at rates reasonably close to their proportion in ChevronTexaco's workforce.

The Task Force praised ChevronTexaco for integrating diversity into all training because it "sends the message that diversity is integral to the Company's business."[40] Nonetheless, the Task Force expressed concern that ChevronTexaco did not make ongoing diversity training for existing supervisors mandatory: "The Company actively encourages diversity training, but, in some instances, the most needy may not be the most likely to respond positively to that encouragement."[41]

ChevronTexaco adopted Texaco's mentoring programs and combined the best practices of both premerger companies' standardized performance evaluation programs. Among the most effective was Texaco's job competency model, which defined the facts, abilities, and skills required to perform specific jobs: "By breaking down the skills required on the job, the competency model avoids stereotypes, presumptions, and assumptions about ability."[42]

ChevronTexaco developed a problem resolution process, based in part on Texaco's program, to help employees resolve workplace concerns at any level of the organization. The program included a confidential telephone hotline and a mailing address for employees to report allegations of wrongdoing without fear of retaliation. Its procedures aimed at the following:

- Solving problems and resolving issues in their early stages

- Ensuring that all employees with work-related issues are treated with respect and dignity

- Helping provide a productive and safe workplace environment

- Making counselors, mediators, and arbitrators available as needed to assist with problem resolution

- Communicating to all employees the company's zero tolerance for discrimination, harassment, and retaliation in any form to alleviate fears of retaliation

ChevronTexaco also retained Texaco's highly successful Ombuds Program, in which workers could contact any one of several ombudspersons to safely and confidentially discuss any work-related issue.

The ombudsperson serves as "a champion for fair process who can advise and assist employees in developing an action plan to address work-related issues."[43]

Noncompliance Is Costly

As ChevronTexaco began reaping the benefits of a diverse workforce with the best candidates in every job, other companies were still learning their own costly lessons about discrimination. The Coca-Cola Company agreed to pay $192.5 million in 2000 to settle racial discrimination charges. According to the complaint, the company's African-American managers were excluded from the global marketing and finance divisions (the most powerful departments offering the best potential for advancement), and they were relegated to low-profile divisions, such as human resources and corporate affairs.[44]

A 1995 report by African-American executives to Coke's then president described an atmosphere in which African-American employees felt "humiliated, ignored, overlooked, or unacknowledged." The report also criticized the absence of African Americans in top management.[45]

Preventing Harassment

No company can retain a high quality work force that reflects the diversity of today's customer base if certain workers are singled out for ridicule, ostracism, unwelcome sexual advances, and other types of abuse because of their race, color, religion, gender, or place of birth. Harassment is degrading not only for the immediate target but also for the coworker who must choose between witnessing it in silence or being branded a troublemaker for complaining.

Recognizing that harassment can make working intolerable, the courts ruled early on that the creation of a hostile work environment based on an employee's race, color, religion, or national origin constitutes unlawful discrimination prohibited under Title VII.[46] Sexual harassment can target males as well as females, and racial or religious bigotry can harm persons of any race or religion.

Title VII also forbids any job-related adverse action (such as denial of a promotion, demotion, discharge, or reassignment to a lesser post) when a person refuses to respond to a supervisor's sexual advances. Such retaliation is known as *quid pro quo harassment*. Quid pro quo harassment also occurs when a supervisor makes an employee submit to sexual advances as a condition for receiving employment benefits.

Employer Liability for Harassment

An employer is absolutely liable for a supervisor's quid pro quo sexual harassment regardless of whether the employer knew what the supervisor was doing or had any reason to be aware of it. The employer is liable even if it had well-distributed policies that prohibited *quid pro quo* harassment.

Even though a supervisor is acting outside the scope of employment when harassing an employee, the authority the employer has given the supervisor makes the harassment possible (and the employer liable). As the Supreme Court explained: "When a fellow employee harasses, the victim can walk away or tell the offender where to go, but it may be difficult to offer such responses to a supervisor" with the power to hire, fire, and set work schedules and pay raises.[47] If the harassing supervisor fires, demotes, or takes other adverse employment action against the harassed employee, then the employer is liable for the supervisor's wrongful conduct even if the employer sought to prevent it.

If, however, the supervisor does not take adverse action against the employee, then the employer may have an affirmative defense against liability for a supervisor's hostile work environment harassment. To avail itself of this defense, the employer must demonstrate two things: (1) management exercised reasonable care to prevent and promptly correct any harassing behavior, and (2) the employee unreasonably failed to take advantage of the preventative or corrective opportunities provided by the employer.[48]

This affirmative defense is designed to encourage employers to do their best to prevent harassment, and it can provide companies a powerful shield in hostile-environment cases. By being proactive, managers can reduce the likelihood that harassment will occur, mitigate the harm caused, and limit or eliminate their vicarious liability.

An employer is liable for hostile environment harassment by a coworker or customer if the employer knew or should have known of the harassment and failed to take prompt and reasonable steps to prevent or remedy it. For example, Pizza Hut was found liable when a rowdy male customer grabbed a waitress and put his mouth on her breast. Before this incident, the waitress had informed the manager that the customer and his companion had made offensive comments to her and pulled her hair, but the manager had ordered her to continue waiting on them, saying, "You were hired to be a waitress. You waitress."[49]

In contrast, the city of San Mateo was held not liable when a male coworker touched a female employee's breast and stomach while she was answering a 911 emergency call. After learning of the incident, the employer immediately investigated the incident and removed the male employee from the workplace.[50] This case demonstrates that even clearly egregious behavior by a coworker does not trigger employer liability if the employer takes prompt and appropriate corrective action.

Prevention Is the Best Defense

Supervisors must make clear to every employee that all forms of racist and sexist behavior and joking are inappropriate in the workplace. Employers should adopt and distribute a clearly written anti-harassment policy, including an effective complaint procedure that specifies company officials other than the employee's direct supervisor to whom complaints can be made.

Senior management, whether through the human resources staff or otherwise, should familiarize themselves with the atmosphere in the workplace and be vigilant about maintaining an appropriate environment where employees can work comfortably. This behavior is especially important when supervisors are physically isolated from top management but have broad authority over their subordinates.

It is also important to develop an atmosphere in which employees feel free to bring a complaint. This policy has two components. First, victims of harassment should be given information and support in identifying and reporting harassment.[51] Providing hot lines and making an ombudsperson available can make it easier for an employee to come forward. Second, because the harasser is often the employee's supervisor, an effective procedure provides more than one person to whom the employee can complain. There should be persons of both genders and of various races and religions designated so employees have a choice.

Employers should do their best to protect employee privacy, but promising the victim confidentiality is a dangerous approach. If the alleged harasser goes on to harass someone else, and that person discovers that the employer knew of the previous claims but did nothing, the failure to act could be used against the employer in a suit by the second victim. For this reason, managers should rarely, if ever, agree to keep the matter confidential.

Managers should also ensure that all complaints are thoroughly investigated. An employer representative should meet with the complaining employee at the employee's earliest convenience and immediately interview the accused person, coworkers, and other witnesses. If the investigation reveals a problem, then the employer should consider whether termination or reassignment of the harasser or a reprimand is in order. Any reprimand should be put in writing and put in the harasser's personnel file. The reprimand should make it clear to the harasser that his or her conduct is unacceptable and that any recurrence will be grounds for severe discipline—including termination. The harasser should also be instructed to avoid having contact with the victim and to refrain from talking about him or her.

A supervisor should follow up with the victim to ensure that there are no continuing problems and to assure him or her that the company will do whatever it can to support the victim's career goals. Even if the investigation is inconclusive, it may be appropriate for the supervisor to offer to reassign the alleged victim.

An employer who fails to respond appropriately to claims or evidence of harassment exposes itself to multimillion-dollar jury awards. Baker & McKenzie, one of the world's largest law firms, learned this the hard way in 1994 after a California jury awarded legal secretary Rena Weeks $50,000 in compensatory damages and $6.9 million in punitive damages for sexual harassment by her supervisor, Martin Greenstein, a former Baker & McKenzie partner. Greenstein, who allegedly grabbed Weeks's breasts and buttocks and dropped M&M candies into her blouse pocket, was ordered to personally pay $225,000 in punitive damages.

At trial, Weeks presented evidence that for several years before Baker & McKenzie hired her, Greenstein had engaged in similar conduct with other women employees. The incidents were reported to the firm's management, but the firm did little in response other than to speak to Greenstein and to document the reports in the women's personnel files. Each time, Greenstein denied the accusation and was warned not to engage in such conduct, but the firm never took further action.

Weeks suggested that the firm hesitated to punish Greenstein for his boorish behavior because he was a major generator of lucrative business. In assessing punitive damages equal to 10 percent of Baker & McKenzie's net worth, the jury was, according to juror Frank Lewis, "sending a message not only to Baker & McKenzie but to corporate America."[52] The trial court reduced the punitive damage award to $3.5 million.

Beware the Holiday Party

The prohibition on harassment applies not only to conduct occurring during normal business hours on the company's premises but to all work-related activities, including company parties, trade shows, and client entertainment. Managers should not require a woman to choose between going to a strip-tease club with the "boys" or staying at the hotel and missing an opportunity to strengthen ties with male mentors or clients.

In 1998, Astra USA, a unit of the pharmaceutical giant Astra AB of Sweden, agreed to pay $9.85 million to more than seventy-five women subjected to a hostile environment and to one man who had been punished for speaking out.[53] An investigative report by

BusinessWeek uncovered a corporate culture in which women employees were regularly groped, expected to go to executives' hotel rooms and have drinks, treated as sex objects at work, and subjected to sexual advances by the president and other members of top management.[54] Those who complained suffered retaliation by being discredited, passed up for promotion, and even discharged. After an internal probe, the president was fired.[55]

Harassment in the Virtual Office

Employers may not disregard offensive messages posted on e-mail systems when the employer knows, or has reason to know, that they are part of a pattern of harassment in the workplace or in related settings. This includes sexually explicit or racist images used as "wallpaper" on computer screens.

Consider the case of Tammy Blakey, the first female captain at Continental Airlines to fly an Airbus 300 widebody jet. Continental's male pilots posted derogatory and insulting remarks about Blakey on the pilots' on-line bulletin board, the Crew Members Forum.[56] Although crew members, not Continental, paid CompuServe an hourly fee to access the forum, the link was an option on Continental's Home Access program, which crew members were required to access to learn their flight schedules.

In analyzing Continental's potential liability, the New Jersey Supreme Court explained that if management knew that a bulletin board at an airport lounge for pilots and crew members contained similar comments, then there would be "little doubt" that the airline would be liable for hostile environment harassment, unless it took prompt corrective action. Similarly, if the insults occurred at a place frequented by senior management, pilots, and crew and were a continuation of a pattern of harassment in the workplace, then the employer "would not be entirely free to ignore" its knowledge of the incident. Thus the virtual bulletin board's "location" outside the workplace did not free Continental from the duty to correct off-site harassment by coemployees.[57]

The court noted the importance of extensions of the workplace where "the relations among employees are cemented or sometimes sundered" and asked "what exactly is the outsider (whether black, Latino, or woman) to do" when the belittling conduct continues in an after-hours setting: "Keep swallowing the abuse or give up the chance to make the team?"

Consider an Apology, Mediation, or Arbitration

As these cases show, it's impossible to overstate the need to take harassment and discrimination charges seriously. Sometimes an employee lawsuit or the threat of a suit stems from misunderstandings or the feeling that management just isn't listening. Although some employees may be interested in only a cash recovery, aggrieved employees often just want the employer to take responsibility for the situation and apologize.[58] The general counsel, who usually has little contact with most employees, may not be the most appropriate choice to listen to their complaints or to apologize on behalf of the employer. Instead, a senior manager may be a better choice. Mediation, which involves using a third party to facilitate discussion and resolution of a dispute, can be particularly effective in the workplace, especially when the employer does not want to lose any of the employees embroiled in the conflict.

Increasingly, employers are requiring employees to agree to submit all work-related disputes to binding arbitration. Mandatory arbitration protects the employer from the often-unpredictable results of a jury trial, and it may provide a faster, less costly, and more private way to resolve disputes. I discuss these processes in detail in chapter 8. Some employers are willing to litigate claims but require employees to waive their right to a jury trial, a practice that has been successfully challenged in several states.[59]

Executive Summary

Fish rots from the head. All the policies in the world will not keep employees out of trouble if the CEO does not set the tone at the top.

Remember the respectful support that Liz Smith received from Jim Kinnear at Texaco? Compare her experience with that of an

African American female consultant working with an airline in South Africa. After being subjected to lewd comments and pinches, she called the partner in charge, only to be told that she should use her own judgment and could come home if she wanted to. Instead of wrapping the lower status person in his mantle of authority and speaking with a senior executive at the client firm, the partner left her swinging in the wind. She finally decided she could not take the abuse any longer after she overheard the client making an extremely lewd and racist comment about her in Africaans. Apparently the client didn't realize that she could understand what he was saying.

The difference between these two incidents can be summed up in one word: leadership. Ultimately, it is not the human resources department that determines whether employees are treated fairly. It's top management.

8

Managing Disputes

D ISPUTES ARE INEVITABLE in business. A vibrant free-market
economy presents countless occasions for companies and
individuals to bump against each other as they strive to create and
capture value. In fact, a firm that never encounters legal challenges
may be missing out on legitimate opportunities by pursuing an
overly cautious legal or business strategy.

Legally astute managers think strategically about their disputes.
Instead of overly delegating or deferring to attorneys, the most successful executives realize that every legal dispute is a business problem requiring a business solution. By becoming actively involved in
the resolution of disputes, business people can often look beyond the
boundaries of the original disagreement. They can put other topics
on the table and find creative, win-win solutions that benefit all parties. In so doing, they convert a zero-sum argument about who is
right into an integrative, variable-sum negotiation in which both
parties trade lower-valued resources for higher-valued ones.[1]

For example, Texaco had contracted to supply oil to a particular
plant at a below-market price. The owner of the plant kept it run-
ning despite its inefficiencies to take advantage of the favorable supply contract. A dispute arose and the plant owner sued Texaco for
breach of contract and various business torts. The heads of the two
companies then conferred and negotiated a settlement. The plant

owner agreed to drop the lawsuit (which could have resulted in hundreds of millions of dollars in damages) in exchange for Texaco's agreement to permit the plant owner to transfer the contract to a more efficient plant. The relationship was salvaged and both companies declared victory.[2]

In the best of worlds, this approach keeps the argument out of court. Litigation is bad news for everyone (except the litigators, of course). Judge Learned Hand told a group of New York lawyers that "as a citizen he would fear litigation beyond anything but sickness and death."[3] Sol Linowitz, former general counsel and CEO of Xerox Corporation, characterized lawsuits as "a defeat for the lawyers and managers just as a war is a defeat for the diplomats."[4] Jerry Jasinowski, head of the National Association of Manufacturers, called trial lawyers "the pariahs of the business community, which is more frightened by them than terrorists, China, or high energy prices."[5] Even the American Bar Association Committee on Professionalism remarked that "litigation today frequently resembles the dance marathons of the 1930s, where the partners or, in this case the adversaries, move as slowly as possible to the music without actually stopping."[6]

Litigation is not only expensive; it is also a serious drain on management time, focus, and energy. Every hour spent in a windowless room being deposed is an hour the manager is not spending executing the business plan.

The win-lose nature of lawsuits usually makes it impossible for both parties to claim satisfaction, save face, or forgive and forget. After a lawsuit, at best one party feels vindicated and the other feels wronged. Even the ostensible winners often feel angry about the time and money spent getting what they felt was their due to begin with.

If a company ends up in court, it has already lost, regardless of the ultimate verdict. Or, as Jay Walker, founder of Priceline.com, put it, "It's not a matter of who wins. It's a matter of who loses less."[7]

Nevertheless, some disputes simply cannot be resolved without third-party help. In such cases, managers almost always need to consult with counsel to understand their rights, their exposure to liability, and the available courses of action. But legally astute managers never just sit back and let the lawyers run the show.

Consider Pennzoil's suit against Texaco for tortious influence with Pennzoil's agreement to buy Getty Oil. Texaco's lawyers were so convinced that Pennzoil had no chance of winning that they persuaded the Texaco board that Texaco should not even dignify Pennzoil's claims by offering any testimony on what damages Pennzoil would be entitled to receive if the jury found that Texaco had wrongfully interfered with Pennzoil's deal with Getty. Left with only the testimony from Pennzoil's damages expert that Pennzoil suffered a loss of $7.5 billion, the jury awarded Pennzoil compensatory damages of $7.5 billion. Had Texaco put a damages expert on the stand, the expert would have testified that, at most, Pennzoil lost the difference between what Texaco paid for Getty Oil in an arm's-length transaction and what Pennzoil had agreed to pay, or roughly $500 million. James Kinnear, vice chair of Texaco at the time of the trial, came away from the experience convinced that managers should never put the company at risk in court or any other place if they can possibly avoid it.[8] According to Kinnear, "The case should have been and could have been settled."[9]

This chapter offers a variety of techniques for managing disputes, beginning with open communication at the most senior levels of the firm. It continues by describing alternative dispute resolution (ADR) techniques, including negotiation, mediation, arbitration, and various combinations of the three, and recommends that companies adopt ADR programs for regular use in all their business activities.

For the times when all ADR mechanisms fail, the chapter sets forth key considerations for managing litigation to obtain the most favorable outcomes at the lowest cost. Finally, it outlines the necessary elements of an effective policy for the creation, retention, and destruction of company documents.

Use Alternative Dispute Resolution Techniques

Alternative dispute resolution techniques, such as negotiation, mediation, arbitration, med-arb, arb-med, minitrials, and summary jury trials, can save valuable management time and money by avoiding litigation. ADR procedures help minimize disruption to the organi-

TABLE 8-1

Models of alternative dispute resolution

	Negotiation	Mediation	Arbitration
How are the disputants represented?	Disputants represent themselves or legal counsel negotiates on their behalf	By themselves	By legal counsel
Who makes the final decision?	Disputants mutually decide	Disputants mutually decide	If binding arbitration, arbitrator decides
How are the facts found and standards of judgment set?	Parties decide ad hoc	Parties decide ad hoc	Arbitrator decides based on preset rules, e.g., those of the AAA
What is the source for the standard of resolution?	Mutual agreement	Mutual agreement	Applicable law and arbitrator's sense of fairness
How will the resolution be enforced?	Agreement usually turned into a contract that is enforceable by the courts	Agreement usually turned into a contract that is enforceable by the courts	By courts, according to the agreement to arbitrate the dispute
Who will pay the dispute resolution fees?	Parties decide ad hoc	Parties decide ad hoc	Parties decide before entering arbitration, often in arbitration clause

Source: Constance E. Bagley, *Managers and the Legal Environment: Strategies for the 21st Century,* 4th ed. (Mason, OH: West Legal Studies in Business, 2002). Used by permission.

zation and increase the likelihood of achieving sound business solutions. Table 8-1 summarizes the varieties of ADR.

Like other business decisions, choosing an alternative dispute resolution mechanism involves many tradeoffs. Managers should think carefully about their own goals and the nature of the various dispute resolution alternatives. Is the right decision more important than quick resolution, or is time of the essence? Will public attention help resolve the conflict, or does the matter require confidentiality? Does the company need to preserve its relationship with the other party, or is this conflict the last interaction with that party? Will mutual

Med-arb/Arb-med	Minitrial	Summary jury trial
By legal counsel	By legal counsel	By legal counsel
Arbitrator if parties can't agree	Disputants mutually decide	Jury
Parties and arbitrator decide	Parties decide ad hoc	Rules of court
Applicable law and arbitrator's sense of fairness if parties can't agree	Mutual agreement	Jury's sense of fairness
By courts, according to the agreement to arbitrate the dispute	Agreement usually turned into a contract that is enforceable by the courts	By courts
Parties decide in advance	Parties decide ad hoc	Parties decide ad hoc

resolution of the conflict enhance the company's reputation as a desirable business partner? Will potential disputants seek conflict if the company appears weak and unwilling to defend itself vigorously?

Parties who have agreed to use ADR usually include a clause to that effect in their contracts. Unfortunately, ADR clauses often do not include details of how mediation or arbitration will proceed, when and where it will take place, who will preside, what (if any) discovery will be available, and what types of damages can be awarded. In some states, such as Illinois, an arbitrator cannot award punitive damages unless the parties expressly authorize it. Parties are therefore better served by including specific provisions concerning these matters in their agreement before a dispute arises.

Try Basic Communication First

Often, communication or the lack of it makes the difference between a minor disagreement and protracted litigation. If managers are willing to discuss the issues at hand, they can often find solutions that make sense to everyone concerned.

Sometimes, as we saw in chapters 6 and 7, what the other party really wants is just an apology. Mike France of *BusinessWeek* dubbed this strategy the "mea culpa defense."[10] Instead of stonewalling, France calls on executives to acknowledge their mistakes and apologize. He offers the following recipe for delivering corporate apologies: apologies should be offered promptly, authoritatively, clearly, and bravely—and spoken in plain honest English. As Merrill Lynch learned when its CEO David H. Komansky apologized for its misleading analyst reports, an apology is less likely to be considered authentic and result in an improved customer relationship if it is accompanied by a disclaimer of liability.[11]

Work with Mediators and Arbitrators

A mediator's role is to suggest ways to resolve the dispute fairly and to guide the parties toward resolution. Unlike a judge or an arbitrator, a mediator cannot enforce a solution. The parties must come to a resolution themselves and then agree to abide by it.

A skilled mediator knows how to bring disputing parties to genuine settlement. An unskilled mediator can push parties into agreements they later regret or, worse, can inflame the situation. According to the Society of Professionals in Dispute Resolution, qualified mediators should be able to:

- Understand the negotiating process and the role of advocacy.

- Earn trust and maintain acceptability.

- Convert parties' positions into needs and interests.

- Screen out nonmediational issues.

- Help parties invent creative options.

- Help parties identify principles and criteria that will guide their decision making.

- Help parties assess their nonsettlement alternatives.

- Help parties make their own informed choices.

- Help parties assess whether their agreement can be implemented.[12]

In contrast to mediation, an arbitrator's ruling is generally binding. While a jury's or a judge's decision can be set aside if it is clearly erroneous, New York's highest court stated nearly two decades ago, "An arbitrator's paramount responsibility is to reach an equitable result, and the courts will not assume the role of overseers to mold the award to conform to their sense of justice. Thus, an arbitrator's award will not be vacated for errors of law and fact committed by the arbitrator."[13]

Parties using mediation/arbitration (med-arb) first try to mediate the dispute. If this is unsuccessful, they proceed to binding arbitration. Parties using med-arb should not designate the same person to serve as mediator and arbitrator because this practice will inhibit the parties' willingness to speak candidly about their case and thus make settlement less likely during the mediation phase.

Parties using arbitration/mediation (arb-med) present their case to an arbitrator who makes an award, but the arbitrator keeps it secret while the parties try to resolve the dispute through mediation. If the mediation fails, then the arbitrator's award is unsealed and becomes binding on the parties.

Implement a Systematic ADR Program

Legally astute management teams often adopt systematic, organizationwide ADR programs to forestall and manage disagreements. Implementing an effective alternative dispute resolution program takes five basic steps:[14]

- *Generate enthusiasm within the company.* High-level management should demonstrate full commitment to the program. Executives should work with corporate counsel to explain its benefits to all employees.

- *Ensure that ADR procedures are followed.* Some companies negotiate ADR clauses into all their standard business agreements. Others work with their attorneys to decide which disputes are best resolved by alternative dispute resolution rather than litigation.

- *Persuade business partners to use ADR techniques.* After deciding that an ADR method is the best way to achieve its goal, the company must persuade the opposing party to participate in the procedure. Most parties readily accept certain forms such as mediation, which is informal and can be terminated at any time. Furthermore, a mediator can protect the confidentiality of sensitive data, which might be made public during litigation.

- *Work with counsel but focus on the business strategy.* As with litigation, managers should not just rely on their lawyers to run the show. The officials with authority to approve monetary settlements should be involved throughout the process, not just at the last minute. This helps keep the legal strategy aligned with the business strategy. Proaction, interaction, and involvement should be the rule rather than an after-the-fact reaction.

- *Monitor, refine, and improve the program.* Once a company has developed an ADR program, all participants should provide continuous feedback and constructive criticism to incorporate the lessons of experience. The company may wish to designate one manager as the ADR "point person" who is responsible for monitoring the program, correcting its flaws, and refining its strengths.

Litigate When Necessary but Be Strategic About It

Sometimes litigation—with all its costs and other disadvantages—is the only way to preserve a firm's first-mover advantage or to protect its assets and rights. But managers should never rush to trial. Before filing a lawsuit, they should consider the following:

- Whether the likelihood of recovery and the amount of recovery are enough to justify the cost and disruption of litigation

- Whether the defendant would be able to satisfy a judgment against it

- Whether the defendant is likely to raise a counterclaim

- Whether suing will cause any ill will among customers, suppliers, or sources of corporate financing

- Whether any publicity accompanying the suit will be harmful

- What impact litigation is likely to have on the company's relationship with the defendant and on its reputation in general

After taking these considerations into account, a manager may decide not to sue the manufacturer of its multimillion-dollar computer system over a $50,000 software problem if the company must rely on this manufacturer for support, service, and parts for the next few years. Instead, it may make more sense to try to persuade the manufacturer to provide additional hardware or software that is worth more to the customer than it costs the manufacturer to provide.

But sometimes no amount of persuasion or negotiation remedies the problem, and litigation becomes the only way to protect the firm's position. For example, after Priceline.com had successfully patented its buyer-driven auction system for the sale of airline tickets, hotel rooms, and other items, Microsoft's Expedia began using a similar system to sell hotel rooms. Notwithstanding Jay Walker's distaste for litigation, when his efforts to resolve the dispute amicably failed, he concluded that Priceline had no choice but to sue Microsoft and Expedia:

> [W]hen we looked at the whole Internet space, the sameness of the commercial offerings is simply breathtaking. Priceline.com's IP gives it a huge advantage—there is no other demand aggregation system like it, and we believed it would continue to

give us a unique product offering that would translate into
revenue and market share. In this case, we concluded that the
IP was at the core of our ability to differentiate ourselves in an
environment of low barriers to entry and ease of imitation.
Once we looked at the issue this way, the decision to sue was
very straightforward.[15]

G. Richard Shell chronicled Sumner Redstone's decision, as Viacom CEO, to sue Time Inc. for refusing to carry Viacom's two premium cable movie channels, Showtime and The Movie Channel.[16]
Time was one of the largest cable operators in the United States and
owned two of its own movie channels, Home Box Office (HBO) and
Cinemax. Although Time was Viacom's biggest customer and car-
ried Viacom's MTV, Nickelodeon, and VH-1 channels in its lineup,
Time refused to carry Showtime and The Movie Channel in New
York or Detroit. Redstone (a graduate of the Harvard Law School
and former appellate advocate for the U.S. Justice Department) had
advised Time that he considered their refusal anticompetitve behavior in violation of the antitrust laws, but Time refused to relent.

Despite the risk that Time might throw all of Viacom's channels
off its cable networks, Redstone decided that he had no choice but to
sue. He explained:

My corporate life was on the line; we were facing a risk that
went to the very core of the long-term viability of Viacom. If
allowed to continue, this boycott could kill Showtime. One
thing you cannot tolerate is someone using raw power to
disenfranchise your company.[17]

Redstone knew that Viacom's profits would take a beating if Time
dropped Viacom's channels. Nevertheless, he considered it unlikely
that Time would risk provoking a congressional inquiry by com-
pounding its arguably anticompetitive conduct, especially when it
was negotiating to merge with Warner Communications. Moreover,
he assumed that Time would want to avoid alienating its own viewers by reducing its channel offerings.

This assessment of Time's motivations allowed Redstone to zero in on his main goal of gaining market share for his movie channels. As a result, he did not get Viacom involved in an ongoing congressional investigation of cable TV rates and regulation. Nor did he sue to enjoin the merger of Time with Warner. Instead, he chose a rifle-shot approach: he sued specifically for the right to include Showtime and The Movie Channel in Viacom's lineup.

After two years of pretrial discovery, during which Viacom collected persuasive evidence that Time was favoring its own programming in violation of the antitrust laws, the parties settled. Time paid a small part of the $2.4 billion in damages Viacom had demanded but agreed to carry both Showtime and The Movie Channel and to buy more advertising on Viacom's other channels.[18]

Similarly, MCI used litigation against American Telephone & Telegraph to open up the market for long-distance telephone services. The lawsuit kept the issue before the public and the regulators. It also gave MCI a measure of credibility and name recognition far greater than its meager profits would have generated.[19]

Sometimes a lawsuit is worth pursuing simply to establish a company's credibility as one that will fight to support a legitimate business position. For example, an employer might sue an employee for a $100 theft to deter others from trying to steal or embezzle much larger amounts. If the problem is a recurring one or if the opposing party is clearly making a frivolous or extortionate claim, then the courtroom may be the most practical alternative.

Although historically companies have viewed class actions as the bane of their existence, legally astute managers have embraced them as strategic management tools. To firms sued for product liability, they offer the ability to resolve millions of claims by both persons already evidencing signs of injury and persons who may exhibit injury in the future.

Don't Let the Lawyers Run the Show

Even if the manager responsible for resolving a dispute concludes that litigation is inevitable, he or she should not rely on the lawyers to make the best business decisions. Litigators often wrongly assume that they call the shots. As a result, they may spend more time and money on a case than the client intended. The key decision makers need to be involved from the outset so that the people motivating the action are in the same room as the people with the power to resolve the dispute.[20]

Before filing the complaint, managers should work with counsel to develop a budget for the lawsuit. The budget should include not only attorney's fees but also the cost of employee time, as well as other hidden expenses such as disruption of business and damage to company morale.

Defendants Need a Litigation Strategy, Too

A defendant receiving a complaint and summons should never let the lawsuit go unattended. The defendant should plan a defense strategy and follow it step by step. Factual and legal preparation should be done promptly so that important evidence—such as the memory of key witnesses—is not lost.

When a company receives a complaint, management should make every effort to determine why the plaintiff felt it necessary to sue. The inquiry should go beyond the specific claims of the suit. For example, managers should find out whether prior bargaining or negotiations with the plaintiff broke down. Perhaps the company's negotiator was pursuing the wrong tactics or following an agenda inconsistent with the company's business strategy. The managers in charge should also ascertain whether the lawsuit resulted from flawed personnel or customer relations practices that the company still needs to correct.

Finally, management should review the specifics of the suit with counsel and evaluate the company's business risks and potential legal exposure. Figure 8-1 provides a framework for estimating a company's legal exposure for its past actions.

The managers of the defendant company responsible for resolving the dispute should decide whether it would be beneficial to discuss the lawsuit with the plaintiff or to apologize. The defendant may also want to suggest mediation or arbitration as alternatives to

FIGURE 8-1

Evaluating legal exposure for past acts

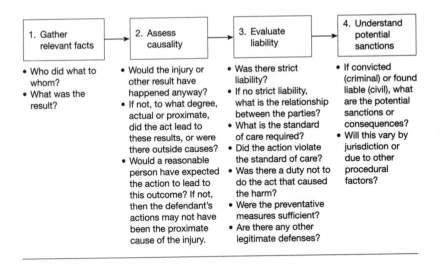

1. Gather relevant facts	2. Assess causality	3. Evaluate liability	4. Understand potential sanctions
• Who did what to whom? • What was the result?	• Would the injury or other result have happened anyway? • If not, to what degree, actual or proximate, did the act lead to these results, or were there outside causes? • Would a reasonable person have expected the action to lead to this outcome? If not, then the defendant's actions may not have been the proximate cause of the injury.	• Was there strict liability? • If no strict liability, what is the relationship between the parties? • What is the standard of care required? • Did the action violate the standard of care? • Was there a duty not to do the act that caused the harm? • Were the preventative measures sufficient? • Are there any other legitimate defenses?	• If convicted (criminal) or found liable (civil), what are the potential sanctions or consequences? • Will this vary by jurisdiction or due to other procedural factors?

an expensive trial. Additionally, if the suit was filed in a state court, the defendant must decide whether it is possible and desirable to move the action to federal court. Out-of-state defendants often feel that they will receive a more impartial hearing in federal court.

Try to Settle Earlier Rather Than Later

More than 95 percent of cases settle before trial, saving all parties the time, cost, and ill will of a trial. Unfortunately, settlement often occurs on the courthouse steps after the parties have spent lots of time and money on discovery and other pretrial wrangling.

All courts urge the parties to confer and settle the case if possible. The judge often acts as a settlement mediator and assists the parties and their counsel in recognizing the strengths and weaknesses of their cases. Indeed, federal and state judges often refuse to schedule a case for trial until the parties have attempted mediation or attended a settlement conference before a specially designated settlement judge.

Litigation—especially before a jury—can have a lottery quality. Juries convinced that a corporate defendant has done something wrong can wreak their vengeance by awarding punitive damages many times higher than the compensatory damages for the plaintiff's actual loss. Thus a claim that seems little more than a nuisance suit designed to extort money from the company can yield a very negative outcome if the case goes to a jury.

Citigroup CEO (and former general counsel) Chuck Prince declared victory when he was able to settle—for a "mere" $2.65 billion—claims that Citigroup and its star analyst Jack Grubman had misled former WorldCom shareholders about WorldCom's prospects. Citigroup thereby avoided what Prince told analysts was a "roll of the dice" that could have resulted in a jury verdict of $54 billion if the case had gone to trial.[21]

Managers should engage in a continuing conversation with counsel to find ways of settling cases cheaply and quickly. This requires identifying and overcoming the litigious working assumptions of both the company and the lawyers. Involving high-level company people in the settlement talks sends the crucial message that the company takes the allegations seriously.

Negotiation expert Roger Fisher notes that emotions, a desire to pass the buck, and partisan bias can create a litigation trap that prevents some conflicts from being settled in a timely manner.[22] Egos must be set aside—by both managers and lawyers—in pursuit of optimal *solutions* to the *problem* of litigation.

Fisher recommends that managers instruct counsel to develop a settlement strategy in addition to a litigation strategy.[23] That is, while litigators are searching for ways to overcome a potential adversary, corporate counsel should also delineate specific settlement options and seek ways to resolve the conflict as soon as possible. Managers should work with counsel to construct a litigation decision tree so that they can determine at each step of the proceeding the chances of prevailing or losing, the costs of going forward, and the potential amount of recovery. Then during each phase of the case, both the managers and the lawyers can discuss the options based on an ongoing cost-benefit analysis.

Such an organized approach enables the responsible manager to keep the conflict in perspective by comparing the costs, advantages, and disadvantages of litigation and settlement. It also assists a manager in identifying situations in which it is worthwhile to go to court, either to establish a beneficial precedent or to limit (or overturn) a disadvantageous one. A postmortem review comparing the accuracy of cost predictions with the results of settlement or litigation may also help reduce legal fees over time.

When All Else Fails

The following kinds of lawsuits are unlikely to settle:

- Cases presenting legal questions—such as the meaning of an ambiguous term in a contract—that the court should clarify to avoid future disputes between the same parties

- Cases that could bring a large recovery if the plaintiff wins and no great harm if it loses

- Cases where one side has acted so unreasonably that settlement is impossible[24]

Having decided to pursue or to defend a lawsuit, top management should carefully select the managers who will act as the contacts for the attorneys and be responsible for managing the litigation strategy. These people should have substantial authority in the company. They should begin by ensuring that the attorneys are given timely access to all necessary information and documents.

Top management should remind all employees not to destroy any documents (including e-mail and other electronic files) that may be relevant to the lawsuit. As explained at the end of this chapter, the improper destruction of documents can be harmful, even illegal.

Furthermore, the managers who will be witnesses in the lawsuit or working with the corporate attorneys should not handle public relations. This practice could lead to the inadvertent waiver of attorney-client privilege.

Employees should be instructed not to discuss the lawsuit with anyone, including family or close friends. Casual comments about bankrupting the opposing party or teaching an opponent a lesson may turn up as testimony at trial, with undesirable consequences.

Adopt a Policy for Document Creation, Retention, and Destruction

When a company is a party in a lawsuit or the subject of a government investigation, it must produce all documents within its control that may be relevant to the dispute or investigation. (One exception is documents protected by the attorney-client privilege, discussed in chapter 9.) Discoverable information includes all documents in employees' physical and computer files, regardless of whether the files are kept in the company's offices or at the employees' homes.

Alert Employees to the Dangers of E-mails and Instant Messages

Managers are often surprised to learn that their private diaries, notebooks, calendars, e-mails, and instant messages are all subject to discovery and can be used to prove liability in court. E-mail and instant messaging are particularly problematic. Because of the informality of the medium and the ease with which e-mail and instant messages can be created, sent, and forwarded, companies can find themselves trying to explain the midnight machismo of a manager (remember the Microsoft employees' e-mails discussing ways to "cut off Netscape's air supply" and "knife the baby") or the road-weary ruminations of a sales rep ("Wouldn't it be great if a couple of us little guys could stop slitting each other's throats so we stand a chance at outbidding the 800-pound gorilla?"). The latter statement, together with a calendar showing a lunch date with a sales rep working for another small competitor, might be enough to prove illegal bid-rigging.

New York attorney general Eliot Spitzer's case against Marsh & McLennan Companies, the world's largest insurance broker, for illegal bid rigging hinged on damning e-mails, such as the one in which a Marsh executive requested an insurance company to send someone to make a phony bid for an insurance policy Marsh had already decided to steer to another insurer that agreed to pay Marsh a kickback: "This month's receipt of our Coordinator of the Month Award requested a body at the rescheduled April 23 meeting. He just needs a live body. Anyone from New York office would do. Given recent activities, perhaps you can send someone from your janitorial staff—preferably a recent hire from U.S. Postal Service."[25]

Even if an employee believes that he or she has deleted an e-mail or instant message, the likelihood is that there is a copy on a hard drive, server, or backup tape somewhere. Forensic experts excel at pulling "deleted" files off hard drives. As a result, no employee should put anything in an e-mail or instant message that he or she would not put in a written memo to the file. Sometimes it makes more sense to just pick up the phone to discuss a sensitive issue rather than to exchange e-mails that later might be misconstrued or taken out of context.

Implement a Document Management Program

Managers cannot be expected to keep track of all the federal and state regulations concerning the preservation of documents. What they can and should do is to seek legal advice to ensure that the company has a well-designed document management program. Counsel should periodically review the program and perform audits to ensure that it is being implemented properly.

A well-designed and well-executed document management program can provide these benefits:

- Ensure that the company retains the documents it is legally required to retain and does not inadvertently destroy documents in the face of a lawsuit or government investigation.

- Reduce corporate liability.

- Protect trade secrets and other confidential information.

- Save on storage costs.

- Reduce litigation expenses.[26]

Time and money are wasted when corporate staff and lawyers are forced to search for documents during discovery. With an organized document management program, a company knows exactly what documents are in its possession and where the documents are located. The program also streamlines company files by eliminating documents that serve no legal or business purpose.

To stand up in court, a document retention policy must satisfy several requirements. Specifically, it must be systematic with well-defined procedures that are applied in a consistent fashion. It must preclude selective destruction. It must also have special procedures for retaining and producing documents in the event of a threatened or pending lawsuit or government investigation.

Plan Well and Create a Systematic Design

Companies usually appoint a senior officer of the organization to be responsible for supervising and auditing the document management program. Specific policies should establish the types of documents to be retained or destroyed, including documents stored on computer or word processing disks. The unnecessary documents should then be systematically destroyed according to an established time frame (for example, when they reach a certain age). Financial and accounting information should be kept for at least seven years.

Avoid Selective Destruction

The importance of a systematic document-management and destruction program cannot be emphasized enough. Courts routinely inquire whether documents were destroyed in the ordinary course of business. Any hint of selective destruction jeopardizes the defensibility of a document management program. It also may constitute obstruction of justice or hindering a government investigation or court proceeding, which the Sarbanes-Oxley Act made federal offenses punishable by up to twenty years in prison.

Forbid Document Destruction in the Face of Potential Lawsuits or Government Investigation

Arthur Andersen is no more because it shredded Enron audit papers after learning that an SEC investigation was imminent. As Andersen learned the hard way, it is illegal to destroy documents when the company has notice of a potential lawsuit or government investigation. A company cannot wait until a suit is formally filed against it to stop destroying relevant documents. A company must halt destruction as soon as it has good reason to believe that a suit is likely to be filed or an investigation started.

In addition, if a court decides that a party to a civil lawsuit has improperly destroyed documents (including electronic files), then the judge can direct a verdict for the other side. For example, in a case involving Piper Aircraft,[27] flight data information essential to the case was missing. The judge did not believe Piper Aircraft's claim that it had not deliberately destroyed the relevant document, so he issued a directed verdict for the plaintiff and awarded $10 million in damages.

Executive Summary

No manager wants to be locked up for days in a windowless conference room being deposed. Similarly, few managers are comfortable putting the fate of their companies in the hands of twelve men and women who may know nothing about the product at issue, the industry, or the intricacies of financial engineering and accounting. Yet it is not uncommon for even very hands-on managers to defer to counsel once a complaint is filed.

A dispute often represents a breach in a relationship. Most managers would not feel comfortable delegating to a third party the task of structuring, nurturing, or modifying a business relationship. Nor should they feel comfortable delegating the job of salvaging or unwinding one. Remember, every legal dispute is a business problem requiring a business solution.

9

Achieving the Advice Advantage

W HAT DO YOU HAVE when you have a lawyer up to her head in sand? Not enough sand.

Managers often express frustration that lawyers are too expensive and not practical enough about what it takes to compete effectively in today's global marketplace. Popular stereotypes of lawyers include "overhead," "Dr. No," "internal cop," "keep us out of trouble," and "get us out of trouble!"[1] In a survey by the Case Western Reserve University Law School, business leaders associated the word *lawyer* with "authoritative," "conservative," "arrogant," "intimidating," and "know-it-all."[2] It needn't be this way.

Ideally, managers and their counsel work together as a team to identify the business and legal risks and opportunities associated with a particular transaction or activity. When managers and lawyers effectively tap each other's areas of professional expertise, the available attractive options increase dramatically.

For example, experienced intellectual property lawyers can help firms protect the trade secrets that create competitive advantage, build valuable brands, and exploit (either internally or through licensing) proprietary technology or original works of authorship. Skilled corporate attorneys can help structure acquisitions or dispositions of assets to achieve the most favorable after-tax return while reducing the downside risk.[3] Yet the plethora of lawyer jokes reflects just how hard it is to forge a strategic alliance between lawyers and their clients.

This final chapter shows managers how to collaborate more effectively with their lawyers to craft the best overall strategy and tactics for achieving core business objectives while minimizing legal risks and costs. It urges managers to bring in the lawyers early in the process of deciding what action to take. Drawing on research from the field of information technology, it suggests ways managers can better integrate legal considerations into the formation and execution of business strategy and create relationships of trust and mutual respect with counsel. The chapter discusses the role of a general counsel and offers guidelines for using attorney-client privilege to protect confidential communications. It concludes by explaining the importance of working with lawyers who view themselves as true counselors and not mere hired guns.

Treat Your Lawyer as a Partner, Not a Necessary Evil

To question existing assumptions and break away from old habits, both lawyers and managers must be creative. As a first step, they should be proactive. Legally astute managers bring in counsel early in the decision-making cycle; they do not wait until the last minute to fight a fire that has already started or to bless a deal that has already been struck. For counsel, being invited to participate in the decision-making or the deal-making stage means something far different than serving as a rubber stamp or a "No man."

While in private practice, I was surprised at the number of times my clients told me that a change in structure that I proposed to dramatically reduce the legal risk would, with some tweaking, make little difference in the business outcome. If my clients had been reluctant to bring me in early, I would have been far less effective. By helping me better understand their business and strategic goals and by listening to my legal concerns, my clients enabled us to tap each other's areas of professional expertise. Working together, we crafted strategies and solutions that were superior to what either of us would have devised acting alone.

Unfortunately, counsel-manager communication often takes the form of reaction-counteraction. Despite their limited legal expertise, managers are often reluctant to ask their attorneys too broad a question for fear that they might receive an answer that would preclude their doing what they really want to do. So instead, the client frames a very technical question to the attorney, and the attorney frames an equally technical answer, without inquiring why the question is being asked or considering the broader business context within which it is being raised. This conventional approach is depicted in figure 9-1.

Consider the board of directors of Enron, who asked Enron's long-time outside counsel Vinson & Elkins whether the board needed to take any action in response to an employee memo claiming accounting irregularities. The board expressly told Vinson & Elkins not to "second guess" Andersen's accounting treatment. Vinson & Elkins duly responded to this very narrow inquiry by acknowledging that the accounting treatment was "creative and aggressive" and that there was a "serious risk of adverse publicity and litigation"

FIGURE 9-1

Conventional approach

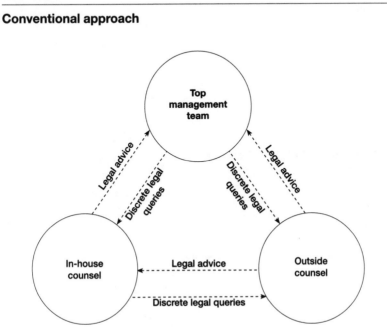

due to the "bad cosmetics" of certain transactions, but they concluded that no further investigation was needed.[4]

It is hard to understand how a lawyer can render meaningful advice about a claim of accounting fraud without considering whether the claim has any merit. Indeed, the special board committee that investigated Enron's accounting debacle faulted Vinson & Elkins for its failure to look at the whole picture.

Legally astute managers call on their lawyers to play a more active role in formulating the corporation's strategy as a whole instead of just being technical consultants brought in when the firm is confronted with a legal problem.[5] This approach is depicted in figure 9-2.

Marshall Clinard and Peter Yeager go so far as to assert, "Business corporations do not have legal problems. They have business problems where legal considerations may be more or less important, depending on the specific circumstances."[6] Clinard and Yeager focused on preventing the value destruction that results from non-

FIGURE 9-2

Legally astute approach

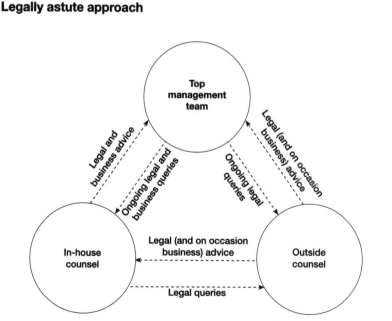

compliance, but their reasoning applies equally to the upside, where managers can create and capture value.[7]

Of course, counsel has to earn management's respect by learning enough about the company's business and strategy to make a creative contribution in the joint problem-solving exercise. Legal advice should be business oriented. It should help managers address business opportunities and threats in ways that are legally permissible,[8] effective, and efficient.[9]

David Andrews, former senior vice president for legal affairs at PepsiCo, stresses to his lawyers the importance of "getting close" to the client—the business units.[10] To further this objective, he instituted the PepsiCo Legal Academy in 2003. PepsiCo's top lawyers met with Indra K. Nooyi, the company's president and chief financial officer, as well as its auditors and others, to discuss the company's strategy, financial performance, and accounting controls. Nooyi encouraged PepsiCo's lawyers to bring both their legal expertise and their business judgment to bear when working with managers, saying, "We can't afford this separation of church and state."[11] She urged the lawyers to speak up if a manager proposed a deal that did not make good business sense to the lawyer instead of just focusing on preparing the perfect legal documentation for a flawed deal.

The goal should be to create what Kim Clark and Steven Wheelwright call "heavyweight teams,"[12] comprising managers and their counsel. Instead of just representing their functional group, members of heavyweight teams act as general managers with responsibility for the success of the entire project. This requires team members to become actively involved in the work of members from other functional areas.

On a heavyweight product development team, for example, members from engineering, production, marketing, sales, and legal take joint responsibility for designing and selling an innovative and differentiated product while also complying with applicable law and avoiding product liability risk. The legal strategy becomes part of the business strategy when top management calls on every team member to consider the business and legal opportunities and risks associated with various designs, methods of production, marketing plans, and sales activities.

To ensure that the top management team receives objective legal advice about the legality of the business strategy crafted by the heavyweight team, it may be appropriate for certain in-house and outside lawyers to be kept separate from the management team designing the strategy. This important monitoring function is akin to that performed by internal and external auditors and requires a degree of independence.

Like Information Technology, Law Is Not a Black Box Best Left to the Experts

In many ways, this book's mantra of integrating legal considerations into business strategy and decision making parallels what is now regarded as best practice for managing information technology (IT) in many industries.[13] Early on, companies tended to view information technology as a black box.[14] IT issues were shuffled off to the IT department or outsourced with a "you take care of it" attitude.

Information technology executives spent the majority of their careers within the IT function. Few were likely to be involved in strategic planning and control. On the other hand, general managers were not expected to understand the technology, and CEOs and other senior executives were not expected to become personally involved in IT decisions. Top managers felt uncomfortable making hard choices about IT yet found that they were not realizing much business value from the high-priced technology they installed.

Today, experts agree that IT is too important to business success to be handled in a vacuum. Research by Lynda M. Applegate and Joyce J. Elam reveals that today the IT function is more closely integrated with general corporate management.[15] IT executives are often external hires with significant experience managing a non-IT function. They are expected to gain experience in business strategy, management, and operations so that they can bring a broad business perspective to the position. An increasing number of IT executives report directly to the CEO and are members of the senior management team or sit on the strategic policy committee.

Jeanne Ross and Peter Weill concluded in a recent study that senior managers in high-performing companies take a leadership role in key IT decisions.[16] Although IT executives should make decisions about IT management, Ross and Weill recommend that they should not be left to make choices (whether by default or by design) that determine the impact of IT on a company's business strategy. Indeed, Mark D. Lutchen, former global CIO of Pricewaterhouse-Coopers, argues that a firm will not reap the expected benefits from technology unless the "CEO and his or her executive leadership team . . . have a conceptual understanding of how technology can support business growth."[17]

So too should the CEO and other senior managers exercise leadership over the business consequences of legal decisions and the legal consequences of business decisions. But it should be *informed* leadership that takes the middle road between complete abdication of responsibility for any legal issues to the legal department, on the one hand, and infrequent consultation with the lawyers on the other.

The CEO and the general counsel can both take valuable lessons from the Applegate and Elam study of the IT function. First, the barriers of overspecialization must come down. Senior managers must learn more about the legal function, and the general counsel and other members of the legal team must learn more about the business function. Second, synergy must be cultivated—it won't grow or happen on its own. Taking the perspective of the other person (or at the very least, learning more about the thought process behind legal or business decision making) can help build a mutually complementary understanding that combines the best expertise from both the legal and the business sides. A general counsel who can articulate "hybrid" business-legal solutions is extremely valuable.

Third, any general counsel who really wants to have an influence on corporate decision making has to earn a place at the table in policy making or strategic planning committees. Hank Barnette, general counsel and then CEO of Bethlehem Steel, attended executive education courses at the Harvard Business School to hone his general management skills. Fourth, the general counsel must educate and groom the legal staff to play a more integrated role with company management.

The decision whether to outsource the IT function also yields insights for companies as they choose between hiring in-house counsel or retaining an outside firm as needed. Outsourcing the IT functions to an outside service provider used to be a popular cost-saving option for many companies. Ross and Weill discovered, however, that many outsourcing arrangements eventually became unsatisfactory as a company's needs changed. Service providers with standard offerings and detailed contracts were not flexible enough to meet changing requirements.

Ross and Weill make the point that outsourcing a function means outsourcing responsibility for critical decisions related to that function. Companies often opted to outsource IT because management was unhappy with their in-house staff, yet the dissatisfaction was often the result of senior management's own lack of involvement.[18] Today firms are more likely to keep their main IT capabilities in-house and also engage in "selective outsourcing" when special skills and expertise may be required for particular problems.

Like internal IT staff, in-house lawyers have intimate knowledge of the company and its policies and objectives, as well as accumulated wisdom in dealing with particular kinds of corporate problems. In-house lawyers are able to participate in strategy and business planning and can often establish a better relationship with top managers. This internal competence can be complemented as needed by an outside law firm's expertise and breadth of experience with many different corporate clients and regulators.[19]

Experienced inside counsel can usually judge when something can and should be done in-house and when it should be farmed out. For example, firms often retain outside counsel to handle peak-time overflow work, litigation, and specialty matters, such as international tax, in which in-house counsel lack the requisite expertise. Regulatory law, antitrust compliance, and intellectual property matters often require collaboration between inside and outside counsel.

Stephen Friedman and Evan Stewart recommend that companies move to a "project team" model, whereby projects are staffed by both inside and outside lawyers, chosen for their experience and ability (even if costly).[20] Typically, when a new project arises inside a company, the first question asked is "Should this project be done by inside or outside counsel?" Friedman and Stewart argue that this question leads to inefficiencies. They would instead ask, "Who is the best person to be responsible for this project?" and "Who should be on the team?"

Thus a project manager (from the company or the outside law firm) directs the team composed of in-house and external counsel. This arrangement could challenge the traditional organizations of both the legal department and the outside law firm, but it works well for people like PepsiCo's associate general counsel, Rob Cox. Cox uses this approach when PepsiCo does a major acquisition. He selects a partner from one of the company's preferred law firms to work with him and his staff to negotiate and close the deal.

The Critical Role of General Counsel

Smaller businesses often cannot afford in-house legal staff, and even some very large corporations elect to retain outside counsel for all their legal work. Regardless of whether a company relies on inside or outside counsel or some combination thereof, every company should have one lawyer who acts as a general counsel with overall responsibility for the legal function. If a company has no in-house general counsel but instead uses a variety of lawyers within one outside law firm, there should be a single partner in the law firm managers can contact to determine which lawyer in the firm would be best suited to handle the matter at hand.

The role of general counsel is more relevant than ever. Indeed, a December 2004 article in *BusinessWeek* titled "A Compelling Case for Lawyer-CEOs" cited the elevation of Charles O. Prince III to head Citigroup and Michael G. Cherkasky to head scandal-ridden Marsh & McLennan as evidence that the number of lawyer-CEOs is only likely to grow.[21] Although *BusinessWeek* is probably correct that the JD degree is unlikely to replace the MBA as the credential of choice for CEOs anytime soon,[22] there has probably never been a time when legal considerations have played such a key role in strategy formulation and execution.

Corporations are facing global, multijurisdictional regulations and challenges, and they are risking large penalties and damage to reputation for noncompliance. Lawyers must teach clients compliance and policy requirements plus practical tactics to keep out of trouble. General counsel must keep abreast of legal trends, pending legislation, and competitive opportunities and risks so that they can step in proactively to shape results, avoid other companies' mistakes, and prevent crises.

Laura Stein, senior vice president and general counsel of Heinz, believes that in-house lawyers develop best relations with senior management by building trust and providing proactive advice.[23] She sees her job as increasing shareholder value.[24] To do so, she interacts frequently with senior management over strategy, growth, risk protection, budget, planning, and operations.

In its *Corporate Executive's Guide to the Role of General Counsel*,[25] the American Corporate Counsel Association (ACCA) identified four goals for the general counsel. First, the general counsel must be aware of the big corporate picture and understand the wider, cumulative, and aggregate risk consequences for the company of individual management decisions. Second, the general counsel should maintain a separate corporationwide information flow that counterbalances the "filtered" information flow upward to the CEO and board of directors. A separate information flow enables the general counsel to serve as a senior adviser capable of giving the most senior levels of the company a clear picture of what is going on.

Third, the general counsel must be viewed as a person who helps guide the chief executive to do the right and wise thing, a role far more broadly defined than ensuring minimum compliance with applicable laws and regulations. To ensure that he received frank and candid advice, Texaco CEO James Kinnear selected a general counsel whose career objective was to be the very best general counsel possible, not the next CEO.[26]

Fourth, the general counsel should adopt a risk assessment approach. There is often no clear right answer, so the challenge is to know enough about what might happen to chart a course that stands the best chance of protecting the company's interests.

General counsel can help the company manage risk with the following actions:

- Identifying and assessing risks

- Counseling senior management and the board

- Managing the actual provision of legal services for the company

- Controlling costs associated with those risks and services

- Performing an internal regulatory function

Furthermore, the general counsel is instrumental in implementing the disclosure and reporting controls required by the Sarbanes-Oxley Act. The CEO and CFO must certify the adequacy of these controls, and they should work with the general counsel to design them, to monitor their adequacy, and to make any necessary refinements or changes.

In the ACCA's 2001 survey of CEOs and other senior managers at 149 companies, the respondents characterized the four most important roles of in-house general counsel:

- Educator regarding legal issues (61 percent)

- Ethics advisor (60 percent)

- Compliance officer (52 percent)

- Sounding board or confidante for the CEO (51 percent)[27]

Only 37 percent of respondents valued in-house counsel as a member of the strategic planning team, only 23 percent as a risk manager, and only 16 percent as a mediator or conflict resolution expert. There is clearly room for improvement.

The ACCA survey identified trustworthiness, confidentiality, and providing accurate, timely, and focused feedback as the most desirable qualities for counsel.[28] Respondents rated as critically important counsel's understanding of company business and his or her ability to focus on prevention and compliance.

The ACCA recommends that the in-house general counsel be free to focus on how to achieve the best legal results, whether via hiring experienced professionals or retaining the best outside counsel. According to the ACCA, if the in-house general counsel is responsible for the costs and results of litigation (including the total amount of settlements and money damage awards) and of transaction-oriented work, then the company should be indifferent to particular legal costs, as long as the overall cost of a project is as low as is practical.

I disagree. If, as I believe is true, every legal dispute is a business problem requiring a business solution, then the lawyers should not be the ultimate decision makers when it comes to deciding whether to settle a case and on what terms.

Similarly, although the general counsel (like the technical IT experts deciding how to staff a project) is usually in the best position to decide when to retain outside counsel and to select the best lawyer for the job, it is important for the general managers involved to have a say in the matter. This is especially critical when negotiating transactions where the style and experience of the outside counsel can seriously affect the likelihood of striking an advantageous deal and creating an enduring relationship. Even in the event of litigation, the responsible manager should ask about the proposed litigator's approach to litigation ("take no prisoners" or try to find a win-win solution to settle the dispute) and ask whether the lawyer has relevant experience dealing with disputes of this kind in this industry.

Involving the managers who will be deciding the business issues in the selection of counsel reinforces the notion that the lawyers and the managers are expected to work as a team. It also makes it clear that outside counsel's real client is the manager, not the general counsel. Certainly the general counsel should be kept informed and consulted when appropriate, but there should be a clear line of communication between the managers with decision-making authority and the lawyers (regardless of whether they are inside or outside of the company).

Managers should require the general counsel to create a realistic budgeting structure for outside work so that the lawyers and managers can make intelligent judgments about what the project or litigation is worth and should cost. For example, the Monsanto legal department requires a budget plan for legal matters expected to exceed $20,000, detailing the scope and sequence of the contracted work and the milestones to be met for each phase of the representation.[29] The budget must also stipulate billing deadlines to satisfy Monsanto's forecasting requirements and to assist the finance department with monthly accrual information. Some extra-contract supplemental costs are allowed, but they require company authorization before reimbursement. The Monsanto legal department has not resorted to using outside auditors to review billing charges, but they have challenged excessive billing or poor performance on occasion.

Most law firms bill Monsanto by the hour, although some offer flat fee or hybrid arrangements (monthly retainer plus discounted hourly fees) as well. Monsanto also negotiates volume discounts, but these sometimes lead to problems of accessibility and responsiveness. To facilitate mutual understanding and to build a strong relationship, Monsanto stresses the need for regular, clear, and open communication with the outside firm.

In allocating legal costs to the various business units, top management should ensure that they do not deter managers from seeking legal advice when they need it. Rather than viewing legal expenses as a cost, companies might be better served to view it as an investment in a valuable dynamic capability that can be a source of competitive advantage.

Centralize or Decentralize Legal Resources?

Another issue is whether a company should have a central law department or distribute the in-house lawyers among their corporate clients, such as by business unit. Considerations of consistency, efficiency, cost, and evaluation must play a part in this decision. For example, in a company with homogeneous products and plans, a centralized legal department might make most sense, whereas decentralization may be preferable in a large, multibusiness company. However, it is important to ensure that decentralized groups of lawyers do not become captives of their business groups or pursue legal strategies at odds with the legal and business strategies of the firm as a whole. Thus, it is often prudent to centralize regulatory functions, such as antitrust, environmental, and securities law compliance, at the firm's executive headquarters and for the board of directors to appoint a chief compliance officer who reports directly to the audit committee of the board.

The ACCA recommends that the general counsel have ultimate authority to evaluate and set up the compensation for the in-house lawyers in either scenario. This seems appropriate as long as the general counsel seeks feedback from the manager-clients about the quality, timeliness, and cost of the legal services provided.

Keeping Communications Confidential: The Attorney-Client Privilege

Since the sixteenth century, the *attorney-client privilege* has promoted justice by protecting confidential communications between clients and their attorneys. Clients are more likely to make a full and frank disclosure of the truth to an attorney if they know that the attorney cannot be compelled to pass the information on to other parties. Lawyers, in turn, are better able to advise and represent their clients if the client honestly discloses the complete facts.

Although many business people believe that they understand which communications are privileged, a survey by Paul Rice of a sample of *Fortune* 100 corporations revealed serious gaps in managers' knowledge of the requirements for maintaining the privilege. Of those surveyed, 72 percent knew that only communications between an attorney and client that relate to legal advice are protected by the attorney-client privilege. But only 58 percent knew that the communications had to be confidential or that confidentiality had to be maintained by limiting distribution to those with a "need to know."[30] Rice found that officers and directors were generally no better informed about the privilege than other employees even though officers and directors have far greater access to confidential communications.[31] To remedy the knowledge gap, managers should understand and apply the following considerations.

Who Is the Client?

The attorney-client privilege belongs to the client alone. The attorney has an obligation to alert the client to the existence of the privilege and, if necessary, to invoke it on the client's behalf. The client can, however, waive the privilege over the attorney's objection if the client so desires.

Because the attorney-client privilege belongs only to the client, it becomes critically important to identify who exactly is the client. This is not an issue when an individual hires a lawyer to give legal advice on a personal matter, but it becomes more problematic when a company hires an attorney.

The general counsel and other in-house lawyers as well as the outside counsel retained by the company represent the *company*, not the managers who may have hired them. Among the Rice survey respondents, more than half the officers and directors erroneously believed that the general counsel represents them personally when they discuss matters relating to their corporate responsibilities.[32]

Because the company is the client, no employee or director (not even the CEO) may invoke the privilege on his or her own behalf. Whatever an employee divulges cannot be kept secret from the executive officers of the company or the board of directors. The board has the ultimate authority to decide whether to assert the attorney-client privilege on behalf of the corporation or to disclose the communication to a prosecutor, court, or other third party.

Companies often seek to defend a criminal or other charge by claiming that the wrong was committed by a "rogue" employee. As a result, individual employees who confessed their role in the wrongdoing often find themselves offered up as sacrifices to take heat off the company.

Management should make it clear to every employee and director that, unless otherwise specified in a written engagement letter, any lawyer hired by the company or serving in the in-house legal department represents the company, not any one individual. As a result, anything divulged by an employee or director can be disclosed to a prosecutor or other third party and used in a court of law.

Which Communications Are Privileged?

Several conditions must be satisfied for communications to be protected by the privilege. First, the communication must be kept confidential. If the client relays the information to others or makes the communication in the presence of others not protected by the privilege, then the communication is not privileged.

All privileged documents should be marked "attorney-client privilege" both to restrict their circulation to those with a "need to know" and to ensure that they are not inadvertently produced in response to a discovery request. A manager should never forward an e-mail or letter from counsel to anyone else without first confirming with counsel that the document can be shared with that person without losing the privilege. Sometimes, it is best for managers to meet face-to-face with counsel or to chat over the telephone and not reduce the conversation to writing to avoid indiscreet disclosure of sensitive discussions.

Consider the following example of how *not* to document legal advice. A partner at Cravath, Swaine and Moore had explained to a client whose business was being seriously affected by price-cutters the difference between refusing to do business with a price-cutter (a legal choice) and entering into agreements with customers not to cut prices (illegal minimum resale price maintenance). When the Federal Trade Commission investigated the client for resale price maintenance, one of the first documents found in the files of the sales manager was a memorandum to his district managers, stating, "Cravath says we can refuse to sell to price-cutters, but can't make agreements to maintain prices. Accordingly, whenever you put a price-cutter back on our list [based] on his agreement not to cut prices, do not send a copy of the agreement to the home office."[33]

Second, the attorney to whom the communication is made must be a practicing attorney at the time of the communication, and the person making the communication must be a current or prospective client seeking legal advice. The attorney-client privilege extends to communications with both in-house and outside counsel as long as the communication occurs while the attorney is acting in a legal capacity. However, if a client is conversing with an attorney about nonlegal matters (such as business strategy), the conversation is not protected.

Throughout this book I have urged counsel to link legal strategy with business strategy. When it comes to attorney-client privilege, however, the lawyers must maintain a clear distinction between their legal services and their role as a business advisor. This can be particularly difficult and dangerous when a lawyer serves as both general counsel and a board member, because it is often not clear whether the attorney is giving business or legal advice. As a result, it is generally not prudent for the general counsel to serve as a member of the board of directors.

Third, the attorney-client privilege does not protect client communications that are made to further a crime or other illegal act. If an executive were to ask an attorney about the best way to embezzle money without getting caught, the conversation would not be privileged.

In July 1997, the Florida Court of Appeals rejected the tobacco companies' claim of attorney-client privilege for eight confidential documents, including attorneys' notes from in-house meetings on legal strategy.[34] The court concluded that because the documents contained evidence that tobacco attorneys participated in an industrywide conspiracy to defraud the public about the danger of smoking, they came within the exception for communications to further commission of fraud or a crime. Disclosure of these documents was pivotal to the successful lawsuits that resulted in the tobacco companies paying more than $200 billion to settle charges of engaging in a conspiracy to mislead the public about the hazards of smoking.

Protecting Corporate Communications

A corporation (or other business entity) can communicate with an attorney only through its officers, directors, or employees. The attorney-client privilege protects the communications of any company employee with counsel as long as the subject matter of the communication relates to the employee's duties and the communication is made at the direction of a corporate superior.[35] Thus, communications between a corporation's attorneys and any of its employees, not just a small, upper-level group, can be protected under the attorney-client privilege as long as the communications pass the subject matter test.

It is not clear whether the attorney-client privilege applies to communications with former employees. There is also an issue of what exactly constitutes a voluntary waiver of the attorney-client privilege by a corporation. Finally, there is still uncertainty about the protection the privilege gives corporations in suits brought against them by their own shareholders.

The corporation's storage and dissemination policies regarding privileged communications should be distributed in writing and explained to all employees. Over half the respondents in Rice's survey were unaware of any corporate policies on the creation, storage, and distribution of privileged communications, 70 percent did not know that the policies were in writing, and a remarkable 90 percent expressed the view that corporate policies were not adequately communicated. Further, almost half of the people surveyed did not think it necessary either to segregate privileged documents or to clearly label them with "attorney-client privilege" to alert potential readers to their confidential nature.

Guidelines for Retaining the Privilege

Experts have offered several suggestions for keeping communications between a corporate employee and counsel within the scope of the attorney-client privilege.[36] First, a communication between an attorney and a corporation is protected when the client is seeking or receiving only legal advice, not business advice. Thus, corporations should usually request legal advice in writing and assign communication with the attorney to a specific employee who has responsibility over the subject matter at issue.

Second, corporations should make sure that senior management directs all communications between employees and corporate counsel and that the employees know they must keep all communications confidential.

Third, corporate employees should deal directly with counsel (not through intermediaries) and maintain separate confidential files and documentation. Communications with counsel must not be shared with anyone outside the corporation or even with other corporate employees unless the subject matter relates to the employee's duties and the communication is shared at the direction of a corporate superior.

Fourth, when a corporation gives a government agency access to its communications or files, the corporation should negotiate a written agreement of confidentiality with the agency or an agreement that the agency will not take physical possession of the documents. The corporation should also investigate the possibility of statutory protection in this situation.

Internal Investigations and Waiver of the Attorney-Client Privilege

If a corporation wants to avoid prosecution for the misdeeds of its employees, it must offer full cooperation in the investigation and prosecution of the individuals involved in the alleged wrongdoing. The U.S. Justice Department has taken the position that cooperation often includes waiving attorney-client privilege for any internal investigations by counsel retained to determine whether wrongdoing has occurred or to identify the individuals involved.

This controversial policy requires top management and counsel to make what can feel like a Hobson's choice. On the one hand, they open the corporation to criminal prosecution if they do not agree to waive attorney-client privilege. On the other hand, if they waive the privilege in hopes of avoiding corporate prosecution, they take the risk that the information thus revealed could lead to a broader corporate indictment.

Arthur Andersen's corporate demise occurred in just such a situation: after Andersen agreed to waive attorney-client privilege in hopes of avoiding a firmwide indictment in the Enron affair, the company released masses of documents to the government. Among these was the "smoking gun" e-mail in which Andersen lawyer Nancy Temple reminded the Enron audit team to honor Andersen's document retention policies—which helped seal Andersen's conviction for obstruction of justice.

Select a Counselor, Not a Hired Gun

Managers are best served by lawyers who provide judicious and informed advice that helps leverage lawful business opportunities into activities that increase realizable value while managing risk. Sometimes that means saying no. So when selecting counsel, legally astute managers consider not only technical expertise but also the reputation the lawyer has for pushing back when the client has proposed a course of action that the lawyer considers unwise.

Elihu Root, a former U.S. secretary of war, secretary of state, and U.S. senator, remarked, "About half the practice of a decent lawyer consists in telling would-be clients that they are damned fools and should stop."[37] As professionals and officers of the court, lawyers are expected to exercise independent judgment and not sell their conscience as well as their services to the client who pays them.[38]

The American Bar Association's *Model Rules of Professional Conduct*, adopted in whole or in part by most states, require a lawyer to "exercise independent professional judgment and render candid advice."[39] When advising a client, "a lawyer may refer not only to law but to other considerations such as moral, economic, social and political factors, that may be relevant to the client's situation."[40] The ABA goes on to explain that a client is entitled to "straightforward advice expressing the lawyer's honest assessment" even when it "involves unpleasant facts and alternatives that a client may be disinclined to confront."[41] Although a lawyer "endeavors to sustain the client's morale and may put advice in as acceptable a form as honesty permits," a lawyer "should not be deterred from giving candid advice by the prospect that the advice will be unpalatable to the client."[42]

Purely "technical legal advice" can sometimes be inadequate. Instead, the ABA calls it "proper for a lawyer to refer to relevant moral and ethical considerations" because these considerations "impinge upon most legal systems and may decisively influence how the law will be applied."[43] The ABA states that a lawyer may accept at face value an express or implicit request for purely technical advice from a client experienced in legal matters, but in my experience clients are rarely best served by such advice.

Consider how Columbia/HCA Healthcare's managers and lawyers responded when Columbia/HCA discovered a $14 million Medicare reimbursement error in its favor. Instead of reporting the error, Columbia/HCA executives sought and obtained a legal opinion that it was not required to disclose the error to the Department of Health and Human Services. They also established a "reserve" of $500,000 per year to repay any money the government might later decide that Columbia/HCA owed.[44] It turned out that the lawyers got it wrong. Columbia/HCA's failure to report the error led to the first criminal indictments against the company's managers for Medicare fraud.

I don't know how Columbia/HCA's lawyers couched their advice, whether they framed their opinion in terms of legal technicalities or some broader principle. Given that Columbia/HCA used the opinion as an excuse for not reporting the error, I suspect it was the former. Perhaps the management team was intent on keeping the error secret regardless of its lawyers' advice.

What I do know is that a client is less likely to push the limits of the law and to engage in unethical conduct if its lawyers go beyond the technicalities of the rules and engage the client in a meaningful dialogue about the ethics of the client's plan and the probable effect on their reputation and their relationships with key constituencies.

A lawyer shouldn't say "no" without first collaborating with the responsible manager to determine both what the objective should be and whether there is a legal way to achieve it, however. Thus, the general counsel of Heinz stated that she never expects a lawyer to approve a transaction that does not meet the requirements imposed by law, but she does want outside counsel to be more "creative and innovative."

Contrast the advice the lawyers gave Enron and Columbia/HCA Healthcare with the collaborative process that created Citigroup, as described in the opening paragraphs of this book. As general counsel at the time, Chuck Prince did not suggest that Chairman Sandy Weill violate the letter or the spirit of the law. Instead, the two worked to change the law while preparing a backup plan to put into place if their lobbying efforts failed.

The Importance of Winning Legally

In his next job as Citigroup's CEO, Chuck Prince faced continuing challenges as he attempted to teach the whole sprawling global organization the importance of winning legally. Perhaps if Citigroup's managers and lawyers had worked together more effectively at the cutting edge of competition and innovation, they could have avoided the analyst scandals, the questionable deals for Enron and World-Com, the predatory mortgage lending practices, and other mistakes of the late 1990s. Certainly Chuck Prince (and Citigroup shareholders) would have preferred to save the roughly $10 billion the group paid in fines and damages to put "the entire era behind us."[45]

But is the struggle ever really over? In September 2004, the financial authorities in Japan shut down Citigroup's lucrative private banking business there, citing "severe legal violations" and "extremely inappropriate transactions" that could indicate a pattern of money laundering. The Japanese government also announced that it would revoke Citibank's private banking license as of September 2005.[46] Six officers left their jobs in the immediate wake of the announcement, out of 238,000 highly capable employees in a worldwide organization that consistently wins awards for being the best and most admired company in its industry.

Citigroup announced in early 2005 that it had taken a $244 million after-tax charge against earnings related to the closing of Japan Private Bank and had set up a $131 million after-tax reserve related to the resolution of a Securities and Exchange Commission investigation of its transfer agent business.[47] Prince characterized the legal and regulatory charges recorded in 2004 as "significant disappointments" and assured investors that "resolving open legal and regulatory issues is a key management priority." Chuck Prince still has work to do—and so does every other CEO, senior executive, manager, and corporate counsel who cares about building an enduring organization that can maximize strategic value while minimizing legal and business risk.

Winning legally requires leadership, persistence, and vigilance, but it is an attainable goal. By studying the game plan and heeding the play-by-play advice contained in this book, managers increase their odds of fielding a winning team.

Notes

Chapter 1

1. Monica Langley, *Tearing Down the Walls: How Sandy Weill Fought His Way to the Top of the Financial World . . . and Then Nearly Lost It All* (New York: Simon & Schuster, 2003), 258–279. See also Laura J. Cox, "The Impact of the Citicorp-Travelers Group Merger on Financial Modernization and the Repeal of Glass-Steagall," *Nova Law Review* 23 (1999): 899–925; Arthur E. Wilmarth Jr., "The Transformation of the U.S. Financial Services Industry, 1975–2000: Competition, Consolidation, and Increased Risks," *University of Illinois Law Review* 2002 (2002): 215–332.

2. See Anthony Bianco, "Citi's New Act," *BusinessWeek*, 28 July 2003, 31.

3. Timothy L. O'Brien, "Fed Assesses Citigroup Unit $70 Million in Loan Abuse," *New York Times*, 28 May 2004, C1.

4. Susanne Craig and Randall Smith, "Last Stock-Case Holdouts to Pay," *Wall Street Journal*, 13 July 2004, C1.

5. Loren Steffy, "Citi Settlement Doesn't Mean Lesson Learned," *Houston Chronicle*, 16 May 2004, 1.

6. O'Brien, "Fed Assesses Citigroup Unit," C1.

7. Steffy, "Citi Settlement," 1.

8. See Richard Breeden, *Restoring Trust*, report to the Hon. Jed S. Rakoff, the United States District Court for the Southern District of New York, filed with the WorldCom bankruptcy court on August 26, 2003.

9. James Willard Hurst, "Problems of Legitimacy in the Contemporary Legal Order," *Oklahoma Law Review* 24 (1971): 224–238: "In deciding what to include as 'law' I do not find it profitable to distinguish 'law' from 'government' or from 'policy.'"

10. See Mark D. Lutchen, *Managing IT as a Business: A Survival Guide for CEOs* (Hoboken, NJ: Wiley, 2004), 43.

11. Patrick M. Wright and Scott A. Snell, "Toward a Unifying Framework for Exploring Fit and Flexibility in Strategic Human Resource Management," *Academy of Management Review* 23 (1998): 756–772.

12. See William A. Sahlman, "Some Thoughts on Business Plans," in William A. Sahlman et al., eds., *The Entrepreneurial Venture*, 2d ed. (Boston: Harvard Business School Press, 1999), 158.

13. See George J. Siedel, "Six Forces and the Legal Environment of Business: The Relative Value of Business Law Among Business School Core Courses," *American Business Law Journal* 37 (2000): 717. See also George J. Siedel, *Using Law for Competitive Advantage* (San Francisco: Jossey-Bass, 2002).

14. Oliver Wendell Holmes Jr., "The Path of the Law," *Harvard Law Review* 10 (1897): 457. Thanks to Hank Reiling for introducing me to this reasoning.

15. For a general discussion, see C. Argyris, *Reasoning, Learning and Action: Individual and Organizational* (San Francisco: Jossey-Bass, 1982).

16. Matthew Parsons, *Effective Knowledge Management for Law Firms* (Oxford and New York: Oxford University Press, 2004).

17. William A. Sahlman, "Some Thoughts on Business Plans," 158.

18. To reap the benefits of a heterogenous team, firms must overcome the barriers to common understanding created by different dialects and stories. See S. L. Keck, "Top Management Team Structure: Differential Effects by Environmental Context," *Organization Science* 8 (1997): 143–156; M. L. Tushman and T. J. Scanlan, "Boundary Spanning Individuals: Their Role in Information Transfer and their Antecedents," *Academy of Management Journal* 24 (1981): 289–305; D. Knight, C. L. Pearce, K. G. Smith, J. D. Olian, H. P. Sims, and P. Flood, "Top Management Team Diversity, Group Process, and Strategic Consensus," *Strategic Management Journal* 20 (1999): 445–465.

19. Richard A. Oppel Jr. and Kurt Eichewald, "Arthur Andersen Fires an Executive for Enron Orders," *New York Times*, 16 January 2002, A1.

20. Thomas A. Schweich, *Protect Yourself from Business Lawsuits (. . . and Lawyers Like Me)* (New York: Scribner, 1998), 54–58.

21. See Garth Saloner, Joel Podolny, and Andrea Shepard, *Strategic Management* (Upper Saddle River, NJ: Prentice Hall, 2002), for a more complete discussion of the internal organization and context of firms.

22. See Jay B. Barney, "Firm Resources and Sustained Competitive Advantage," *Journal of Management* 17 (1991): 99–120, for a general discussion of the resource-based view of the firm.

23. Ibid.

24. David J. Teece, Gary Pisano, and Amy Shuen, "Dynamic Capabilities and Strategic Management," *Strategic Management Journal* 18 (1997): 509–533.

25. Tom Hinthorne, "Predatory Capitalism, Pragmatism, and Legal Positivism in the Airline Industry," *Strategic Management Journal* 17 (1996): 251–270.

26. Adam M. Brandenburger and Barry J. Nalebuff, *Co-opetition* (New York: Currency Doubleday, 1996), viii. For example, although American Airlines and Delta are competitors for passengers and landing slots and gates at airports, they are complementors for Boeing, a key supplier of aircraft. It is much cheaper for Boeing to design a new plane for both airlines together than to design one for each of them separately. Design and development costs can be shared, and the demand for more units helps Boeing move along the learning curve more quickly.

27. Michael E. Porter, "How Competitive Forces Shape Strategy," in Michael E. Porter, *On Competition* (Boston: Harvard Business School Press, 1996), 21–22. For an excellent discussion of the law's impact on the five forces, see G. Richard Shell, *Make the Rules or Your Rivals Will* (New York: Crown Business, 2004).

28. Robert Kaplan and David Norton, *Strategy Maps* (Boston: Harvard Business School Press, 2004), 322.

29. Ibid., 326.

30. Ibid., 329–332.

31. Ibid., 332–344.

32. Irwin Ross, "How Lawless Are Big Companies?" *Fortune* (1 December 1980): 56–64.

33. Mike H. Ryan, Carl L. Swanson, and Rogene A. Buchholz, *Corporate Strategy, Public Policy and the Fortune 500: How America's Major Corporations Influence Government* (Oxford and New York: Blackwell, 1987), 167–168.

34. Michael Porter and others have argued that "nonmarket relationships are best accounted for by folding them into the analysis of market relationships—by looking at the role of government, for instance, solely in terms of how it shapes the five (or [if one includes the role of complementors] six) forces." Pankaj Ghemawat, *Strategy and the Business Landscape: Core Concepts* (Upper Saddle River, NJ: Prentice Hall, 2001), 35. Pankaj Ghemawat cautions, however, that "folding nonmarket considerations into the analysis of market relationships tends to focus on the effects of non-market variables . . . at the expense of systematic analysis of their evolution, including efforts to influence them." Pankaj Ghemawat, "Notes on Non-market Strategy," Harvard Business School Globalization Note Series (Boston: Harvard Business School Publishing, 2002). David Baron has proposed a framework for "nonmarket strategy" that looks at the impact of government on business separately from the market forces then attempts to develop integrated strategies that explicitly address both market and nonmarket relationships. David P. Baron, "Integrated Strategy: Market and Nonmarket Components," *California Management Review* 37 (Winter 1995): 47–65. This book takes a more integrated approach that encompasses both the effect of law on the institutional environment and the institutional arrangements law makes available to managers.

35. Stevenson, Roberts, and Grousbeck break down the entrepreneurial process into five steps: (1) evaluating the opportunity; (2) developing the business concept; (3) assessing required resources both human and capital; (4) acquiring needed resources; and (5) managing and harvesting the venture. Howard H. Stevenson, Michael J. Roberts, and H. Irving Grousbeck, *New Business Ventures and the Entrepreneur*, 2d ed. (Homewood, IL: Irwin, 1985), 17–21. The five steps in table 1-3 are based on this model with modifications to reflect the fact that very different but significant legal issues arise in the course of marshaling human resources and raising money and in the course of managing the development, production, marketing, and sale of the product or service and in harvesting the venture.

36. See the general discussion in Saloner et al., *Strategic Management*, 40.

Chapter 2

1. Michael E. Porter, "Enhancing the Microeconomic Foundations of Prosperity: The Current Competitiveness Index in World Economic Forum," in *The Global Competitiveness Report 2001–2002* (New York: Oxford University Press, 2002), 59–61.

2. Theodore J. Lowi, "Risks and Rights in the History of American Governments," *Daedalus* 119, no. 4 (Fall 1990): 17–40.

3. Howard H. Stevenson, *Do Lunch or Be Lunch* (Boston: Harvard Business School Press, 1998), 22.

4. Douglass C. North, *Institutions, Institutional Change and Economic Performance* (Cambridge, UK: Cambridge University Press, 1990).

5. David A. Moss, *When All Else Fails: Government as the Ultimate Risk Manager* (Cambridge, MA: Harvard University Press, 2001), 4.

6. Ibid., 7.

7. Ibid.

8. Ibid., 9

9. Ibid.

10. Debora Spar, *Ruling the Waves: Cycles of Discovery, Chaos and Wealth from the Compass to the Internet* (New York: Harcourt, 2001).

11. *Diamond v. Chakrabarty*, 447 U.S. 303 (1980).

12. Pub. L. 107–204, 116 Stat. 745 (2002).

13. *Greenman v. Yuba Power Products, Inc.*, 377 P.2d 897 (Cal. 1963).

14. See, for example, Rafael La Porta, Florencio Lopez-de-Silanes, Andrei Shleifer, and Robert W. Vishny, "Legal Determinants of External Finance," *Journal of Finance* 52 (1997): 1131–1150; Simon Johnson, Rafael La Porta, Florencio Lopez-de-Silanes, and Andrei Shleifer, "Tunneling," *American Economic Review* 90, no. 2 (2000): 22–27.

15. This topic is discussed further in Constance E. Bagley and Diane W. Savage, *Managers and the Legal Environment: Strategies for the 21st Century*, 5th ed. (Mason, OH: West Legal Studies in Business, 2006), 723–724.

16. Michael E. Porter, *On Competition* (Boston: Harvard Business School Press, 1996), 183–184.

17. For example, Germany seeks to promote economic growth by facilitating the capital markets, but its goal of protecting workers has led to the system of codetermination whereby half the members of the supervisory boards of large German corporations are elected by the workers and unions, and half are elected by the shareholders.

18. As hedge-fund operator and financier George Soros warned in the mid-1990s, unbridled capitalism can result in political backlash that could jeopardize the entire free-market system. George Soros, "The Capitalist Threat," *Atlantic Monthly*, February 1997, 45.

19. For example, as mentioned in chapter 1, a company being investigated by the Securities and Exchange Commission for improperly booking certain transactions might end up deciding that it is better to sign a consent decree and change its accounting policies than to continue to fight an investigation that has put a pall over its stock price.

20. Although policy makers often equate greater intellectual property protection with more innovation, economist Josh Lerner argues that this view is overly simplistic. Amy Harmon, "In the 'Idea Wars,' a Fight to Control a New Currency," *New York Times*, 11 November 2001, Section 3, 1. Professor Lerner studied sixty developing countries and found no statistically significant relationship between the role of innovation and the strength of patent protection provided in the different countries.

21. Thomas C. McCraw, ed., *Creating Modern Capitalism: How Entrepreneurs, Companies, and Countries Triumphed in Three Industrial Revolutions* (Cambridge, MA: Harvard University Press, 1997), vi.

22. Hernando de Soto, *The Mystery of Capital: Why Capitalism Triumphs in the West and Fails Everywhere Else* (New York: Basic Books, 2000), 156.

23. Ibid., 7.

24. Ibid., 8.

25. Ibid., 6.

26. Douglass North and Barry Weingast, "Constitutions and Commitments: The Evolution of Institutions Governing Public Choice in Twentieth-Century England," *Journal of Economic History* 49 (1989): 803.

27. For a general discussion, see Myron S. Scholes et al., *Taxes and Business Strategy: A Planning Approach*, 2d ed. (Upper Saddle River, NJ: Prentice Hall, 2002).

28. Thomas K. McCraw, "American Capitalism," in McCraw, ed., *Creating Modern Capitalism*, 316.

29. Ibid.

30. Although the federal Superfund law relieves current owners and operators of liability if they can prove that they were in no way responsible for the waste and that they were unaware of it notwithstanding having done all appropriate due diligence before acquiring the property, in practice, this so-called innocent landowner defense can be difficult to establish. Even if it is available at the federal level, some states (such as Massachusetts) do not recognize it. Federal and some statutes do, however, offer some protection for developers of so-called brownfields, known contaminated waste sites such as landfills.

31. *General Electric Co. v. Environmental Protection Agency*, 360 F.3d 188 (D.C. Cir. 2004).

32. However, as Adam B. Jaffe and Josh Lerner warn in *Innovation and Its Discontents: How Our Broken Patent System Is Endangering Innovation and Progress, and What to Do About It* (Princeton, NJ, and Oxford: Princeton University Press, 2004), overly broad patent protection can actually stifle innovation.

33. Moss, *When All Else Fails*, 6.

34. *International Shoe Co. v. Washington*, 326 U.S. 316 (1945).

35. *State Farm Mutual Automobile Ins. Co. v. Campbell*, 538 U.S. 408 (2003).

36. *Reno v. ACLU*, 521 U.S. 844 (1997).

37. 33 U.S.C. §§ 1351 et seq.

38. 42 U.S.C. §§ 6901 et seq.

39. *Berman v. Parker*, 348 U.S. 26, 33 (1954).

40. See Constance E. Bagley and Gavin Clarkson, "Adverse Possession for Intellectual Property: Adapting an Ancient Concept to Resolve Conflicts Between Antitrust and Intellectual Property Laws in the Information Age," *Harvard Journal of Law & Technology* 16, no. 2 (Spring 2003): 327–393; Constance E. Bagley and Gavin Clarkson, "Crossing the Great Divide: Using Adverse Possession to Resolve Conflicts Between the Antitrust and Intellectual Property Regimes," in *Intellectual Property and Entrepreneurship, Advances in the Study of Entrepreneurship, Innovation and Economic Growth*, Vol. 15, ed. Gary D. Libecap (Oxford: Elsevier JAI, 2004): 149–199.

41. For an excellent discussion of both the importance of government to business and ways managers can help shape the regulatory environment, see Michael Watkins, Mickey Edwards, and Usha Thakrar, *Winning the Influence Game* (New York: Wiley, 2001).

42. Ibid., 2. See also G. Richard Shell, *Make the Rules or Your Rivals Will* (New York: Crown Business, 2004), 13–84.

43. Frank Shipper and Marianne M. Jennings, *Business Strategy for the Political Arena* (Westport, CT: Quorum Books, 1984), xviii.

44. Arthur Levitt, *Take on the Street* (New York: Pantheon Books, 2002), 131–133, 140–143. Former SEC chair Levitt commented that "the Enron/ Andersen audit failure is a perfect example of what I was trying to prevent" by requiring greater auditor independence. Ibid., 143.

45. Porter, "Enhancing the Microeconomic Foundations," in *Global Competitiveness Report*, 59.

46. Yuki Noguchi, "FCC Asserts Role as Internet Phone Regulator," *Washington Post*, 10 November 2004, E1. In the course of accepting Vonage's request for relief from regulation by state telecommunications authorities, FCC Chair Michael K. Powell declared, "This landmark order recognizes that a revolution has occurred. Internet voice services have cracked the 19th-century mold to the great benefit of consumers." Ibid.

Chapter 3

1. Associated Press, "Charges of Fraud Cost HCA," *Deseret Morning News* (Salt Lake City), 27 June 2003, D10.

2. See Lucette Lagnado, "Columbia/HCA Graded Its Hospitals on Severity of Their Medicare Cases," *Wall Street Journal*, 30 May 1997, A6.

3. Ibid.

4. Ibid.

5. Ibid.

6. Ibid.

7. Ibid.

8. Ibid.

9. Graham Brink, "Deal Ends HCA's Criminal Probe," *St. Petersburg Times*, 26 January 2001, 1E.

10. See Lucette Lagnado, "Columbia Taps Lawyer for Ethics Post; Yuspeh Led Defense Initiative of 1980s," *Wall Street Journal*, 14 October 1997, B6.

11. Ibid.

12. See Andy Pasztor and Lucette Lagnado, "Ethics Czar Aims to Heal Columbia," *Wall Street Journal*, 26 November 1997, B1, B6.

13. K. Schnatterly, "Increasing Firm Value Through Detection and Prevention of White-Collar Crime," *Strategic Management Journal* 24 (2003): 587–614. See also Jay B. Barney, "Organizational Culture: Can It Be a Source of Sustained Competitive Advantage?" *Academy of Management Review* 11, no. 3 (1986): 656–665.

14. Jay B. Barney and M. H. Hansen, "Trustworthiness as a Source of Competitive Advantage," *Strategic Management Journal* 15 (1994): 175–190.

15. Jay Barney, "Firm Resources and Sustained Competitive Advantage," *Journal of Management* 17, no. 1 (1991): 99–120. According to the resource-based view (RBV) of the firm, "a firm develops competitive advantage by not only acquiring but also developing, combining, and effectively deploying its physical, human, and organizational resources in ways that add unique value and are difficult for competitors to imitate." Barry A. Colbert, "The Complete Resource-Based View: Implications for Theory and Practice in Strategic Human Resource Management," *Academy of Management Review* 29, no. 3 (2004): 341–358.

16. The same is true of failure to implement the correct corporate government practices. Jay Barney, Mike Wright, and David J. Katchen Jr., "The

Resource-Based View of the Firm: Ten Years after 1991," *Journal of Management* 27 (2001): 625–641.

17. Lynn Sharp Paine, "Managing for Organizational Integrity," *Harvard Business Review*, March–April 1994, 106–107.

18. Mark Maremont, "Executives on Trial: Next Evidence for Kowzlowski Jurors: Party Video," *Wall Street Journal*, 28 October 2003, C1.

19. See Constance E. Bagley and Karen L. Page, "The Devil Made Me Do It: Replacing Corporate Directors' Veil of Secrecy with the Mantle of Stewardship," *San Diego Law Review* 38 (1999): 897–945.

20. Robert S. Kaplan and David P. Norton, *Strategy Maps: Converting Intangible Assets into Tangible Outcomes* (Boston: Harvard Business School Press, 2004), 165.

21. Michael E. Porter, "How Competitive Forces Shape Strategy," in Michael E. Porter, *On Competition* (Boston: Harvard Business School Press), 75–98.

22. *United States v. Park*, 421 U.S. 658 (1975).

23. *United States v. Gel Spice Co.*, 773 F.2d 427 (2d Cir. 1985) (quoting *United States v. New England Grocers Co.*, 488 F. Supp. 230 (D. Mass. 1980)).

24. *Otis Engineering Corp. v. Clark*, 668 5.W.2d 307 (Tex. 1983).

25. David A. Moss, *When All Else Fails* (Cambridge, MA: Harvard University Press, 2003).

26. *Meinhard v. Salmon*, 164 N.E. 545 (N.Y. 1928).

27. The corporate opportunity doctrine is discussed further in Constance E. Bagley and Diane W. Savage, *Managers and the Legal Environment: Strategies for the 21st Century*, 5th ed. (Mason, OH: West Legal Studies in Business, 2006), 758–759.

28. *In re The Walt Disney Co. Derivative Litigation*, 825 A.2d 275 (Del. Ch. 2003).

29. *Smith v. Van Gorkom*, 488 A.2d 858 (Del. 1985).

30. *Hanson Trust PLC v. ML SCM Acquisition, Inc.*, 781 F.2d 264 (2d Cir. 1986).

31. *In re W.R. Grace & Co.* [1997 Transfer Binder], *Federal Securities Law Reporter* (CCH) ¶85, 963 (8 October 1997).

32. The business judgment rule and the standards applicable to the use of defensive tactics, such as poison pills, to defeat unsolicited tender offers are discussed more fully in Bagley and Savage, *Managers and the Legal Environment*, 742–771.

33. *In re Caremark International Derivative Litigation*, 698 A.2d 959 (Del. Ch. 1996).

34. Robert Simons, *Levers of Control* (Boston: Harvard Business School Press, 1995).

35. See Constance E. Bagley and Richard H. Koppes, "The Leader of the Pack: A Proposal for Disclosure of Board Leadership Structure," *San Diego Law Review* 34 (1997): 149, 152.

36. Elizabeth P. Smith, interview with the author, Boston, Massachusetts, 27 September 2004.

37. Quoted in William S. Laufer, "Corporate Liability, Risk Shifting, and the Paradox of Compliance," *Vanderbilt Law Review* 52 (October 1999): 1343, 1372 n. 127.

38. Quoted in ibid.

39. William S. Laufer, "Corporate Prosecution, Cooperation, and the Trading of Favors," *Iowa Law Review* 87 (January 2002): 653, n. 47.

40. See Kaplan and Norton, *Strategy Maps*, 163–191.

41. *Basic v. Levinson*, 485 U.S. 224 (1988).

42. Jeffrey Krasner, "Nov. Fund Outflows Punish," *Boston Globe*, 30 December 2003, C1.

43. "Securities Class Action Settlement Average Increased to $24.3 Million, Research Finds," *Corporate Counsel Weekly* 18 (16 April 2003): 1.

44. Mark Maremont, "Rite Aids's Ex-CEO Sentenced to 8 Years for Accounting Fraud," *Wall Street Journal*, 28 May 2004, A3.

45. *Mueller v. Sullivan*, 141 F.3d 1232 (7th Cir. 1998).

46. Kurt Eichenwald, "Warning to Executives: Honesty Is the Best Policy," *New York Times*, 10 July 2004, C1.

47. See *Virginia Bankshares v. Sandberg*, 501 U.S. 1083 (1991), which holds that a statement about beliefs or opinions may be actionable if the opinion is known by the speaker at the time it is expressed to be untrue or to have no reasonable basis in fact.

48. Quoted in Alan Murray, "CEO Responsibility Might Be Right Cure for Corporate World," *Wall Street Journal*, 13 July 2004, A4.

49. Ibid.

50. Securities Exchange Act Rule 10b5-1 defines *insider trading* as buying or selling securities of any issuer on the basis of material, nonpublic information about the security or the issuer in breach of a duty of trust or confidence owed directly, indirectly, or derivatively to (1) the issuer or its security holders or (2) any other person who is the source of the material nonpublic information. 65 Fed. Reg. 51,716, 51,737 (24 August 2000). A *material fact* is one that a reasonable investor would have considered important in deciding whether to buy or sell. *TSC Industries v. Northway, Inc.*, 426 U.S. 438 (1976).

51. Constance L. Hays, "Former Chief of ImClone Is Given 7-Year Term," *New York Times*, 11 June 2003, C1.

52. *Dirks v. Securities and Exchange Commission*, 463 U.S. 646 (1983).

53. *United States v. O'Hagan*, 521 U.S. 642 (1997).

54. Securities Exchange Act Rule 10b5-1.

55. Harry First, "Antitrust at the Millennium (Part II): The Vitamins Case: Cartel Prosecutions and the Coming of International Competition Law," *Antitrust Law Journal* 68 (2001): 11.

56. "Vitamin Cartel Fined for Price-fixing," *Guardian*, 21 November 2001.

57. Ibid.

58. Ibid.

59. *United States v. Topco Assocs., Inc.*, 405 U.S. 596 (1972).

60. Jeffrey Sonnenfield and Paul R. Lawrence, "Why Do Companies Succumb to Price-Fixing?" *Harvard Business Review* 56, no. 4 (July–August 1978): 145–157.

61. Ibid.

62. *State Oil Co. v. Khan*, 522 U.S. 3 (1997).

63. Ibid.

64. *United States v. Aluminum Co. of America*, 148 F.2d 416, 430 (2d Cir. 1945).

65. David Yoffie, *Judo Strategy* (Boston: Harvard Business School Press, 2000), 201.

66. As of April 2005, Microsoft had agreed to pay more than $1.5 billion to settle antitrust actions by nine states and the District of Columbia and another $1.6 billion to settle a private antitrust and related intellectual property claims by its longtime rival Sun Microsystems. Laurie J. Flynn, "Preliminary Settlement Reached in Microsoft Case," *New York Times*, 20 April 2004.

67. Louis V. Gerstner Jr., *Who Says Elephants Can't Dance?* (New York: Harper Business, 2002), 118.

68. Ibid.

69. "Playboy Interview: Bill Gates," *Playboy*, July 1994, 63. See also John Heilemann, "The Truth, the Whole Truth and Nothing but the Truth: The United Story of the Microsoft Antitrust Case," *Wired*, November 2000, 261–311.

70. For example, William A. Sahlman calculated that the financial rewards Microsoft reaped from its anticompetitive conduct were so great that they made even a multibillion dollar fine an inadequate penalty. William A. Sahlman, *Financial Analysis of Microsoft*, Harvard Business School Note N9–802–194 (Boston: Harvard Business School Publishing, 2002).

71. See *In re Caremark International Derivative Litigation*, 698 A.2d 959 (Del. Ch. 1996), which stated that directors may be held personally liable for a corporation's noncompliance with applicable legal standards unless they have adequate procedures in place to ensure compliance with law.

72. Sonnenfeld and Laurence, *Why Do Companies Succumb to Price-Fixing?*

73. P. R. Lawrence and N. Nohria, *Driven: How Human Nature Shapes Our Choices* (San Francisco: Jossey-Bass, 2002).

74. S. J. Fox-Wolfgramm, K. B. Boal and J. G. Hunt, "Organizational Adaptation to Institutional Change: A Comparative Study of First-Order Change in Prospector and Defender Banks," *Administrative Science Quarterly* 43, no. 1 (1998): 87–126.

75. Ibid.

76. Ibid.

77. Ibid.

78. Ibid.

79. Ibid.

80. Indeed, Cisco Systems used Microsoft's e-mail messages as examples of what not to do when training its employees. Scott Thurm, "Safe Conduct, Microsoft's Behavior Is Helping Cisco Learn How to Avoid Trouble," *Wall Street Journal*, 1 June, 2000, A1.

81. Max Bazerman and Michael Watkins, *Predictable Surprises* (Boston: Harvard Business School Press, 2004).

82. See, e.g., *United States v. Beusch*, 596 F.2d 871 (9th Cir. 1979); *State v. Hy Vee Food Stores, Inc.*, 533 N.W.2d 147 (S.D. 1995).

83. Laufer, "Corporate Prosecution," 643, 645 n. 12.

84. Details of the *Darling International* case are drawn from Dean Starkman, "Pollution Case Highlights Trend to Let Employees Take the Rap," *Wall Street Journal*, 9 October 1997, 1.

85. Laufer, "Corporate Prosecution," 653.

86. Ibid., 659–660.

87. Ibid., 660.

Chapter 4

1. *Apple Computer, Inc. v. Microsoft Corp.*, 799 F. Supp. 1006 (N.D. Cal. 1992).

2. *Apple Computer, Inc. v. Microsoft Corp.*, 717 F. Supp. 1428 (N.D. Cal. 1989).

3. Ibid.

4. Ibid.

5. Quoted in John Seabrook, "A Reporter at Large: E-Mail from Bill," *New Yorker*, 10 January 1994.

6. For a general discussion, see Garth Saloner, Andrea Shephard, and Joel Podolny, *Strategic Management* (New York: Wiley, 2001), 39–40.

7. Jay B. Barney and M. H. Hansen note that companies can gain advantage through the skillful management of contractual forms of governance. Jay B. Barney and M. H. Hansen, "Trustworthiness as a Source of Competitive Advantage," *Strategic Management Journal* 15 (1994): 175–190.

8. Adrian J. Slywotzky et al., *Profit Patterns: 30 Ways to Anticipate and Profit from Strategic Forces Reshaping Your Business* (New York: Times Business, 1999), 111–112.

9. See Howard Stevenson, *Do Lunch or Be Lunch* (Boston: Harvard Business School Press, 2000).

10. As Oliver Williamson explained, "Rather than reply to opportunism in kind, the wise [bargaining party] is one who seeks both to give and receive 'credible commitments.'" Oliver E. Williamson, *The Economic Institutes of Capitalism: Firms, Markets and Relational Contracting* (New York: Free Press, 1985), 48–49.

11. *Vizcaino v. Microsoft Corp.*, 173 F. 3d 713 (9th Cir. 1999), *cert. denied*, 528 U.S. 1105 (2000); *Vizcaino v. Microsoft Corp.*, 97 F. 3d 1187 (9th Cir. 1996), *aff'd on reh'g*, 120 F. 3d 1006 (9th Cir. 1997), *cert. denied*, 522 U.S. 1099 (1998).

12. See, for example, C. Hill, "Cooperation, Opportunism, and the Invisible Hand: Implications for Transaction Cost Theory," *Academy of Management Review* 15 (1990): 500–513.

13. Laura Poppo and Todd Zenger, "Do Formal Contracts and Relational Governance Function as Substitutes or Complements?" *Strategic Management Journal* 23 (2002): 707–725.

14. Quoted in S. Macauly, "Non-contractual Relatives in Business: A Preliminary Study," *American Sociological Review* 28 (1963): 58–59.

15. Danny Ertel, "Getting Past Yes: Negotiating as if Implementation Mattered," *Harvard Business Review* 82 (November 2004): 60–68.

16. Darin Bifani, "Win the Battle or Build a Relationship: How Japanese Style Could Help American Negotiators," *Business Law Today* 12, no. 5 (May/June 2003): 25. Darin Birani, of the law firm of Baker and McKenzie, calls on American negotiators to pay more attention to the Japanese values of *ningen kankei*—human relationships—and *wa*—harmony. Japanese lawyers and managers are more likely to focus on the business relationship and, according to Bifani, "bend over backwards to correct business mistakes without being asked to, often at great corporate and personal cost and sacrifice." Ibid. To maintain the appearance of harmony, conflicting positions are avoided, and people and their actions are very rarely, if ever, criticized in public.

17. Ibid., 65.

18. Ibid.

19. Ibid.

20. Ibid., 67.

21. William M. Carley, "Ties That Bind: CEO Gets Hard Lesson in How Not to Keep His Top Lieutenants—International Paper's Chief, Frustrated by Poaching, Pushed Noncompete Pact—Pressuring the Nonsigners," *Wall Street Journal*, 11 February 1998, A1.

22. *CTA Inc. v. United States*, 44 Fed. Cl. 684 (Fed. Cl. 1999).

23. *Brass v. American Film Technologies, Inc.*, 987 F.2d 142 (2d Cir. 1993).

24. *Schipper v. Levitt & Sons, Inc.*, 207 A.2d 314 (N.J. 1965).

25. *Strawn v. Canuso*, 657 A.2d 420 (N.J. 1995).

26. *Wharf (Holdings) Ltd. v. United International Holdings, Inc.*, 532 U.S. 588 (2001).

27. *Marsu B.V. v. Walt Disney Co.*, 185 F.3d 932 (9th Cir. 1999).

28. *Rissman v. Rissman*, 213 F.3d 381 (7th Cir. 2000).

29. *Reiss v. Financial Performance Corp.*, 764 N.E.2d 958 (N.Y. 2001). Accord *Lohnes v. Level 3 Communications, Inc.*, 272 F.3d 49 (1st Cir. 2001).

30. *Reiss v. Financial Performance Corp.*

31. *Rissman v. Rissman*, 213 F.3d 381 (7th Cir. 2000).

32. *Smith v. Van Gorkom*, 488 A.2d 858 (Del. 1985).

33. Mary Jane Auer, "The High Cost of Terminating a Deal," *Daily Deal*, 14 April 2000.

34. Ibid.

35. See *Omnicare Inc. v. NCS Healthcare Inc.*, 818 A.2d 914 (Del. 2003): "[D]irectors have a continuing obligation to discharge their fiduciary responsibilities, as future circumstances develop, after a merger agreement is announced."

36. See William G. Schopf et al., "When a Letter of Intent Goes Wrong," *Business Law Today* 5 (January/February 1996): 31.

37. *Texaco, Inc. v. Pennzoil Co.*, 729 S.W.2d 768 (Tex. Ct. App. 1987), *cert. dismissed*, 485 U.S. 994 (1988).

38. James Kinnear, *The Man Who Wore the Star: Real-time Perspectives on a Business Leader's Changing World* (Albany, NY: The Business Council of New York State, 2001), 32.

39. The *New York Times* blasted the Texas Supreme Court for refusing to review the case. "In Texas, Contempt by Court," *New York Times*, 5 November 1987, A34.

40. James W. Kinnear, correspondence with the author, 1 April 2003.

41. James Shannon, *Texaco and the $10 Billion Jury* (Englewood Cliffs, NJ: Prentice Hall, 1988), 344–345.

42. Acquisition agreements are discussed in more detail in Constance E. Bagley and Craig E. Dauchy, *The Entrepreneur's Guide to Business Law*, 2d ed. (Mason, OH: West Legal Studies in Business, 2003), 585–649.

43. See, for example, *Richmond v. Peters*, 1998 U.S. App. LEXIS 30114 (6th Cir. Nov. 20, 1998), holding that there is no implied duty to maximize the return for the seller.

44. See Lucien J. Dhooge, "A Previously Unimaginable Risk Potential: September 11 and the Insurance Industry," *American Business Law Journal* 40, no. 4 (Summer 2003): 687, 700–703.

45. David A. Moss, *When All Else Fails: Government as the Ultimate Risk Manager* (Cambridge, MA: Harvard University Press, 2001), 231.

46. *Gonzalez v. A-1 Self-Storage, Inc.*, 795 A.2d 885 (N.J. Super. 2000).

47. As explained by what finance scholars refer to as real options theory, there is value inherent in the right to delay a decision. On the value of options to defer, see, for example, Robert McDonald and Daniel R. Siegel, "The Value of Waiting to Invest," *Quarterly Journal of Economics* 101 (November 1986): 707–727; J. E. Ingersoll and S. A. Ross, "Waiting to Invest: Investment and Uncertainty," *Journal of Business* 6 (January 1992): 1–30.

48. V. G. Narayanan and Ananth Raman, "Aligning Incentives in Supply Chains," *Harvard Business Review* 82 (November 2004): 94–102.

49. Ibid., 99.

50. Ibid., 100.

51. See Bagley and Dauchy, *Entrepreneur's Guide*, 445–472.

52. *Norcon Powers Partners, L.P., v. Niagara Mohawk Power Corp.*, 705 N.E. 2d 656 (N.Y. App. 1998).

53. William Eagan, "The Westinghouse Uranium Contracts: Commerical Impracticability and Related Matters," *American Business Law Journal* 18 (1980): 281.

54. Ibid.

55. This ability to accept or reject contracts applies only to executory contracts, which are contracts that require further performance from each party.

56. *In re Computer Communications, Inc.*, 824 F.2d 725 (9th Cir. 1987).

57. Macauly, "Non-Contractual Relatives."

58. Benjamin Klein and Keith B. Leffler, "The Role of Market Forces in Assuring Contract Performance," *Journal of Political Economy* 89 (1981): 615–641.

Chapter 5

1. Sabra Chartrand, "Patents: A Federal Agency, in Transition, Reaches Out to Independent Inventors with a New Department," *New York Times*, 5 April 1999, C2. See also Michael Montembeau, "In Pursuit of Patents: Patent Strategy and Management," *Patent Strategy & Management* 4 (2004): 7.

2. As Dorothy Leonard explained, corporate knowledge, capabilities, and relationships are increasingly important sources of firm value creation. Management of these strategic knowledge assets determines the company's ability to survive, adapt, and compete. Dorothy A. Leonard, *Wellsprings on Knowledge: Building and Sustaining the Sources of Innovation* (Boston: Harvard Business School Press, 1998).

3. William Rodarmor, "Prosecution Complex," *California Lawyer* (December 2001): 23, 27.

4. Louis V. Gerstner Jr., *Who Says Elephants Can't Dance?* (New York: Harper Business, 2002), 147–149.

5. Lawrence Ingrassia and James S. Hirsch, "Polaroid's Patent-Case Award, Smaller than Anticipated, Is a Relief for Kodak," *Wall Street Journal*, 11 October 1990, A3

6. See *Community for Creative Non-Violence v. Reid*, 490 U.S. 730 (1989).

7. *Diamond v. Chakrabarty*, 447 U.S. 303 (1980).

8. *State Street Bank & Trust Co. v. Signature Financial Group, Inc.*, 149 F.3d 1368 (Fed. Cir. 1998).

9. *J. E. M. Ag Supply Inc. v. Pioneer Hi-Bred*, 534 U.S. 124 (2001).

10. Ibid.

11. Pui-Wing Tam, "More Patents, Please! Tech Companies Urge Staffers to Submit Innovative Ideas; Cash Awards, Plaques at H-P," *Wall Street Journal*, 3 October 2002, B1.

12. Ibid.

13. Ibid.

14. Clayton Christensen, *The Innovator's Dilemma* (Boston: Harvard Business School Press, 2001).

15. See, for example, Don Clark, "Microsoft's Other Legal Headache," *Wall Street Journal*, 3 October 2002, B1.

16. Morgan Chu, "A Giant-Killer Should Limit Scope of Attack," *National Law Journal* (13 March 1995). Large firms, including Unisys and NCR, have successfully defended patent infringement claims by so-called patent trolls, shell companies usually run by lawyers that are formed with the purpose of pressing infringement claims based on questionable patents they purchased from entrepreneurs at bargain prices. Thomas Adcock, "IP Pain Puts Heat on Shell Firms and Their 'Patent Trolls,'" *Broward Daily Business Review*, 20 April 2005, 10.

17. Ian Fried, "Intel to Pay Intergraph for Patent Dispute," ZDNN (15 April 2002), available at http://zdnet.com.com/2100-1103-882764.html (accessed 16 April 2002). In 2005, Research in Motion Ltd., maker of the BlackBerry wireless e-mail device, agreed to pay NTP Inc. $450 million to settle a patent infringement suit involving NTP's radio communications technology. Associated Press, "450 Million Payout to Settle BlackBerry Suit," *National Law Journal*, 21 March 2005, 16.

18. Geoff Winestock and Helene Cooper, "WTO Envoys Agree to Ease Access to Key Drugs," *Wall Street Journal*, 13 November 2001.

19. Amy Harmon, "In the 'Idea Wars,' a Fight to Control a New Currency," *New York Times*, 11 November 2001, Section 3, 1.

20. Ibid.

21. Ibid.

22. Ibid.

23. Ibid. For a critical look at business process patents, see Adam B. Jaffe and Josh Lerner, *Innovation and Its Discontents: How Our Broken Patent System Is Endangering Innovation and Progress, and What to Do About It* (Princeton, NJ, and Oxford: Princeton University Press, 2004).

24. See, for example, *Pro CD v. Zeidenberg*, 86 F.3d 1447 (7th Cir. 1996).

25. *A&M Records, Inc. v. Napster*, 239 F.3d 1004 (9th Cir. 2001).

26. Pub. L. No. 105–304, 112 Stat. 2860 (1998).

27. John Seabrook, "A Reporter at Large: E-Mail from Bill," *New Yorker*, 10 January 1994.

28. Ken Bensinger, "Film Companies Take to Mexico's Streets to Fight Piracy," *Wall Street Journal*, 17 December 2003, B1.

29. *Sony Corp. of America v. Universal City Studios*, 464 U.S. 417 (1984).

30. *American Geophysical Union v. Texaco, Inc.*, 60 F.3d 913 (2d Cir. 1994).

31. *Fonovisa, Inc. v. Cherry Auction, Inc.*, 76 F.3d 259 (9th Cir. 1996).

32. The U.S. Supreme Court ruled that Grokster Ltd. and StreamCast Networks, which distribute peer-to-peer file-sharing computer networking software used to share music and movie files, were liable for copyright infringement by their users because they actively induced illegal sharing of files. *Metro-Goldwyn-Mayer Studios, Inc. v. Grokster Ltd.*, 2005 U.S. LEXIS 5212 (27 June 2005).

33. *Morlife, Inc. v. Perry*, 66 Cal. 2d 731 (Cal. Ct. App. 1997).

34. See Constance E. Bagley and Craig E. Dauchy, *The Entrepreneur's Guide to Business Law*, 2d ed. (Mason, OH: West Legal Studies in Business, 2003), 328–339, for a sample independent contractor agreement.

35. *PepsiCo, Inc. v. Redmond*, 54 F.3d 1262 (7th Cir. 1995).

36. Patrick McGeehan, "Arbitrator Rules That a Bell South Executive Can Join Sprint," *New York Times*, 19 March 2003, C5.

37. 15 U.S.C. §§ 1051–1072 (1994).

38. *Two Pesos, Inc. v. Taco Cabana, Inc.*, 505 U.S. 763 (1992).

39. *Goto.com Inc. v. Disney Co.*, 202 F.3d 1199 (9th Cir. 2002).

40. Interbrand used publicly available marketing and financial data to calculate the projected net earnings, which it discounted to a present value based on how risky the projected earnings were.

41. George Weigel, "Whatever You Do with This Article, Don't 'Xerox' It," *Chicago Sun-Times*, 7 October 1990, 57.

42. Sol M. Linowitz and Martin Mayer, *The Betrayed Profession: Lawyering at the End of the Twentieth Century* (New York: Scribner, 1994), 75.

43. *Quality King Distrib., Inc. v. L'anza Research Int'l, Inc.*, 523 U.S. 135 (1998).

44. See Edward Felsenthan, "Copyright Protection for Firms That Export Is Limited by Court," *Wall Street Journal*, 10 March 1998, A1.

45. Gerstner, *Who Says Elephants Can't Dance?* 149.

46. Ibid., 148.

47. Ibid.

48. Adrian J. Slyworthy et al., *Profit Patterns: 30 Ways to Anticipate and Profit from Strategic Forces Reshaping Your Business* (New York: Times Books, 1999), 232.

Chapter 6

1. Mike Moser, *United We Brand, How to Create a Cohesive Brand That's Seen, Heard, and Remembered* (Boston: Harvard Business School Press, 2003), 177.

2. Quoted in Gerry Khermouch, "The 100 Top Brands," *BusinessWeek*, 4 August 2003, 72–74.

3. "F.T.C. Accord on Volvo Ads," *New York Times*, 22 August 1991, 19.

4. Moser, *United We Brand*, 16.

5. Bruce Horowitz, "Volvo, Agency Fined $150,000 Each for TV Ad Commercials," *Los Angeles Times*, 22 August 1991, 2.

6. Joshua Levine, *Forbes*, 27 May 1991, 319–321

7. Moser, *United We Brand*, 45.

8. Ibid., 147.

9. Quoted in ibid., 156, n.1.

10. Peter S. Goodman, "China Serves as Dump Site for Companies," *Washington Post*, 24 February 2003, A1.

11. Ibid.; P. J. Huffstutter, "Recycled Electronics Pose a Health Hazard in Asia," *Los Angeles Times*, 26 February 2002, C1.

12. Goodman, "China Serves as Dump Site."

13. John Markoff, "2 PC Makers Given Credit and Blame in Recycling," *New York Times*, 27 June 2003, C3.

14. Dee DePass, "Prudential Will Pay $35 Million Fine and Restitution," *Star Tribune* (Minneapolis), 10 July 1996, Metro 1A; Amanda Levin, "Pru Violates ADR Process, Suits Allege," *National Underwriter, Property & Casualty/ Risk and Benefits Management Edition*, 15 November 1999, 10.

15. *WarnerLambert Co. v. FTC*, 562 F.2d 749 (D.C. Cir. 1977), *cert. denied*, 435 U.S. 950 (1978).

16. *In re Novartis Corp.*, FTC Docket No. 9279 (March 9, 1998), 66 U.S.L.W. 2582 (March 31, 1998).

17. *Coca-Cola Co. v. Tropicana Prods., Inc.*, 690 F.2d 312 (2d Cir. 1982).

18. See, for example, *Walker v. American Cynamid Co.*, 948 P.2d 1123 (Idaho 1997).

19. Melissa S. Baucus and David A. Baucus, "Paying the Piper: An Empirical Examination of Longer–Term Financial Consequences of Illegal Corporate Behavior," *Academy of Management Journal* 40 (1997): 129–151.

20. *Conway ex rel. Roadway Express Inc. v. White Trucks*, 639 F. Supp. 160 (M.D. Pa. 1986).

21. *Grimshaw v. Ford Motor Co.*, 119 Cal. App. 3d 757 (1981).

22. Frank Swoboda and Caroline E. Mayer, "A $4.8 Billion Message: Jury Hits GM with Historic Crash Verdict," *Washington Post*, 10 July 1999, A1.

23. Jeffrey Ball and Milo Geyelin, "GM Ordered by Jury to Pay $4.9 Billion," *Wall Street Journal*, 12 July 1999, A3.

24. Melvyn A. J. Menezes, "Ethical Issues in Product Policy," in N. Craig Smith and John A. Quelch, *Ethics in Marketing* (Homewood, IL: Irwin, 1993), 284.

25. In contrast, a statute of limitations begins to run only at the time an injury occurs. Thus, if a state had a one-year statute of limitations and a ten-year statute of repose for product liability claims, then a person injured eleven years after the product was delivered would be time-barred from suing by the statute of repose, even though the statute of limitations had not yet run.

26. Allen Michel et al., "Protecting Future Product Liability Claimants," *American Bankruptcy Institute Journal* 1 (December 1999): 3–4.

27. Paul D. Rheingold, "The Future of Product Liability: The Plaintiff's Perspective," *Product Safety & Liability Report* (BNA) 17 (1989): 711.

28. Smith and Quelch, *Ethics in Marketing*, 285.

29. E. Marla Felcher, "Children's Products and Risk," *Atlantic Monthly*, November 2000, 36–42.

30. See, for example, *Herrnreiter v. Chicago Housing Authority*, 281 F.3d 634 (7th Cir. 2002).

31. Smith and Quelch, *Ethics in Marketing*, 365–366.

32. Ibid.

33. Myron Levin, "Tire Maker to Add Safety Features to Settle Suits; Bridgestone/ Firestone Also Agrees to Fund a $15-Million Consumer Education Campaign," *Los Angeles Times*, 25 July 2003, A36.

34. Stephen Power, "Update Needed for Tire Rules, Activists Argue," *Wall Street Journal*, 8 September 2000, B1.

35. Todd Zaun, Joseph White, and Timothy Appel, "Firestone Parent Will Set Aside Cash for Claims—Bridgestone Says Lawsuits Won't Force U.S. Unit into Bankruptcy Court," *Wall Street Journal*, 6 December 2000, A6.

36. Martha Neil, "Confidential Settlements Scrutinized—Recent Events Bolster Proponents of Limiting Secret Case Resolutions," *ABA Journal*, July 2002, 20–22.

37. Mark Magnier, "Bridgestone's Top Man Resigns, a Victim of Firestone Scandal," *Los Angeles Times*, 12 January 2001, C1.

38. Ibid.

39. Milo Geyelin, "Squabbles Between Ford and Firestone May Hurt Their Legal Defense," *Wall Street Journal*, 9 October 2000, B1.

40. Ibid.

41. Caroline E. Mayer and Frank Swoboda, "A Corporate Collision; Ford-Firestone Feud Accelerated after Effort to Head It Off Failed," *Washington Post*, June 20, 2001, E1.

42. Ibid.

43. Ibid.

44. Ibid.

45. Keith Bradsher, "Advertising: 2 Different Approaches in Aftermath of Tire Recall," *New York Times*, 5 April 2001, C1.

46. Zaun, White, and Appel, "Firestone Parent Will Set Aside Cash for Claims."

47. Geyelin, "Squabbles Between Ford and Firestone."

48. *United States v. Park*, 421 U.S. 658 (1975).

49. Adrian J. Slyworthy et al., *Profit Patterns: 30 Ways to Anticipate and Profit from Strategic Forces Reshaping Your Business* (New York: Times Books, 1999), 282–284.

50. Assembly Bill 1950 (2004).

51. Lisa Burden, "Report Says Privacy Laws Cost Big Bucks without Calming Customer Fears," *Financial News*, 29 January 2001.

52. *Eli Lilly & Co.*, 67 Fed. Reg. 4963 (1 February, 2002); *In re Eli Lilly & Co.*, 2002 FTC LEXIS 3 (1 February, 2002).

53. Mike France, "Mea Culpa Defense," *BusinessWeek*, 26 August 2002, 77.

54. Andrea Gerlin, "A Matter of Degree: How a Jury Decided That a Coffee Spill Is Worth $2.7 Million," *Wall Street Journal*, 1 September 1994, A1.

55. Rachel Zimmerman, "Doctors' New Tool to Fight Lawsuits: Saying 'I'm Sorry,'" *Wall Street Journal*, 18 May 2004, A1.

56. Quoted in ibid.

Chapter 7

1. James W. Kinnear, correspondence with the author, 1 April 2003.

2. Elizabeth P. Smith, interview with the author, Boston, Massachusetts, 9 November 2003.

3. Ibid.

4. Peter Bijur, Keynote Address, Stanford Law School General Counsel Institute, Palo Alto, California, 14 January 1998.

5. Elizabeth P. Smith, interview with the author.

6. *Texaco Task Force on Equality and Fairness, Fifth Annual Report* (September 30, 2002), available at http://www.texaco.com/texaco/texaco/search/redirector .asp?url=/sitelets/diversity/index.hrml [hereinafter *Final Report*].

7. Peter F. Drucker, "They're Not Employees, They're People," *Harvard Business Review* 83, no. 2 (February 2003): 70, 71.

8. Ibid., 73.

9. Ibid., 74 (italics added).

10. For a general discussion, see Constance E. Bagley, "Risky Business: Understanding and Reducing Employer Risk," *Advances in the Study of Entrepreneurship, Innovation, and Economic Growth, Vol. 10* (1998): 123–166. Greenwich, CT: JAI Press.

11. For an excellent discussion of good hiring practices, see Pierre Mornell, *Hiring Smart* (San Francisco: Ten Speed Press, 1998).

12. *Fortune v. National Cash Register Co.*, 364 N.E.2d 1251 (Mass. 1977).

13. Jeffrey Pfeffer, *Competitive Advantage Through People: Unleashing the Power of the Work Force* (Boston: Harvard Business School Press, 1994), 132.

14. Ibid., 147–148.

15. Quoted in ibid., 146.

16. Ibid., 157.

17. Ibid., 155.

18. *Reeves v. Sanderson Plumbing Products, Inc.*, 530 U.S. 133 (2000).

19. "Employment Discrimination Settling Claims: Plaintiff, Defense Experts Provide Advice on Negotiating Agreements, Releases, Payment, Apologies," *Corporate Counsel Weekly* 18 (12 March 2003): 87–88.

20. For a discussion of the matters that should be covered in an employment agreement, see Constance E. Bagley and Craig E. Dauchy, *The Entrepreneur's Guide to Business Law*, 2d ed. (Mason, OH: West Legal Studies in Business, 2003), 306–310.

21. For a sample independent contractor services agreement, see ibid., 328–339.

22. National Workrights Institute, "On Your Tracks: GPS Tracking in the Workplace," available at http://www.workrights.org/issue_electronic/NWI_GPS_Report.pdf.

23. *Clackamas Gastroenterology Associates P.C. v. Wells*, 537 U.S. 1169 (2003).

24. Riva D. Atlas, "Fund Inquiry Informant Discloses Her Identity," *New York Times*, 9 December 2003, C1. See also Michael J. Gundlach, Scott C. Douglas, and Mark J. Martinko, "The Decision to Blow the Whistle: A Social Information Processing Framework," *Academy of Management Review* 28 (2003): 107–123.

25. Charles Haddad and Amy Barrett, "A Whistle-Blower Rocks an Industry," *BusinessWeek*, 24 June 2002, 126.

26. Ibid., 128.

27. Ibid., 126.

28. Drucker, "They're Not Employees," 74.

29. David A. Thomas and Robin J. Ely, "Making Differences Matter: A New Paradigm for Managing Diversity," *Harvard Business Review* 74, no. 9 (September–October 1996): 3–14.

30. Ibid.

31. *Grutter v. Bollinger*, 539 U.S. 306, 334 (2003): "[M]ajor American businesses have made clear that the skills needed in today's increasingly global marketplace can only be developed through exposure to widely diverse people, cultures, ideas and viewpoints."

32. *Final Report*, 9.

33. Hanna Rosin, "Cultural Revolution at Texaco," *New Republic*, February 1998, 18.

34. Ibid.

35. *Final Report*, 28.

36. Ibid., 9.

37. Ibid., 32.

38. Adam Bryant, "How Much Has Texaco Changed?" *New York Times*, 2 November 1997, Section 3, 1.

39. *Final Report*, 37.

40. Ibid., 30.

41. Ibid., 29.

42. Ibid., 71.

43. Ibid., 80.

44. Davan Maharah, "Coca-Cola to Settle Workplace Racial Bias Lawsuit: Soft Drink Giant Agrees to Pay $192.5 Million Over Allegations It Treated Blacks Unfairly," *Los Angeles Times*, 17 November 2000, A1.

45. Greg Winter, "Coca-Cola Settles Racial Bias Case," *New York Times*, 17 November 2000, A1.

46. *Meritor Savings Bank, FSB v. Vinson*, 477 U.S. 57 (1986).

47. *Faragher v. City of Boca Raton*, 524 U.S. 775 (1998).

48. Ibid.

49. *Lockard v. Pizza Hut, Inc.*, 162 F.3d 1062 (10th Cir. 1998).

50. *Brooks v. San Mateo, Calif.*, 229 F.3d 917 (9th Cir. 2000).

51. See Bernice R. Sandler, "Handling Sexual Harassment," *Women in Medicine and the Medical Sciences* (Fall 1997): 1 (discussing strategies that victims may use to address workplace sexual harassment).

52. Rachel Gordon, "Amount of Award Split Harassment Jury," *San Francisco Examiner*, 3 September 1994.

53. Associated Press, "Drug Firm to Pay Record $9.85 Million," *San Francisco Chronicle*, 6 February 1998.

54. Mark Maremont, "Abuse of Power: The Astonishing Tale of Sexual Harassment at Astra USA," *BusinessWeek*, 13 May 1996, 86.

55. Laura Johannes, "Astra USA Fires Bildman from Top Post," *Wall Street Journal*, 27 June 1996, A3.

56. *Blakey v. Continental Airlines, Inc.*, 751 A.2d 653 (N.J. 2000).

57. For a general discussion, see Diana J. P. McKenzie, "Information Technology Policies: Practical Protection in Cyberspace," *Stanford Journal of Law, Business and Finance* 3 (1997): 84.

58. "Effective Advocacy in Mediation, Arbitration Requires Understanding Goals, Limitations," *U.S. Law Week* 71 (15 October 2002): 2254.

59. Jane Spencer, "Waiving Your Right to a Jury Trial," *Wall Street Journal*, 17 August 2004, D1.

Chapter 8

1. See Howard Raiffa, *The Art and Science of Negotiation* (Cambridge, MA, and London: Belknap Press, 1982), for a classic treatment of negotiating strategies. For example, suppose a supplier fails to deliver computer chips on time. The buyer could sue the supplier for monetary damages equal to the extra cost it incurred buying the chips from another supplier. Alternatively, the buyer could negotiate a transaction whereby the supplier agrees to expedite shipment of the next generation chips to the disappointed buyer. Having access to the new chips may be worth more to the buyer than the extra cost it incurred when it had to fill its original order elsewhere. Providing the new chips may cost the supplier less than what it would have had to pay in monetary damages in a breach of contract suit.

2. James Kinnear, interview with the author, Boston, Massachusetts, 10 November 2003.

3. Sol M. Linowitz and Martin Mayer, *The Betrayed Profession: Lawyering at the End of the Twentieth Century* (New York: Scribner, 1994), 93.

4. Ibid., 172.

5. Richard A. Oppel Jr. and Glen Justice, "The 2004 Election: The Response: Kerry Gains Campaign Ace, Risking Anti-Lawyer Anger," *New York Times*, 7 July 2004, A15.

6. Ibid., 174

7. Jay Walker, interview with the author, Boston, Massachusetts, 2003.

8. James W. Kinnear, correspondence with the author, 1 April 2003. For a further discussion of the case, see James W. Kinnear, *The Man Who Wore the Star: Real-time Perspectives on a Business Leader's Changing World* (Albany, NY: The Business Council of New York State, 2001).

9. Ibid.

10. Mike France, "The Mea Culpa Defense," *BusinessWeek*, 26 August 2002, 77.

11. Patrick McGeehan, "How Settlement Is Worded Could Be Costly to Merrill," *New York Times*, 10 May 2002, C4. Philip M. Aidikoff, a plaintiff's lawyer who is president of the Public Investors Arbitration Bar Association, stated, "An apology is not worth anything unless Merrill Lynch is prohibited from denying the wrongdoing when investors bring claims."

12. National Institute of Dispute Resolution, *Dispute Resolution Forum*, 9 May 1989.

13. *Sprinzen v. Nomberg*, 389 N.E. 2d 456, 458 (N.Y. 1979).

14. This discussion is based on Center for Public Resources, "Mainstreaming: Corporate Strategies for Systematic ADR Use," *Practical Guide Series*, looseleaf (New York, 1989), Section E.

15. Michael J. Roberts and Constance E. Bagley, *Priceline.com v. Microsoft(B)*, Harvard Business School Case No. 802-082 (Boston: Harvard Business School Publishing, 2001), 1–3.

16. G. Richard Shell, *Make the Rules or Your Rivals Will* (New York: Crown Business, 2004), 85–87.

17. Quoted in ibid.

18. Ibid., 86–87.

19. David Yoffie, "Corporate Strategy for Political Action: A Rational Model," in A. Marcus, A. Kaufman, and D. Beam, eds., *Business Strategy and Public Policy* (New York: Quorum, 1987), 92–111.

20. "Presence of Decision-makers Key to Mediating Bias Claims," *Corporate Counsel Weekly*, 3 April 2002, 109.

21. Timothy L. O'Brien, "Citigroup Assesses a Risk and Decides to Settle," *New York Times*, 11 May 2004, C2.

22. Aspects of this discussion are drawn from Roger Fisher, "He Who Pays the Piper," *Harvard Business Review* 63, no. 3 (March–April, 1985): 150.

23. Ibid.

24. For an economic analysis of decisions to settle or litigate, see Peter Siegelman and Joel Waldfogel, "Toward a Taxonomy of Disputes: New Evidence Through the Prism of the Priest/Klein Model," *Journal of Legal Studies* 28 (1999): 101; Chris Guthrie, "Better Settle than Sorry: The Regret Aversion Theory of Litigation Behavior," *University of Illinois Law Review* 1999 (1999): 43. For a more psychological approach, see Jeffrey J. Rachlinski, "Gains, Losses, and the

Psychology of Litigation," *Southern California Law Review* 70 (1996): 113. Thanks to Gregory Todd Jones of Georgia State University for bringing this literature to my attention.

25. Alex Berenson, "Once Again, Spitzer Follows E-Mail Trail," *New York Times*, 18 October 2004, C1. The scandal caused Marsh & McLennan's stock to drop almost 50 percent and prompted the board to fire both the CEO and the general counsel.

26. Aspects of this discussion of document retention are based on John Ruhnka and Robert Austin, "Design Considerations for Document Retention/Destruction Programs," *Corporate Confidentiality and Disclosure Letter* 1 (1988): 2.

27. *Carlucci v. Piper Aircraft Corp*, 102 F.R.D. 472 (S.D. Fla. 1984).

Chapter 9

1. Stephen J. Friedman and C. Evan Stewart (eds.), *Corporate Executive's Guide to the Role of the General Counsel* (Chicago, IL: American Corporate Counsel Association, 2000). According to Ben Heineman, General Electric's senior vice-president, law and public affairs, "Nowdays every firm should have its own in-house lawyer-statesman" who supplies practical wisdom and not just technical mastery, understands long-term effects, and evinces a deep concern for the public interest as well as for the private good of the firm. *Economist*, 20 March 2004.

2. Milo Geyelin, "More Law Schools Are Teaching Students Value of Assuming Clients' Point of View," *Wall Street Journal*, 17 September 1991, B1.

3. Ronald J. Gilson, "Value Creation by Business Lawyers: Legal Skills and Asset Pricing," *Yale Law Journal* 94 (1984): 239–311.

4. Richard A. Oppel Jr. and Kurt Eichewald, "Arthur Andersen Fires an Executive for Enron Orders," *New York Times*, 16 January 2002, A6.

5. Marshall B. Clinard and Peter C. Yeager, *Corporate Crime* (New York: Free Press, 1980), 20

6. Ibid.

7. Ibid.

8. Ibid., 18.

9. "Effective" is used here to refer to the aspect of strategy implementation that focuses on doing the right things. "Efficient" refers to doing things right. Mike H. Ryan, Carl L. Swanson, and Rogene A. Buchholz, *Corporate Strategy, Public Policy and the Fortune 500: How America's Major Corporations Influence Government* (Oxford and New York: Blackwell, 1987), 18.

10. David Andrews, interview with the author, Purchase, New York, 30 October 2005.

11. Indra K. Nooyi, interview with the author, Purchase, New York, 30 October 2005.

12. Kim B. Clark and Steven C. Wheelwright, "Organizing and Leading Heavyweight Development Teams," *California Management Review* 34 (Spring 1992): 9–28.

13. See Michael E. Porter and Victor E. Millar, "How Information Gives You Competitive Advantage," in Michael E. Porter, *On Competition* (Boston: Harvard Business School Press, 1996), 77.

14. The discussion of the evolution of information technology management that follows is drawn from Lynda M. Applegate and Joyce J. Elam, "New Infor-

mation Systems Leaders: A Changing Role in a Changing World," *MIS Quarterly* 16, no. 4 (December 1992): 469–490.

15. Ibid.

16. Jeanne W. Ross and Peter Weill, "Six IT Decisions Your IT People Shouldn't Make," *Harvard Business Review* 81, no. 11 (November 2002): 84–91.

17. Mark D. Lutchen, *Managing IT as a Business: A Survival Guide for CEOs* (Hoboken, NJ: Wiley, 2004), 8.

18. Ibid.

19. Friedman and Stewart, *Corporate Executive's Guide*.

20. Ibid.

21. Mike France and Louis Laville, "A Compelling Case for Lawyer-CEO's," *BusinessWeek*, 13 December 2004, 88.

22. According to the headhunting firm SpencerStuart, 10.8 percent of the CEOs of companies in Standard & Poor's 500-stock index have law degrees. They include Sumner M. Redstone (Viacom), Kenneth I. Chenault (American Express), and Richard D. Parsons (Time Warner).

23. P. Clendenen, "General Counsel for Changing Times," *Business Lawyer*, May/June 2002.

24. Ibid.

25. Friedman and Stewart, *Corporate Executive's Guide*.

26. James Kinnear, interview with the author, Boston, Massachusetts, 27 September 2004.

27. American Corporate Counsel Association, *In-house Counsel for the 21st Century* (Chicago, IL: American Corporate Law Association, 2001).

28. Friedman and Stewart, *Corporate Executive's Guide*.

29. "Interview: D. C. Yu—Corporation's Retention and Management of Outside Counsel," *Corporate Counsel Weekly*, 20 September 2000, 8.

30. Paul Rice, "Corporate Attorney-Client Privilege: Study Reveals Corporate Agents Are Uninformed; What They Don't Know Can Destroy the Privilege," American Corporate Counsel Association, August 1988, available at http://www.acca .com/vl/privilege/rice.html.

31. Ibid.

32. "Protecting the Privilege," *Corporate Counsel Weekly*, 21 August 2002, 261.

33. Robert Swaine, *The Cravath Firm*, vol. 2 (New York: Ad Press, 1948), 696.

34. *U.S. Law Week*, 19 August 1997.

35. *Upjohn Co. v. United States*, 449 U.S. 38 (1981).

36. This discussion is based in part on Dennis Block and Carol Remz, "After 'Upjohn': The Uncertain Confidentiality of Corporate Internal Investigative Files," in *American Bar Association Section on Litigation, Recent Developments in Attorney-Client Privilege, Work-Product Doctrine and Confidentiality of Communications Between Counsel and Client* (Chicago: American Bar Association, 1983).

37. Linowitz and Mayor, *The Betrayed Profession*, 4.

38. Ibid., 16.

39. "Rule 2.1," *American Bar Association Model Rules of Professional Conduct* (Chicago: American Bar Association Center for Professional Responsibility, 2002), 70.

40. Ibid.

41. Ibid.

42. Ibid.

43. Ibid.

44. See Andy Pasztor and Lucette Lagnado, "Ethics Czar Aims to Heal Columbia," *Wall Street Journal*, 26 November 1997, B1.

45. Mitchell Pacelle, "Don't Bet on Citigroup Being in the Clear Yet," *Wall Street Journal*, 14 May 2004, C1.

46. Mara Der Hovanesian, Paula Dwyer, and Stanley Reed, "Can Chuck Prince Clean Up Citi?" *BusinessWeek*, 4 October 2004, 32–35.

47. Ken Magill, "Citigroup 4Q Profits Hit Record," *New York Sun*, 21 January 2005. In the wake of a controversial European government bond trade that disrupted the electronic market and other regulatory problems, the Federal Reserve Board instructed Citigroup not to plan to do any big new mergers or acquisitions until it addresses "the deficiencies in compliance risk management." David Wighton, "Fed Calls on Citigroup to Boost Controls," *Financial Times* (London), 18 March 2005, 23. On March 1, 2005, Citigroup kicked off its "Five Point Plan" for new management training, tighter financial controls, and improved communications between employees and executives. Although the plan includes a mandatory online ethics training course for all 300,000 employees, it is not clear whether Citigroup also plans to increase the legal literacy of its employees. Attaining Chuck Prince's articulated goal of turning Citigroup into the most respected global financial service company (Hamilton Nolan, "Citigroup Kicks Off Internal Efforts to Clarify Standards," *PR Week*, 4 April 2005, 3) will almost certainly require a higher degree of legal astuteness than certain of Citigroup's managers have exhibited in the past.

Index

abandonment, 142
Acme Markets, 56, 167
acquisition contracts
   benefits of, 107–108
   need for, 103–106
actual abandonment, defined, 142
Adelphia Communications
   collapse of, 3
   conflicts of interest at, 58
advocacy, for legal change, 43–45, 46
Age Discrimination in Employment
   Act (ADEA), 182, 190–191
agency law, 34
AllSport, 137, 138
alternative dispute resolution (ADR),
   205
   benefits of, 205–206
   ground rules of, 207–208
   models of, 206–207
   preludes to, 208
   systematization of, 209–210
   tradeoffs involved in, 206–207
   types of, 205
America Online, 122
America West Airlines, customer
   service by, 170
American Film Technologies, 97
American Home Products, 102, 103
American Telephone and Telegraph,
   litigation against, 213
Americans with Disabilities Act of
   1990 (ADA), 192–193
Amgen, 119, 149
Andreas, Michael, 91
Andrews, David, 227

antitrust, 13, 38
   compliance issues, 75–76
   and conflict of laws, 42–43
   education about, 80–81
   and monopolies, 74–75
   and price restrictions, 71–74
apology
   to customers, 170–171
   to employees, 201
   power of, 208
apparent authority, 90
Apple Computer
   iTunes of, 132
   and PARC intellectual property, 118
   suit against Microsoft, 87–88
Applegate, Lynda, 228, 229
arbitration
   employer-employee, 183
   features of, 206–207
   hybrid with mediation, 206, 209
   of international contracts, 91
   of personnel issues, 201
   result sought by, 209
Arthur Andersen
   collapse of, 45
   and Enron, 8, 49, 220, 225, 241–242
   legal troubles of, 3, 49, 220–221
Astra, sexual harassment at, 199–200
attorney-client privilege, 236
   client control over, 237
   and criminal acts, 239
   in internal investigations, 241–242
   prerequisites for, 238
   and privileged communications,
   239–240

attorney-client privilege (*continued*)
  retention of, 240–241
  scope of, 238–239
  waiver of, 237, 240, 241–242
at-will employment, 36, 178–181
authority, delegating, 62
authority, to enter into contract, 90
automobile industry, opportunity
    creation in, 77
Avanti Corporation, intellectual
    property violations by, 118

bait-and-switch, 157
Baker & McKenzie, sexual harassment
    at, 199
Balanced Scorecard Management
    System, 54
Bank Holding Company Act, 1, 2
bankruptcy
  and contracts, 115
  laws regarding, 22, 31
Barnette, Hank, 229
BASF, price-fixing by, 71
Bazerman, Max, 82
BellSouth, 138
benchmarking, of risks, 64
Berkshire Hathaway, ethical
    reputation of, 49
best efforts, distinguished from
    reasonable efforts, 98–99
Betamax, 132
Bijur, Peter, 175, 176–177
biotechnology industry, 23
Blakey, Tammy, 200
Blockbuster Video, 111
Boeing, 49
boilerplate, in contracts, 100
Boisi, Geoff, 104
bracketing, of patents, 125
brand equity
  building and loss of, 153–154
  and customer trust, 153, 154–158
  importance of, 140–141, 153
  protection through trademarking,
    140–142
breach of contract, 113
  remedies for, 114–115
break-up fees, 102–103

Bridgestone Tires, 165
Broadout, Tony, 154
Buffett, Warren, 51
bundling, 75
Burger King, 89
Burke, James, 165
business entity, choice of, 30
business judgment rule, 60
business strategy. *See* strategy

Cadence Design Systems, 118
Campbell Soup, deceptive advertising
    by, 157
capacity, to enter into contract, 90
capital markets, facilitation of, 30–31
Capital One, 168
Cendant, 6
  securities fraud at, 64
Cessna, 161
Cetus Corporation, 149
Cherkasky, Michael, 231
Chevron Texaco
  diversity at, 192–194
  Ombuds program at, 194–195
Chicken of the Sea brand name, 141
Chiron, 119
Christensen, Clayton, 124
Cisco Systems, legal advocacy by, 44
Citibank, 1
Citicorp
  merger with Travelers, 1, 2
CitiFinancial, legal issues of, 2
Citigroup
  formation of, 2
  Japanese legal issues in, 244–245
  legal issues of, 2–3, 243–244
  litigation against, 216
  success of, 2
civil law countries, 25
civil rights, in workplace, 37
Civil Rights Act of 1866, 190–191
Civil Rights Act of 1964, 188,
    190–191
Civil Rights Act of 1991, 192–193
Clark, Kim, 227
Clean Water Act, 41–42
Clemenceau, Georges, 5
Clinard, Marshall, 226

Coca-Cola Company
  brand name protection of, 142–143
  brand name value of, 140
  discrimination at, 195
  litigations by, 157
  trade secrets of, 134
  trademarks of, 139
code of ethics, 50–51, 62
  creation of, 52
Cole, Sheryl, 170
collective bargaining, 36
Columbia/HCA
  ethical and legal compliance by,
    47–49
  inappropriate incentives at, 63
  Medicare fraud by, 47–48, 243
common law system, 25
communication
  for compliance, 62
  with counsel, 7–8, 113–115,
    224–225
  privileged, 239–240
Community Reinvestment Act, 77
complete customer solutions strategy,
  11
compliance
  with antitrust provisions, 75–76
  approaches to, 52
  and business risk, 61–63
  coping with failures, 82–84
  duties and, 56–60
  education for, 80–82
  ethics and, 50–56
  fair competition and, 71–76
  feedback and, 62–63
  importance of, 48–49
  incentives for, 63
  internal controls and processes for,
    60–64
  preventing value destruction,
    227–228
  prevention of securities fraud and,
    64–71
  risks and, 56–60, 79
  steps for assuring, 85–86
  strategic aspects of, 49–50
Comprehensive Environmental
  Responsibility Compensation and
  Liability Act (CERCLA), 32

Compton's New Media, 122
computers
  harassment via, 200–201
  use by employees, 183
conflict of interest, avoiding, 58–59
consideration, 89
constitutional rights, 40–41
constructive abandonment, 142
consumer databases, 168
  controls on, 168
consumer protection laws, 22–23
Consumer Product Safety
  Commission, 163
  authority of, 172
Continental Airlines, 200
contracts
  acquisitions, 106–108
  alignment of incentives by, 110–112
  authority to negotiate, 90
  bankruptcy and, 115
  benefits of, 92–94
  boilerplate in, 100
  breach of, 114–115
  caveats regarding, 93
  under changed circumstances,
    112–114
  clarity in, 93–94
  drafting errors in, 100
  elements of, 89–91
  enforceable vs. nonenforceable, 91
  enforcement of, 29–30, 41
  good faith in, 98–99
  honesty in, 96–98
  insurance, 108–109
  international aspects of, 90–91
  language of, 101–103
  management and, 26
  managerial liability in, 101–103
  as meeting of the minds, 94–96
  options offered by, 110
  oral vs. written, 99–100
  preliminary agreements and,
    103–106
  public policy issues in, 91–92
  as relationships, 88–89
  and risk allocation, 106–107
  role of counsel in, 94
  and supply chain, 110–111
contributory infringement, 133

Convention on the International Sale
    of Goods (CISG), 90–91
copyright, 34
    advantages of, 144
    assignment of, 120
    categories of, 128
    characteristics of protection offered
        by, 146–148
    of digital material, 130–133
    and fair use, 130
    international aspects of, 129
    ownership of, 119–120
    requirements of, 144
    scope of, 128–129
    violations of, 131–133
Corporate Executive's Guide to the Role of
    General Counsel, 232
counsel
    advisory role of, 232, 239
    and attorney-client privilege,
        236–242
    attitudes towards, 223–224
    centralizing or decentralizing,
        235–236
    client identification, 237
    communication with management,
        7–8, 113–115, 224–225
    general, 231–235
    importance of, 224–228
    in-house, 230
    "project team" model of, 230–231
    relationship of management with,
        6–7, 223–228
    risk aversion of, 7
    roles of, 213–214, 223
    selection of, 242–245
Cox, Rob, 231
Cravath, Swaine and Moore, 238
criminal action
    dealing with, 82–84
    employee reaction to, 82
    honesty in face of, 82, 84
    manager responsibility and, 82
criminal violations
`   attorney-client privilege, 237
    avoiding, 62
    corporate, in 1970s, 13
    reasons for, 13
cross-licensing, 119, 149

CTA, Inc., 96
customer trust, 140–141, 153
    importance of, 154–158

Daiichi Pharmaceuticals, price-fixing
    by, 71
Darling International, 83–84
databases, as intellectual property, 129
de Soto, Hernando, 28, 29
deceptive advertising, 156–157
deceptive pricing, 157
deCrane, Al, 175, 176
defendant, litigation strategy of,
    214–215
Dell Computer
    computer waste recycling by, 155
    legal advocacy by, 44
    patent holdings of, 121
design defects, 159–160
design patents, 121
Digital Millennium Copyright Act of
    1998 (DMCA), 44, 130
direct copyright infringement, 133
Direct Marketing Association, 172
disabilities, legislation regarding,
    192–193
disclosure
    duty of, 97
    full, 65–66
    selective, 66–67
discrimination, 175–177
    costs of, 195
    eradicating, 188–195
    legislation regarding, 188, 190–193
    policies regarding, 183
    suits alleging, 188–189
disparate impact, 191
disparate treatment, 191
dispute resolution
    alternative, 205, 206–210
    business solutions for, 203–204
    litigation, 210–215
    settlement, 215–217
diversity
    case study of, 189–195
    issues regarding, 176–177
    policies regarding, 188
    promotion of, 188–189

Do Not Call list, 172
Doan's Pills, deceptive advertising by, 157
document management
  benefits of, 219
  design of, 220
  and selective destruction, 220–221
document retention
  of electronic materials, 218–219
  legal requirements for, 217, 220–221
  policy for, 8, 184
domain registration, 140
Drexel Burnham, 49
Drucker, Peter, 177
due care, 32
due diligence, 63–64
due process, 40
  recent interpretations of, 41
DuPont, 142
Durand, Doug, 187
duty
  of care, 59–60
  fiduciary, 58–60, 102–103
  of loyalty, 58–59
  of oversight, 60
duty to disclose, 96–97

Easterbrook, Frank, 99, 100
education
  for compliance, 80–82
Eisai, price-fixing by, 71
Eisner, Michael, 59
Elam, Joyce, 228, 229
Electronic Signatures in Global and National Commerce Act, 23
Eli Lilly, consumer privacy issues and, 168–170
Ely, Robin, 188
e-mail and instant messaging
  dangers of, 218–219
  harassment via, 200–201
  policies regarding, 183
employee benefit plans, 36
employee relations
  consistent application of policy, 184–185
  costs associated with, 177

documentation requirements for, 182
gender equity, 175–176
good faith, 179–180
hiring, 178–179, 180–181
key policies for, 183–184
outsourcing issues, 187–188
performance issues, 185–186
race equity, 176–177
termination, 179–180, 181–182
whistleblowers, 186–187
Employee Retirement Income Security Act (ERISA), 36
Enron, 8, 49, 220, 241, 243
  collapse of, 3, 45
  conflicts of interest at, 58
  pension funds of, 36
  relations with counsel, 225–226
  whistleblowers at, 186
environmental laws, 23, 41–42
environmental liability, 32–33
Environmental Protection Agency, 32
equal protection, 40
Equal Pay Act of 1963, 190–191
Erbitux, 67
Ertel, Danny, 93
ethics
  accountability and, 54–55
  code of, 50–52
  decision tree for, 52–54
  importance of, 50–56
  managerial example and, 51
exit interviews, trade secrets and, 136
Expedia, litigation against, 211–212
Exxon, brand name, 144

facts, noncopyrightability of, 129
failure to warn, 160–161
fair use doctrine, 130
Family and Medical Leave Act of 1993, 192–193
Fastow, Andy, 58
Federal Express, legal advocacy by, 44
Federal Sentencing Guidelines, 83–84
Federal Trade Commission
  act authorizing, 39
  functions of, 156

fiduciary duties, 58–60, 102–103
Financial Performance Corporation, 100
Finkelstein, Julius, 118
Firestone, Harvey, 166
Firestone
  quality control plans of, 166–167
  tire recall by, 165–166
firm
  organization of, 8–9
  resource-based view of, 9
first-sale doctrine, 143
Fisher, Roger, 216
folding-box industry, price-fixing scandal at, 81
Food and Drug Administration, 23, 37
Food, Drug, and Cosmetic Act, 56
force majeure clause, 112–113
Ford, Henry, 166
Ford, William Clay, Jr., 166
Ford Explorer, tire recall of, 165–166
Ford Motor Company
  and Firestone recall, 165–166
  product liability issues of, 160
Ford Pinto, design defects of, 159–160
Foreign Corrupt Practices Act, 23–24
France, Mike, 208
fraud
  described, 96–97
  promissory, 97–98
free-trade agreements, 35, 43
freedom of speech, 40, 41
Friedman, Stephen, 230, 231
Frito Lay products, 77
full disclosure, 65–66

Gates, Bill, 76, 88, 131
Gatorade, 137, 138
gender equity, 175–176
  preventing harassment, 195–201
General Aviation Revitalization Act, 161
general counsel
  advisory role of, 232
  attitudes towards, 233–234
  budgetary role of, 234–235
  global focus of, 232
  importance of, 231–232
  informational function of, 232
  integration with corporate picture, 232
  relations with management, 234
  risk assessment approach of, 232–233
  roles of, 232
General Electric
  brand name value of, 140
  environmental liability of, 32–33
General Electric Credit Corporation, 101, 102
General Motors Corporation, 137
  product liability issues of, 160
Georges, John, 95
Gerstner, Lou, 76, 145
Getty, Gordon, 104, 105
Getty Museum, 104
Getty Oil, 104, 205
Getty Trust, 104
Glass-Steagall Act, 1, 2
Go.com, 139
Goldman Sachs, 59
good faith, 98–99
  in employee dealings, 179–180
GoTo.com, 139
governance
  importance of, 61
Grand Met PLC, 58
Grass, Martin, 64
Grasso, Richard, 61
gray market, 143
Greenspan, Alan, 1, 66
Greenstein, Martin, 199
Grubman, Jack, 216
Gruner, Richard, 63

Hand, Learned, 74, 204
harassment
  electronic, 200–201
  employer liability for, 196–197
  at holiday parties, 199–200
  investigation of, 198
  need for policy regarding, 183
  prevention of, 197–199
  quid pro quo, 196
Health Insurance Portability and Accountability Act (HIPAA), 183

HealthSouth, 6
heavyweight teams, 227–228
Heinz, H. J., 31, 243
Hewlett-Packard
  computer waste recycling by, 155
  encouragement of inventions by, 122
Hinthorne, Tom, 9
Hoffman-La Roche, price-fixing by,
  13, 71
holiday parties, as scene of
  harassment, 200
Holmes, Oliver Wendell, 6
honesty
  in contract negotiations, 96–97
  in criminal investigations, 82, 84
  with employees, 180–181
  and product safety rules, 163–164
horizontal price-fixing, 72
hostile work environment, 196–197,
  200–201
HP Services, 94
Huhm, Steve, 94
human capital
  development of, 177
  diversity, 175–177, 188–195
  key employment
Hurst, James Willard, 4
Hyundai Electronics, patent
  infringements of, 126

IBM
  antitrust issues with, 76
  brand name value of, 140
  encouragement of inventions by,
    122
  intellectual property holdings of,
    118, 145, 149
  relations with Microsoft, 88
ImClone Systems, 3
  insider trading at, 67, 69
Immigration Reform and Control Act
  of 1986 (IRCA), 190–191
implied warranty of fitness for
  purpose, 158
incentives, for compliance, 63
independent contractors, 185
  benefits paid to, 91–92
  copyright ownership by, 120

written agreements for, 183
inevitable disclosure doctrine,
  137–138
infomercial industry, self-regulation
  by, 172
information technology
  attitudes toward, 228
  importance of, 229
  outsourcing of, 230
infrastructure improvements, 34–35
innovation, incentives to, 34
The Innovator's Dilemma, 124
insider trading, 67
  decision tree analysis of, 70
  prevention of, 68–69, 71, 184
  tipping, 67–68
insurance contracts, 108–109
Intel
  antitrust compliance by, 74
  brand name value of, 140
  patent infringement by, 127
intellectual property
  avoiding violations, 118
  as bargaining chip, 119
  copyright, 119–120, 128–133
  encouraging development of,
    121–122
  importance of, 117
  laws regarding, 38
  licensing of, 118–119, 145, 149–151
  offensive and defensive use of,
    118–119
  ownership of, 119–120
  patents, 118, 120–128
  protection of, 143–145, 146–148
  trade secrets, 133–138
  trademarks, 138–143
  ubiquity of, 117–118
intent to be bound, 103
Intergraph, patent holdings of, 127
internal controls
  corporate governance, 60–61
international contract law, 90–91
International Paper Company, 95
Internet Corporation for Assigned
  Names and Numbers (ICANN),
  140
Itanium chip, 127
iTunes, 132

Jackson, Jesse, 176
Jamail, Joe, 105
Jasinowski, Jerry, 204
Jenner, Bruce, 157
job security, 36
Johns Hopkins, customer service at,
    170
Johnson & Johnson, ethical reputation
    of, 49
jury trial, right to, 40
justice, effective administration of, 39

Kaizaki, Yoichiro, 165, 166
Kaplan, Robert, 10, 54
Kinnear, James, 175, 205, 232
Kleenex, brand name protection of,
    142
Kodak, 119
    brand name, 141
    and digital cameras, 124
Komansky, David, 208
Kotler, Philip, 164
Kozlowski, Dennis, 51

labor markets, promotion of, 34
land use laws, 42
language, ambiguities of, 7–8
Laufer, William S., 84
law
    ambiguities in, 6
    business and, 4–5
    and competitive strategy, 8–13
    conflicts and overlaps in, 42–43
    conservatism in dealing with, 77–80
    and consumer welfare, 37–39
    defined, 4
    dynamic nature of, 22–26
    and economic growth, 28–35
    evolution of, 21–22
    importance of, 4, 5
    judicial interpretation of, 25
    mutability of, 10
    opportunity creation by, 77
    private, 26
    public priorities and, 22–23
    and public welfare, 39–42
    reasons for violating, 10, 13

responsible advocacy and, 43–45, 46
    as underpinning of economic
        system, 21–22
    and value chain, 10, 12
    worker protection by, 35–37
Lay, Kenneth, 65
leave policies, 183
    laws regarding, 192–193
Leeson, Nick, 84
legal astuteness, 5, 7, 9
Lemelson, Mark, 125
Lerner, Josh, 128
Levers of Control, 60
Levitt, Arthur, 45
licensing
    advantages to licensee, 150
    advantages to licensor, 145, 149
    disadvantages to licensee, 150–151
    disadvantages to licensor, 149–150
    profitability of, 118
Liebeck, Stella, 171
limitations of liability, 109, 158
limited liability laws, 22
Linowiz, Sol, 204
Lipton, Marty, 105
Listerine, deceptive advertising by,
    156–157
litigation
    alternatives to, 205–210
    attitudes towards, 204
    defendant strategy for, 214–215
    hidden effects of, 7
    indications for, 210–213, 217
    jury effect in, 215–216
    management of, 213–214
    strategies for, 217
    tips for, 211
lobbying, 43–44
    purpose of, 45
lock-in strategy, 11
Louisiana-Pacific, 95
low total cost strategy, 11
loyalty, duty of, 58–59
Lutchen, Mark, 229

Macintosh
    graphical interface of, 87, 118
    operating system of, 87

Macy, R. H., 31
Madrid Protocol, 143
management
  communication with counsel, 7–8,
    113–115, 224–225
  and contract law, 26
  fiduciary duties of, 101–102
  influencing governance structure,
    26
  and lawmaking, 26
  legal understanding of, 6, 9, 226,
    228–231
  relationship to counsel of, 6–7,
    213–214, 223–228, 234
Mantrala, Murali, 164
manufacturing defects, 159
Marlboro, brand name value of, 140
Marsh & McLennan Companies,
    218–219
Marsu B.V., 98
Martin, David, 153
Matrix films, 131
Mauna Loa Macadamia Nut
    Corporation, trademarks of, 139
McCraw, Thomas, 31
McDonald's
  brand name value of, 140
  Russian enterprises of, 89
  tort case against, 171
MCI, litigation against AT&T, 213
McKinley, John, 104, 175
mediation
  employer-employee, 183
  features of, 206–207
  features of mediators, 208–209
  hybrid with arbitration, 206, 209
Medicare, 37
Medicare fraud, 47–49
  investigations of, 48–49
meeting of the minds, 94–96
merchantability, warranty of, 158
Merck, 150
Merrill Lynch, 59
Meyer, Andrew, 171
Microsoft, 122, 141, 218
  antitrust issues with, 75, 76
  brand name value of, 140
  bundling by, 75
  customer education by, 131

employment contract issues at, 92
Expedia product of, 211
intellectual property of, 118,
    121–122
litigation against, 87–88, 211–212
patent infringements by, 126–127
minimum wage laws, 35
  and conflict of laws, 43
minitrial, features of, 207
misappropriation, of trade secrets,
    136–137
misappropriation theory, 68
mistakes
  of fact, 95
  of judgment, 95–96
Model Rules of Professional Conduct
    (ABA), 242–243
monopolization, allowable vs. illegal,
    74–75
Monsanto, legal budgeting of,
    234–235
Moser, Mike, 154
movie rental industry, incentive
    alignment in, 111
Mystery of Capital, 28

Napster, 130, 133
Narayanan, V. G., 110
Nasser, Jacques, 166
National Highway Traffic Safety
    Administration, 37
NBC, trademarks of, 139
negligence, 57
negotiation, features of, 206
Netscape Communications, 122
Nokia, brand name value of, 140
noncompete agreements, 137, 183
nondisclosure agreements, 135, 183
nonprice constraints, allowable, 73–74
Nooyi, Indra K., 227
Norton, David, 10, 54

Occupational Health and Safety Act
    (OSHA), 35
offer and acceptance, 89
offshoring, and ethics, 55
O'Hagan, James, 68

one person, one vote, 40
options, 110
oral contracts, 99
outsourcing, 187–188
outsourcing contracts, 94
oversight, duty of, 60
Ovitz, Michael, 59

PARC (Xerox Palo Alto Research
 Center), 118
Park, John, 167
Parks, Rosa, 13
Patent Cooperation Treaty, 120
patent laws, 23, 34
 and conflict of laws, 42
 and public interest, 43
patent pool, 149
patent thickets, 125
patents, 118, 120, 143
 alternatives to, 144
 application for, 122–123
 assignment of, 183, 184
 cost and benefits of, 124–126
 design, 121
 characteristics of protection offered
  by, 146–148
 competing claims for, 123–124
 costs of litigating, 127–128
 encouraging, 121–122
 infringement of, 125, 126–127
 international aspects of, 123
 plant, 121
 prior art and, 122
 public policy aspects of, 127–128
 searches on, 125–126
 utility, 120–121
Pauley, William, 67
Pennzoil, litigation with Texaco, 104,
 105, 205
Pennzoil v. Texaco, 103
Pentium chip, 127
PepsiCo, 137–138
 Legal Academy of, 227
 legal philosophy of, 231
 opportunity creation at, 77
performance issues, employee,
 185–186
 documentation of, 186

Pfeffer, Jeffrey, 180, 182
Pfizer, 102, 150
Pillsbury Company, 68
Pioneer Hi-Bred, 121
Piper Aircraft, 221
piracy, 131–133
 combating, 133
 of compact discs, 132
 of movies, 131
 and videotape industry, 132
Pizza Hut, 197
plant patents, 121
Polaroid, patents of, 119, 124
policies, 183–184
 team building, 178–188
Porter, Michael, 10
preliminary agreements, 103
 intent issues with, 103–106
 tips for, 103
price-fixing
 in chemical industry, 91
 in folding-box industry, 81
 prohibitions against, 72–73
 in vitamin industry, 71–73
Priceline.com, 128
 litigation against Microsoft by,
  211–212
PricewaterhouseCoopers, 168
Prince, Charles, 1, 2, 3, 216, 231,
 244–245
prior art, 122
Pritzker, Jay, 101, 102
privacy
 and attorney-client privilege,
  238–240
 of consumer data, 168–170
 of employees, 183, 198
 EU legislation on, 172
product defects, 159–161
product leadership strategy, 11
product liability, 32
 managing risk of, 158–161
 reduction of, 161–162
product safety laws, 37–38
product safety programs
 candor in, 163–164
 designing, 162
 features of, 162
 and recalls, 164–167

to reduce liability, 161–162
responsibility for, 162, 167–168
safety audits, 162–163
Progressive Insurance, 156
promise, distinguished from contract, 89
promissory fraud, 97–98
property rights, protection of, 28–29
prospectuses, language requirement of, 101
Prozac.com, 169
Prudential Insurance, trade practices of, 156
Public Company Accounting Oversight Board, 25
public health, patents and, 127
public policy
  and consumer welfare, 37–39
  and economic growth, 28–35
  laws to enforce, 22–23, 26–42
  and protection of workers, 35–37
  and public welfare, 39–42
public safety, responsibility for, 167–168
public welfare
  constitutional rights, 40–41
  justice and, 39–40
  taxation and, 40
purpose, of contract, 90
  illegal, 91
Putnam Investments, 6
  securities fraud at, 64

Quality Films, 131
quid pro quo harassment, 196

race equity, 176–177
  case study of, 189–195
  legislation regarding, 188, 190–193
  promotion of, 188–189
racial discrimination, prevention of, 37
Raman, Ananth, 110
reasonable care, duty to use, 57, 59–60
reasonable efforts, distinguished from best efforts, 98–99
recalls
  case study of, 165–166

criteria for, 164
planning for, 164
recycling services, 155
Redmond, William, Jr., 137, 138
Redstone, Sumner, 212, 213
Reed, John, 1, 2
Regina Corporation, reduction of liability exposure by, 160
regulation
  legal aspects of, 23–25
  systems approach to, 14–17
  underlying rationales of, 27
Regulation Fair Disclosure (FD), 66, 67
releases, characteristics of, 109
religious discrimination, prevention of, 37
rent control, 41
Rentrak, 111
Replay TV, 131
repose, statute of, 161
resale price maintenance, prohibitions against, 73
Resource Conservation and Recovery Act (RCRA), 42
respondeat superior, 33, 57
responsible corporate officer doctrine, 56
revenue-sharing, 111
Rhône-Poulenc, whistleblowing by, 71
RIAA, 133
Rice, Paul, 236
Rigas, John, 58
risk allocation
  contracts and, 106–110
  insurance and, 108–109
  under law, 31–34
risk management
  compliance and, 61–63
  by general counsel, 232–233
  legal tools for, 16–17
  and legal uncertainty, 77–80
  product safety programs and, 161–168
  prospective evaluation for, 79
Rite-Aid, securities fraud at, 64–65
Root, Elihu, 242
Ross, Jeanne, 229, 230
Ruling the Waves, 23

safety audits, 162–163
Salomon Brothers, 1, 49
Salomon Smith Barney, legal issues of, 2
San Mateo, California, sexual
    harassment in, 197
Sanka, brand name protection of, 142
Sarbanes-Oxley Act, 23, 45
  provisions of, 24–25, 36, 40,
    186–187, 220
Scali, McCabe, Sloves, 154
Schmidt, Joette, 170
SCM, 59
Scully, John, 87
Sears, automobile repair scandal at, 63
secondary meaning, defined, 140
Section 16600 (California Business
    and Professions Code), 38
securities (*See also* Sarbanes-Oxley Act;
    securities fraud; selective
    disclosure)
  laws regarding, 22
  regulation of, 30–31
Securities Act of 1933, 39
Securities Exchange Act of 1934, 24,
  39
Securities and Exchange Commission,
  22, 25, 30
securities fraud
  effects of, 64
  examples of, 64–65
  preventing, 66–71
selective disclosure, 66–67
self-regulation, value of, 172
separation agreement, 182
service marks, 139
settlement, 203–204, 215
  strategy for, 216–217
sexual harassment, prevention of, 37
shareholder value, and ethics, 53–54,
  55
Shell, G. Richard, 212
Shuyler, Marc, 122
Simons, Robert, 60
Smith Barney, 1
Smith, Elizabeth P., 175, 176
social effect of laws, 22–23
Social Security taxes, 37
Sony, 132
Sony Pictures, 111

Spar, Debora, 23
Spitzer, Eliot, 218
Sprint, 138
Stac Electronics, 126–127
standards, enforcement, 62
Steamboat Willy, 44
Stein, Laura, 232
Steinberg, Andrew, 128
Stewart, Evan, 230, 231
Stewart, Martha, 69
strategic compliance management, 50,
  85–86
strategy
  influence of law on, 5
  legal aspects of, 11–12
Strategy Maps, 10
strict liability, 32
  legislative relief against, 161
submarine patents, 125
subsidies, 34
summary jury trial, 207
Superfund, 32
Suwyn, Mark, 95
systems approach to business
  regulation, 14–15
  legal tools for, 16–17

Takeda Chemical Industries, price-
  fixing by, 71
TAP Pharmaceutical Products, fraud
  by, 187
tariffs, 35
tax incentives, 34
taxation
  nonconfiscatory aspect of, 31
  and public welfare, 40
Temple, Nancy, 8, 242
temporary workers, 92
termination
  due care in, 181
  improper, 179
  separation agreement, 182
Texaco
  acquisition of Getty, 104, 205
  contract dispute resolution at,
    203–204
  copyright infringement at, 133
  culture of compliance at, 62

diversity issues at, 175–177
litigation with Pennzoil, 104–105, 205
Task Force on Equality and Fairness, 189–195
Texas Instruments, 126
Thirteenth Amendment, 34
Thomas, David, 188
Thomsen, Linda Chatham, 65
3Com Corporation, encouragement of inventions by, 122
Time Inc., litigation against, 212–213
tips, insider, 67–68
Title VII (Civil Rights Act), 188, 190–191, 195–196
TiVo, 131
tobacco industry, attorney-client privilege citation of, 239
tort law, 40
Toyota, brand name value of, 140
trade dress, 139
trade secrets, 133, 143
    advantages of, 144
    characteristics of protection offered by, 146–148
    disadvantages of, 145
    and exit interviews, 136
    identification of, 135
    misappropriation of, 136–137
    nondisclosure agreements and, 135
    policy regarding, 134
    protection of, 134–136
    security of, 136, 145
    types of, 134
trademarks, 34
    characteristics of protection offered by, 146–148
    choice of, 140–141
    creating rights in, 141
    defined, 138–139
    international dimensions of, 143
    loss of rights in, 142–143
    root of value of, 139–140
trading, preclearing of, 69, 71
training, for compliance, 62
Trans Union, 101–102
Travelers
    merger with Citicorp, 1, 2

Tropicana, deceptive advertising by, 157
Truth-in-Lending statutes, 39
Tyco International, 49
    ethics issues at, 51
tying (bundling), 75
Tylenol recall, 165

ultrahazardous activities, 33
unconscionability doctrine, 34
unconscionable, defined, 91
unfair trade practices, 156
Unicor, 155
Universal Studios, 111, 132
utility patents, 120–121

value chain, law and, 10, 12
value creation, legal tools for, 16–17
vertical nonprice restrictions, allowable, 73–74
Veterans Reemployment Act of 1974, 190–191
Viacom, litigation against Time, 212–213
vicarious infringement, 133
Videomax SA, 131
videotape industry, 132
Vinson & Elkins, 225–226
vitamin industry, price-fixing in, 71–73
Vocational Rehabilitation Act of 1973, 190–191
voice over Internet protocol (VOIP), 46
Volkswagen AG, 137
Volvo, brand equity issues, 153–154
Vonage, opportunity creation at, 77

Waksal, Samuel, 67, 69
Walker, Jay, 128, 204, 211
Walt Disney Company
    brand name value of, 140
    conflicts of interest at, 58–59
    contract disputes at, 98
    legal advocacy by, 44
    trademark disputes at, 139

Warner Communications, 212
Warner-Lambert, acquisition of,
    102–103
warnings, inadequate, 160–161
warranties, 157–158
Watkins, Michael, 45, 82
Watson, Thomas, Jr., 61
Weeks, Rena, 199
Weill, Peter, 229, 230
Weill, Sanford, 1, 2, 3, 244
Welch, Jack, 61
Westinghouse, contract issues with,
    113–114
Wheelwright, Steven, 227
whistleblowers, 62
    protection of, 183, 186–187
Wickselman, Martin, 114
Windows operating system
    brand name value of, 141
    as intellectual property, 118
    litigation regarding, 87–88
Winning the Influence Game, 45
worker protection, 35
    civil rights, 37
    collective bargaining ability, 36
    and employee benefits, 36, 37
    and job security, 36

minimum wage laws, 35
    workplace safety laws, 35–36
workers' compensation, 37
workplace safety laws, 35–36
World Trade Center, insurance issues
    regarding, 109
World Trade Organization, 35
WorldCom, 49, 216
    collapse of, 2, 3
    whistleblowers at, 186
written contracts, 99
    importance of, 99–100
Wuu, Stephen, 118

Xerox
    brand name protection of, 142
    intellectual property of, 118

Yeager, Peter, 226
Yuspeh, Alan, 48–49

zoning laws, 42

About the Author

Constance E. Bagley is an Associate Professor of Business Administration at the Harvard Business School, where she teaches Legal Aspects of Management. Before joining the HBS faculty in 2000, she taught for more than ten years at the Stanford University Graduate School of Business, where she received Honorable Mention for the Distinguished Teaching Award. Before teaching at Stanford, she was a corporate securities partner in the San Francisco office of Bingham McCutchen.

Professor Bagley is the coauthor of *The Entrepreneur's Guide to Business Law* (2d ed. 2003) and *Managers and the Legal Environment: Strategies for the 21st Century* (5th ed. 2006). She is a member of the National Adjudicatory Council of the National Association of Securities Dealers and was on the faculty of the Young Presidents Organization International University for Presidents in Hong Kong and Prague. She is on the editorial board of the *Journal of Internet Law*, a staff editor of the *American Business Law Journal*, and a member of the advisory board for the Bureau of National Affairs Corporate Practice Series. She is a member of the State Bar of California and the State Bar of New York.